The Transmedia Vampire

ALSO OF INTEREST AND FROM MCFARLAND

Vampires from Another World: The Cinematic Progeny of H.G. Wells'
The War of the Worlds and Bram Stoker's Dracula, Simon Bacon (2021)

Eco-Vampires: The Undead and the Environment, Simon Bacon (2020)

Dracula as Absolute Other: The Troubling and Distracting Specter
of Stoker's Vampire on Screen, Simon Bacon (2019)

Growing Up with Vampires: Essays on the Undead in Children's Media,
edited by Simon Bacon and Katarzyna Bronk (2018)

To Boldly Go: Essays on Gender and Identity
in the Star Trek *Universe,* edited by
Nadine Farghaly and Simon Bacon (2017)

The Transmedia Vampire

*Essays on Technological
Convergence and the Undead*

Edited by SIMON BACON

Foreword by John Edgar Browning

McFarland & Company, Inc., Publishers
Jefferson, North Carolina

This book has undergone peer review.

Library of Congress Cataloguing-in-Publication Data

Names: Bacon, Simon, 1965– editor. | Browning, John Edgar, author of foreword.
Title: The transmedia vampire : essays on technological convergence and the undead / edited by Simon Bacon ; foreword by John Edgar Browning
Description: Jefferson, North Carolina : McFarland & Company, Inc., Publishers, 2021 | Includes bibliographical references and index.
Identifiers: LCCN 2021039168 |
ISBN 9781476675749 (paperback : acid free paper) ∞
ISBN 9781476643359 (ebook)
Subjects: LCSH: Vampires in mass media. | Mass media—Technological innovations. | Convergence (Telecommunication) | BISAC: LITERARY CRITICISM / Horror & Supernatural | PERFORMING ARTS / Television / Genres / Science Fiction, Fantasy & Horror
Classification: LCC P96.V35 T73 2021 | DDC 809/.93375—dc23
LC record available at https://lccn.loc.gov/2021039168

British Library cataloguing data are available
ISBN (print) 978-1-4766-7574-9
ISBN (ebook) 978-1-4766-4335-9

© 2021 Simon Bacon. All rights reserved

No part of this book may be reproduced or transmitted in any form or by any means, electronic or mechanical, including photocopying or recording, or by any information storage and retrieval system, without permission in writing from the publisher.

Front cover image: Poster art for *Dracula Untold* (2014) (Universal Pictures/Photofest).

Printed in the United States of America

McFarland & Company, Inc., Publishers
Box 611, Jefferson, North Carolina 28640
www.mcfarlandpub.com

Table of Contents

Acknowledgments — vii

Foreword: We Are, All of Us, Renfields
   JOHN EDGAR BROWNING — 1

Introduction
   SIMON BACON — 3

Part I—*Dracula*: Adaptations and Re-Creations

We Are Dracula: *Penny Dreadful* and the Dracula Megatext
   JEFFREY ANDREW WEINSTOCK — 20

"Better Parts": Redemptive Portrayals of Count Dracula as Vlad the Impaler in Selected Film Adaptions of Stoker's *Dracula*
   WAYNE DEREK PIGEON-COOTE — 35

"I've crossed oceans of versions to find you": Remediating Mina from Novel to Screen in *Bram Stoker's Dracula* (1992)
   CATHLEEN ALLYN CONWAY — 47

Part II—Across Mediums, Platforms and Levels of Engagement

Byzantium Stage to Screen
   GINA WISKER — 60

Pixel Parasites: The Virtual Vampire as Enemy, Ally and Self in Video Games
   SHAWN EDREI — 76

Vampire as Doll: Transformations of Meaning Through Play in the *Vampirina* and Draculaura (*Monster High*) Franchises
   DEREK NEWMAN-STILLE — 88

"Do Vampires Get Their Periods?": The *Carmilla* Web Series and the Politics of Bleeding Women
 ALEXANDRA HELLER-NICHOLAS   103

Part III—Transnational Transmedia

Vampire Tourism: Transmedia Narratives, Cultural Histories and Locating the Undead
 LORNA PIATTI-FARNELL   120

Thinking in Connections: A.A. Carr's *Eye Killers* and F.W. Murnau's *Nosferatu*
 SVETLANA SEIBEL   134

From Revenants to Vampires: The Transmedia Evolution of the *Jiangshi*
 KATARZYNA ANCUTA   146

Part IV—Interventions, Fandom, Ownership

Transmedia Interventions and Palimpsestuous Relations: *Carmilla* Meets Carmen Maria Machado
 NATALIE WILSON   162

The Originals and Family History Two-Fold: Caught Between Two Worlds
 VERENA BERNARDI   174

Transmedia Vampire Stories and Their Consumers in Anne Rice's *The Vampire Chronicles*
 LAURA DAVIDEL   187

First-Person Gothic: Anne Rice, Vampirism, Authorship and Identity
 EVAN HAYLES GLEDHILL   201

About the Contributors   217

Index   221

Acknowledgments

This collection has been something of an odyssey, from its original conception seven years ago to final reality, and many thanks are due to all involved in getting it to this stage. I would also like to thank all those involved in these final stages of completing the collection (The Vampire Scholars and Horror SIG Groups on Facebook), the peer reviewers for their invaluable comments, corrections, and suggestions. And last, but never least, the never-ending patience of the always wonderful Mrs. Mine, Seba and Majki and the constant support (and sernik Magdy) of Mam i Tata Bronk.

Foreword

We Are, All of Us, Renfields

JOHN EDGAR BROWNING

The essays in this book, which Simon Bacon has carefully selected, edited, and introduced, clearly demonstrate, as we enter the third decade of the twenty-first century, the proverbial, Tuberculosian "vampire's grasp" on global media and markets. Key to the present book, just as it has been to the vampire itself, is transcendence. Each section in *The Transmedia Vampire—Dracula*: Adaptations and Re-Creations; Across Mediums, Platforms and Levels of Engagement; Transnational Transmedia; and Interventions, Fandom, Ownership—demarcates in crucial ways the vampire's transcendence from story to story, medium to medium, country to country, and author to reader. As the vampire rises beyond the grave, beyond mortality, so has it risen beyond any limit or categorization we can devise to contain or master it. We are beholden to the vampire, whether we like it or not.

The vampire's promise is an unattainable one—life immortal. Yet, this hasn't stopped artists, writers, readers, musicians, programmers, or pornographers from revisiting time and time again through metaphor the desire that beckons so many of us: to be without death, without limits; what we do when we get there has been the *foci* of vampire narratology. In many ways, vampires help us to understand ourselves, bringing to the fore the secrets we hide deep within us to project and displace upon the vampires of the world. This isn't a new phenomenon though—*Dracula* (1897), for example, may well have been, as I will show in a forthcoming reference work, one of the most reviewed books of the entire Victorian literary canon, certainly of the Gothic canon.

Indeed, the figure of the vampire ubiquitously traverses the world and nearly every language. It is worth noting, too, that the scholarly contributions of Montague Summers—the result of his extensive researches throughout Europe—to the critical methodologies used for studying vampires helped to solidify over the course of nearly a century how we have come to understand the vampire and its antecedents throughout the world. We also owe to Summers the globalized approach to vampire studies that we use today.

Unfortunately, whereas excerpts from the work of early vampire scholars like Augustin Calmet or Dudley Wright routinely appear in modern studies and anthologies on the subject, Summers's work often remains curiously absent. No doubt this owes to Summers's tenacity for and (supposedly fervent) belief in the vampire. But are we vampire scholars today, tenacious as we are, really much different from Summers? The scholars whose works are collected here go far in answering that very question, and I'd like to think Summers would be impressed.

In short, offered here is a volume that aims to provide considerable insight into the vampire, suggesting in its pages new and innovative ways of re-reading and re-examining, among other things, the evolution of the vampire's public image. Resulting is a volume that is sure to make for a timely addition to the multitude of recent studies on *Dracula*, Bram Stoker, the Gothic, and vampires generally.

We are, all of us, Renfields in our slavish devotion to the vampires of our age, and I'm not so sure we mind.

John Edgar Browning is a professor of liberal arts at the Savannah College of Art and Design. He has over fifteen contracted or published books and over 75 shorter works, including a recent book with Darren Elliott-Smith, New Queer Horror Film and Television (Horror Studies) (University of Wales Press), *as well as the forthcoming book* Dracula—An Anthology: Critical Reviews and Reactions, 1897–1920 (Edinburgh University Press). *He also recently coedited, with David J. Skal, the second Norton Critical Edition of* Dracula.

Introduction

Simon Bacon

Transmedia and technological convergence are very much at the forefront of cultural analysis at the start of the twenty-first century, and with the increase in emerging media devices, informational interfaces, and virtual technology it is hardly surprising. What *is* surprising is that while there are many studies covering the way fictional narratives and characters are of vital importance to transmedia, none have focused solely on that hugely popular figure that is itself continually transforming across all formats and mediums, and continues to fascinate contemporary culture: namely, the vampire.[1] This timely study focuses on how fictional vampire characters are made more "real" or complete through their depiction in narratives produced in/across different mediums and platforms, and how the immersive "vampire world" so created can be seen to impinge on our own, and vice versa. As such, this work is an investigation into how immersion blurs the boundaries between real and imaginary worlds, the ways in which identity is created through technology, and why the undead world of the transmedia vampire is so well suited to life in the twenty-first century.

It is misleading to think of transmedia as a specifically twenty-first century phenomenon when narratives, and the characters that populate them, have been shared via multiple media since these stories were first recorded or performed in some way—indeed, as argued by Mark J.P. Wolf, such acts of "world building" are fundamental to what it is to be human (2012, 1–2). Movement or adaptation (re-adaptation)[2] across media, such as in novels, films, graphic novels, etc., will inherently introduce changes not only due to the act of retelling in itself but also because of the inherent

---

1. See Simon Bacon, 2014, "The Transmedia Vampire: From Bram Stoker's Dracula to HBO's True Blood," in Tawnya Ravy and Eric Forcier, eds, *Words, Worlds, Narratives: Transmedia and Immersion* (Leiden: Brill), pp. 55–75. https://doi.org/10.1163/9781848881945_004.
2. Re-adaptation and re-creation are used here to denote the ongoing and continual process of change caused in a narrative due to its movement across, or within, mediums.

properties of each new platform. Stories will often be further augmented through advertising, social media, blogs, etc., with the more well-known texts/narratives/franchises being adapted specifically for performance/engagement in other media as part of their process of world creation. The use of other platforms, such as comic-cons, conventions, cosplay, virtual participation, and even intersections with other narratives and their own discrete immersive worlds, promotes greater levels of fan/audience involvement. Arguably this is something that has always happened to popular texts adapted for other media, for instance John Polidori's *The Vampyre* (1819), which was quickly adapted into a series of successful plays, operas and musical theater, then further adapted back into novels again. More famously Bram Stoker's *Dracula* (1897) has been adapted to many more media; an unofficial film in 1922: *Nosferatu* (Murnau); a play in 1924: *Dracula* (Hamilton Deane); the first talking horror film in 1931: *Dracula* (Browning) among many, many others. The 1931 film in particular was popularized through widespread national and international advertising and marketing and subsequently spawned comic books, Halloween costumes, ballets, children's shows, and many other examples. In this vein, theorist Henry Jenkins begins his notion of "convergence culture" (2006) around the arguably vampiric *Matrix* franchise (The Wachowski Brothers 1990–2003)[3] that utilized extensive advertising and marketing, video games, and online fan communities to "world build."

All of these examples are based on the concepts of audience engagement and immersion where the viewer/reader/player becomes familiar with other texts or adaptations of a narrative and its characters, often through social networking, to construct a more rounded or complete picture of them. This often involves investigative work of some kind to "discover" less accessible sections of a narrative, parts that have subsequently been deleted or those no longer under the control of the original creator/author. As such, the more detail provided across multiple mediums, including those that are contradictory, the more "real" the characters and the world they inhabit becomes. An important distinction for Jenkins arises when the audience is no longer seen as passive in this configuration but becomes, or is encouraged to be, active agents in the story/character/world-building process. In particular this encourages greater levels of engagement and intersectionality between mediums—ways in which each can be seen to resonate with and inform others—so that the borders between audience and stage, reader and text, are no longer as strong as they once were.

3. *The Matrix* utilizes many vampiric tropes such as a dream world to contain its victims, *Dark City* (Proyas: 1998), and the farming of humans that features in the earlier Australian vampire film *The Thirst* (Hardy: 1979).

An interesting example of this phenomenon featuring the transmedia vampire is *The Strain Trilogy* by Guillermo del Toro and Chuck Hogan. The franchise began with three novels, *The Strain* (2009), *The Fall* (2010) and *The Night Eternal* (2011), although the story was originally imagined as a television series. In fact, promotional trailers were created after the publication of the last book in 2011,[4] which were seemingly unsuccessful in convincing a network to take-up the series, and it next appeared as a series of graphic novels written by David Lapham and drawn by Mike Huddleston (2011–2015). During the run of the graphic novels, the series was adapted for the FX television channel in 2014. It was created by del Toro and Hogan and ran for four seasons, ending in 2017.[5] While the comics stay very close to the narrative of the novels, the television series makes some rather large departures, based in part on audience response. This, in turn, has led to further tie-in novels with the televised narrative, single issue comics as well as video games,[6] online teasers, and appearances at comic-cons and fan events.[7] This, of course, only lists some of the in-franchise media jumps and narrative resonances/dissonances, and does not delve into the connections and references to other vampire stories/franchises that abound in the narrative world of *The Strain*.

The vampire genre is particularly self-referencing both in copying and purposely *not* copying earlier texts (Auerbach 1994 and Gelder 2012). *The Strain Trilogy* is no different and much of it can be seen to reference Stoker's *Dracula* and del Toro's own earlier excursions into the genre such as *Cronos* (1993) and *Blade II* (2002). These citations and ex-citations (Gelder 2012) with earlier vampire texts not only more fully construct the world and characters of *The Strain Trilogy* in differing mediums and levels of engagement, but are further reinforced through resonance with real world locations, organizations, and events such as New York, Ground Zero, 9/11, the War on Terror, and the Centers for Disease Control (CDC), which appear within the fictional tale.

All these aspects then come together to transform a text/character/world from a one-off manifestation to a multifaceted one that can be more fully engaged with and, possibly, interacted with on a meaningful, often emotional and physical level. The transmedia vampire exists

4. Jail Scene from *The Strain* as released on YouTube, September 2011: https://www.youtube.com/watch?v=nqefQ-jJpW8.
5. It should be noted that both del Toro and Hogan are involved in both the comics and TV series.
6. The cast of *The Strain* television series appeared at San Diego Comic-Con in 2017, https://codex.online/news/inside-the-strain-comic-con-vr-experience.
7. The San Diego Comic Con in 2017 also featured virtual reality walkthroughs of the sets and locations of the television series, https://codex.online/news/inside-the-strain-comic-con-vr-experience.

on multiple platforms that imbue it with a rounded, or three-dimensional identity, and that makes it more engaging (believable) and potentially more open to further levels of meaningful interaction.[8] This applies equally to the world the characters inhabit and through more explicitly immersive mediums such as gaming and virtual reality, that allow the audience to enter the world of the vampire in some way. This also works in the other direction when the characters and environments are recreated in the real world—often described as extraction—allowing for real-time and physical audience participation and engagement. This last is most clearly seen in the recreation of fictional locations in the real world with examples such as the vampire bar Fangtasia from *True Blood* (Ball 2008–14), Dracula Tours around Whitby in the United Kingdom, or Castle Dracula in Transylvania, Romania (Stoker never identifies what real castle it was based on). These in particular offer examples of the ways in which the barriers between the fictional and the real bleed into each other, dissolving the boundaries that ordinarily separate them.

Transmedia

In Henry Jenkins' world of media convergence, the driving force is ultimately economic, as media companies utilize as many different platforms as possible to get consumers to come to them through active engagement and participation. However, as Jenkins further states, "rather than talking about media producers and consumers as occupying separate roles, we may now see them as participants who interact with each other according to a new set of rules none of us fully understands. Not all participants are created equal" (2006, 23). This does not lessen the importance of the meaningful worlds created in this process of gaining a loyal, and growing, fan base of consumers, but those at the top of the hierarchy of participants that come together within the created world often control the direction and outcome as it evolves. As Jenkins notes in *Convergence Culture* (2006), it is the ability of the created world to produce many and diverse narrative threads, so that the audience/players/readers can also interact meaningfully with each other, that determines its ultimate success. As such, the greater the detail of a world's characters, environments, and narrative threads, the more likely it is that the audience will be able to interact with it—though sometimes this information can also

---

8. The Facebook site for the television series *True Blood* allowed users during the run of the series to contact characters online and even arranged for telephone conversations between fans and actors from the series, who remained in character. Since the series ended it has become more of a standard fan site.

be contradictory. Of equal importance here is not just the ability of participants to be able to enter the narrative world (immersion) but also for elements of that world to be brought out into our own (extraction). Jenkins writes about *Star Wars* merchandising: "They are evocative objects that shape the imagination in particular ways. They are authoring tools that grant to the purchaser the right to retell and extend the story that they saw on the screen" (18).[9] Here, he is specifically talking about action figures related to the sprawling space saga, but it equally applies to any item one can remove from the narrative and manipulate beyond the domain of its source medium. "Each new extension of the Star Wars text adds potentially more depth or appreciation of the world depicted on screen ... the mastery built up through the extracted elements can result in greater attention or a greater sense of immersion into the world when we return to the film" (19).

Consequently, this can be seen to apply to fan-related materials and interactions such as cosplay, fanzines, blogs, etc., where the audience/consumers gain individual agency in the ongoing negotiation between participants and which some authors/creators are not always happy about.[10] In many ways, this becomes the point at which a fictional world enters the real one and when it is no longer under the control of those who created it. Fan-fiction and cosplay are good examples of this.[11] What these examples of fan involvement also highlight is the performative nature of transmedia narratives: it is when the players/actors/participants enact/create and re-enact/re-create the story and its characters that the fictional world gains solidity and the ability to remain in one's memory, or gains what those in marketing call "stickiness." This stickiness is very much predicated on the performances between actors/participants and in the way that the audience/participants' engagement with a text/character/world becomes not only memorable in its immediacy but through continued repetition and re-creation. Necessarily, then, the transmedia vampire survives on being re-created, re-adapted, and resurrected over and over again. One almost immediately thinks of Hammer Films and Christopher Lee as Dracula, where no matter how dramatically or finally he seems to have been killed at the end of the film—seven films in total—he is miraculously re-created in the next installment making him "stick" in our imaginations all the more.

    9. Though as noted by Derek Newman-Stille in this volume, this is not always the case and users of toys and dolls often create very different stories to those envisioned by the original authors.
    10. The author Anne Rice is famously hostile to outside interference and contrary readings of her narratives and characters.
    11. See Stephenie Meyer's thoughts on the *Twilight* fan-fiction creation *50 Shades of Grey* by E.L. James, at "Access Hollywood Interview with Stephenie Meyer," *YouTube*, 12 November 2012, https://www.youtube.com/watch?v=14qT8Xv49eE. Accessed 2 August 2020.

The Transmedia Vampire

In many ways it is the core qualities of adaptation, re-enactment, and re-creation occurring across platforms and in the ongoing engagements between narratives and performers that make vampires uniquely suited to transmedia study. As noted by Gelder (2012) and Weinstock (2012) among others, vampires and the vampire genre as a whole are amazingly transformational yet self-referential. Figures such as Count Dracula, and indeed the storyline of Stoker's seminal novel itself, have been continually re-adapted and re-created—as a whole or in part—since the novel's publication in 1897. Possibly the most successful vampire narrative since *Dracula* and that exemplifies a more obvious (contemporaneous) version of the transmedia vampire as Jenkins would understand it, is *The Twilight Saga*.

The Twilight Saga, by Stephenie Meyer, is a text which is itself a re-adaptation of earlier narratives, with hints of *Romeo and Juliet*, *The Vampyre*, *Wuthering Heights*, *Dracula*, and *The Vampire Diaries*.[12] The popularity of the four books—*Twilight*, 2005; *New Moon*, 2006; *Eclipse*, 2007; and *Breaking Dawn*, 2008—was immense, capturing a huge worldwide audience that included both teenage girls and middle-aged women, and the books were translated into at least 38 different languages. Cinematic versions of the books were inevitable.[13] The films increased the furor around the novels with its growing fan-base sharing enthusiasm over social media, fan-forums, and merchandising—much was made of the in-narrative conflict between Edward Cullen and Jacob Black, prompting the promotion of many items for either "Team Edward" or "Team Jacob."[14] The first film was released in 2008 (with a graphic novel debuting a year later in 2010), making overnight stars of the actors—Kirsten Stewart as Bella Swan and Robert Pattinson as Edward Cullen—and the town of Forks in which the story was set. Subsequently, a franchise was created that reached into all areas of merchandising, branding, and product placement. It was a narrative that was not only transmedial, but transnational and trans-narrative as well. It was featured in many other

---

12. The original series of four novels in *The Vampire Diaries* series by L.J. Smith (*The Awakening*, 1991, *The Struggle*, 1991, *The Fury*, 1991, and *Dark Reunion*, 1992) appeared 14 years before Meyer's novels and share many features though it was not until the success of *Twilight* that Smith's novels received a similar level of popular success, and was also adapted into a television series.

13. Twilight "Moms" became something of a phenomenon during the publication and release of the books and films, see Leslie Paris, 2016, "Fifty Shades of Fandom: The Intergenerational Permeability of *Twilight* Fan Culture," in *Feminist Media Studies*, vol. 16, no. 4, pp. 678–92.

14. See Claudia Bucciferro, 2013, *The Twilight Saga: Exploring the Global Phenomenon* (Latham, MD: Scarecro), and Melissa A. Click, Jennifer Stevens Aubrey, Elizabeth Behm-Morawitz, eds, 2010, *Bitten by Twilight: Youth Culture, Media, & the Vampire Franchise* (Bern: Peter Lang).

narratives on different platforms, i.e., computer games such as *The Sims*, television shows, and other paranormal romance novels. Tie-ins with product placement saw advertising for real-world items in the fictional world and even products launched within the film—the Volvo S60R for instance—as well as real-estate promotion with the Cullen's ultra-modern house offered for sale after the films. Indeed, even its fan-fiction created further franchises, as was seen in the *Fifty Shades of Grey* franchise based on the books by E.L. James (the first novel was published in 2011).[15]

What is equally interesting about *Twilight* is the importance of its dissonance to the wider vampire genre. As noted previously, resonance is very important with genre fictions in general and vampire texts in particular—the way we know that a narrative is part of a larger already existing world is through the details that correlate between them, what we might call signposts that identity it as such—for vampire texts this can be a preference for nighttime, reliance on human blood, fangs etc. This builds familiarity and recognition, all qualities that can allow us to know where we are or "feel at home" within a created world. Within a genre, these new worlds should also feature novelty of some kind that marks it as different but which also adds to the details or characteristics of the vampire and it's world that can make it seem more real or relevant to a particular generation/historical moment. This is possibly most strikingly seen in Murnau's *Nosferatu* where, in a burgeoning age of film, sunlight became lethal to the vampire, quite literally turning it to ash, just like the highly flammable nitrate film on which the vampire appeared. Stoker's Count Dracula was only slightly weaker during the daylight hours. *Twilight* makes much of such dissonance though often not in terms of the wider, historical world of the vampire but rather the popularly perceived one of the early 2000s. Meyer's vampires are extremely strong, pale and cold, and hugely wealthy—all familiar traits—though they seem to be made of a marble-like substance when they are killed; more of a link to the Medusa myth, though turning to a crumbling stone-like or ashy substance in death is not uncommon in vampire films. However, the most marked difference is that of sparkling vampires, a characteristic that is not totally original but one which has ensured continuing infamy of the *Twilight* narrative world.

As mentioned previously, migrations across mediums is not new and can even be seen to have caused the vampire panic that spread across Europe

---

15. This is without the various other fan related projects such as *Twilight in Forks: Saga of the Real Twilight* (Brown: 2009) or *Destination Forks: The Real World of Twilight* (Brown: 2010) and even the many spoofs that followed the franchises global popularity like *Vampires Suck* (Friedberg and Seltzer: 2010), *Nightlight* (The Harvard Lampoon: 2009) and *New Moan: The First Book in the Twishite Saga: A Parody by Stephfordy Mayo* (The Harvard Lampoon: 2009).

in the early eighteenth century. It was the intrusion of the "enlightened" Austro-Hungarian empire into the superstitious homelands of Serbia that saw the oral history of the local peoples and their narratives of vampires being taken up by the more sophisticated medium of writing, and medical officers' reports, that sparked the sensational stories in the popular press of the day. Suddenly newspapers across Europe, the social media of the day, told of vampires in the East, to such a level that the word "vampire" itself made it in to the Oxford English Dictionary in 1734.[16] This example of the transmedia vampire saw the figure transform from localized oral ghost story into a pan–European panic that entered the imagination, and the nightmares, of those that read the sensational newspaper articles and books that followed.[17] The next "outbreak," almost a century later, was to consolidate the vampire's place in the hearts and minds of Western Europe and beyond.

In 1819, John Polidori published *The Vampyre*, a brief story that would not necessarily even be recognized as a vampire tale in the twenty-first century as it is more a tale of dishonor, corruption, and deceit than it is about blood-sucking. However, what impelled the story's rise to popularity, or infamy, was the fact that gossip and the popular press thought it was written by Lord Byron and not the unknown young doctor who had been his traveling companion in Switzerland a few years previously. Subsequently, it was not long before the work appeared in other media; the first of these was the 1820 play *Le Vampire* by Charles Nodier. This was so successful that re-adaptations of it began to appear, one even in the same year by James Robinson Planché entitled *The Bride of the Isles*. Curiously, in these various moves across media and countries—from London, to Paris and back again—the lead character, Lord Ruthven, stayed roughly the same but the surroundings altered, moving the action from London and the Grand Tour, as in Polidori, to the Scottish Highlands and beyond. The world of the vampire (vampyre) was not only expanding in re-adaptation and new mediums, but the characteristics of the undead villain grew as well. While Polidori suggested the restorative powers of moonlight, the later theatrical works altered the plot to see the vampire as under a curse (Dumas, *Le Vampire* 1851), trapped in a promise to dark forces that could only be broken by the life, or love, of an innocent, dragged to hell for his wickedness (Nodier, *Le Vampire*), or even vulnerable to special bullets (Boucicault, *The Phantom* 1861).

The nineteenth century also saw the publication of James Malcolm

---

16. Here though it was described as "a ghost who leaves his grave at night to suck the blood of the living" (Twitchell, 7). It is not totally surprising that the vampire is given a male identification as all of the cases noted in the vampire plague were men.

17. Such as Augustine Calmet, 1751, *The Phantom World: Or, The Philosophy of Spirits, Apparitions* published in French but not translated into English until 1850.

Rymer and Thomas Peckett Prest's *Varney the Vampire: or, the Feast of Blood* (1845–7) and Sheridan Le Fanu's *Carmilla* (1872). Both are important works that appeared, in part, due to the popularity of the vampire figure still fueled by Polidori's story and its later re-adaptations. *Varney the Vampire*, a large sprawling work that appeared in installments in penny dreadfuls—inexpensive weekly pamphlets—widened the vampire's audience and sensationalized the character. Essentially, these pamphlets were the equivalent of the Hammer Horror Dracula films of the late 1950s to the 1970s, creating a vivid, brash and romanticized vampire catering to a thrill-seeking readership. With this was also established many of the tropes of the genre instantly recognizable by contemporary audiences, such as a thirst for blood, two fang-like teeth, and a growing call on the audience's sympathy—all missing from the kith and kin of Polidori's Ruthven. It also helped to establish the vampire as a creature that thrives on popular appeal, beyond any critical acclaim, increasing its levels of audience participation and engagement (stickiness). This is one of the vital aspects of the transmedia vampire in that it finds its life energy through its audience and their engagement with it. This engagement, which might also be called entanglement, involves all aspects of audience participation such as easily accessible platforms and media, and ones that allow for physical, psychological, and emotional response. These then come together in a fully integrated unit—an ongoing process of maximized or focused intersectionality to bring life, or believability, to the transmedia vampire.

Carmilla (1872) is a very different work than *Varney* though, arguably, much more important in terms of how it continues to influence the genre. Its tale of an illicit female relationship which consolidated the female vampire as a power beyond patriarchal control and more recently has inspired many re-adaptations across multiple media.[18] If Ruthven and his later ilk are fueled by repressed homosexuality, then *Carmilla*'s lesbianism is on show for all to see—the sexually transgressive nature of the undead becomes one of its defining characteristics, creating a creature that inhabits its victims' dreams as much as their waking nightmares. Both *Varney* and *Carmilla* influenced the most well-known vampire story of the nineteenth century, and indeed arguably the most important one so far to the genre as a whole: Bram Stoker's *Dracula*. Stoker's *Dracula* has already been mentioned but possibly one of its most important features, apart from the continual re-adaptations, re-creations, echoes, and resonances of its characters and plot since its publishing, is the use of information technology within the story itself. *Dracula* is full of different forms of technology, and though not all of it is as "new" as the narrative suggests, it paints

---

18. Female vampires were not uncommon in the nineteenth century and ranged from the beautiful courtesan Clarimonde (Gautier 1836) to the aged Lady Ducayne (Braddon 1896).

the British Empire as a center of science, innovation, and invention—a modern, sophisticated, and civilized society to contrast the out-of-date, superstitious, and barbaric world of the vampire. Consequently, most of the forms of information technology are placed out of the vampire's reach, ostensibly because of his "child mind" but also because they are configured as the means to defeat, if not ultimately destroy, him. The audience/reader is shown photographs, a cinematograph, telegrams, a stenograph, train timetables (as the vampire hunters are shown traveling to and fro across Europe), blood transfusions, typewriters, and even shorthand writing all as ways in which an industrialized society communicates and transfers life-saving information.[19] The irony is that while the vampire itself is excluded from such technologies, its vampiric world, that of the novel, is consumed, disseminated, and engaged with through these very mediums (see Wicke 1992). This again reveals the symbiotic relationship between the vampire and transmediality in the way that the vampire is both a construct of, but also a mirror to, technological convergence. This mirror is one which reveals the consumerist/capitalist vampire at its heart, as noted by Jenkins,[20] and reveals cross-platform worldbuilding and engagement driven by corporate entities looking to create willing participants/customers from which they can continually drain money (blood)—a metaphor clearly represented in the vampire films *Thirst* (Hardy 1979), *The Matrix*, and *Daybreakers* (Speirig Brothers 2009). This has set the mold for subsequent vampire narratives that aggressively promote high levels of engagement and cross-platform penetration, as seen in The Twilight Saga in particular.

The entanglement between vampires and wealth is one that has become ever stronger since the nineteenth century; since the late 1960s this has been correlated with their increasing physical beauty with glittering eyes, teeth and fingernails as well, so that their victims are as likely to be "glamoured" by the look of the vampire as by its hypnotic stare. Meyer's vampires make this literal, portrayed as seemingly constructed from diamonds that glitter in the sunlight—interestingly Dracula similarly "bled" gold coins at the end of Stoker's novel. Edward and his extended vampire "family" are the perfect consumerist, neoliberal vampires of the early 2000s: young, beautiful, extremely wealthy and

19. It is worth noting that Count Dracula has his own methods of "dark" technology that while often more immediate than those of the hunters—mesmerism, mind-control, blood-memory, physical transformation and mind reading—they are all considered as negatives exampling a degenerative past.
20. See also Franco Moretti, 1988, *Signs Taken for Wonders: Essays in the Sociology of Forms*, trans. Susan Fischer, David Forgacs and David Miller (London: Verso), and David McNally, 2012, *Monsters of the Market: Zombies, Vampires and Global Capitalism* (Chicago: Haymarket Books).

environmentally aware.[21] And while they could not be more different from the folkloric vampires from Eastern Europe from which they, arguably, began—poor, fat, and bloated with blood—or the feral, violent monsters from narratives like *30 Days of Night* (Slade 2007) they define the times that created them and highlighted characteristics that have remained "sticky" within the wider narrative world. This further points out an interesting feature of the wider narrative world around the vampire, in that it has become so extensive that it allows for very different fan bases to find and create their own version of the vampire to identify with; to paraphrase Nina Auerbach's idea of there not being a single Dracula but many Draculas, there is not one type of transmedia vampire but many. The *Twilight* franchise is the perfect example of this in terms of both the created world and the individual characters within it. Seeing it exist beyond the boundaries of the original story and films that allowed participants to enter and engage meaningfully with the vampiric world and own actual items from it, revealing that the borders between the two were not only permeable, but at times non-existent.

Something of the same was seen for the television series *True Blood* (Ball 2008–14), based on Charlene Harris's *Southern Vampire Mysteries* series of novels (2001–2013) which utilized many and varied forms of audience/participant engagement as well as exploited ways in which to meaningfully encroach on the real world. While much of its cross-platform world-building and modes of participation and engagement are similar to those discussed previously, maybe more than other vampire narratives, *True Blood* resonated with Goth subcultures and minority groups that have a strong belief in the "vampiric" or alternative lifestyles. Indeed, one of *True Blood*'s notable re-interpretations from earlier vampire narratives was its positivizing of non-normative sexualities and gender identities, which it utilized to engage more meaningfully with its audiences. Forums and "confessional" sites linked to the program and its characters—Baby Vamp Jessica being of particular note[22]—created audience identification and loyalty which further promoted franchise "stickiness."

While these communities do not make up a large proportion of the

---

21. There is much within the *Twilight* narrative world that speaks to both the transnational nature of the vampire and its audience, especially in terms of reception and engagement of "global" franchises in particular cultural locations—differing audiences engaging with different aspects and interpretations of the story world and its characters—as well as direct engagement or intersection with versions of vampires or vampire-like entities from other cultures. *Twilight* rather "white-washes" its views of vampires from other cultures, although many chances to engage with them appear in the final installments of the Saga.

22. See the series of blog posts; https://www.youtube.com/playlist?list=PLVMduFfrL_xdtxWwLaCrkHqZw2tGrebBp as well as an online discussion group https://jessicahamby.wordpress.com.

franchise's total audience/participants it is enough to illustrate the ways in which the transmedia vampire is not limited to any one platform or the virtual boundaries of the fictional narratives from which it arose, and that it creates an active presence in our world just as it invites us into its own.[23]

The Intersecting Worlds of the Transmedia Vampire

This volume is divided into four sections that focus on important areas within the study of the transmedia vampire, ranging from a consideration of the characters and world created in Stoker's seminal novel through to more recent examples of cross-platform vampires, to those that also cross cultural borders, and finally those where engagement and extraction come to the fore. "Part I: *Dracula*: Adaptations and Re-Creations" looks at Stoker's *Dracula* and the first surviving cinematic adaption from it to consider the ways that the story world developing from it has changed and evolved over time, sometimes positively and sometimes not. In "We Are Dracula: *Penny Dreadful* and the Dracula Megatext," Jeffrey Andrew Weinstock looks at the development of Dracula himself using the idea from science fiction of the "megatext." This sees the transmedia vampire as an ongoing accruement of details and characteristics creating the megatext that is "Dracula"; an entity that is the sum of all its parts, resonant and dissonant. In "'Better Parts': Redemptive Portrayals of Count Dracula as Vlad the Impaler in Selected Film Adaptions of Stoker's *Dracula*," Wayne Derek Pigeon-Coote discusses the humanizing of Stoker's vampire as a means to increase our identification with it and thus imbuing it with a greater reality. This, he explains, has been attempted through the linkage of the fictional Count and the actual historical figure of Vlad Țepeș (or Vlad the Impaler), achieving a humanizing that includes romanticizing the vampire and equating immortality with eternal love. Cathleen Allyn Conway's "'I've crossed oceans of versions to find you': Remediating Mina from Novel to Screen in *Bram Stoker's Dracula* (1992)" shifts the focus to the character of Mina Harker, who is neither alive nor dead at various points in the story and arguably, more abject than the vampire itself. Mina, as with Dracula, has undergone a revisionist connection to Vlad Țepeș but has potentially lost more than she gained in the process across centuries and mediums.

"Part II: Across Mediums, Platforms and Levels of Engagement" looks at

---

23. Curiously the shows links to "underground" subcultures reinforces one of the narratives major themes of hidden societies of vampires. Something also picked up with Anne Rice's *Vampire Chronicles*.

the specific effects of moving across mediums that have very different qualities and how it changes the construction of the vampire and our engagement with it. In "*Byzantium* Stage to Screen," Gina Wisker discusses how the play by Moira Buffini was adapted for the movies but also modified to suit the vampire credentials and intentions of the film's director Neil Jordan. Alongside these adjustments, Wisker also shows the weight of genre expectation and precedent that necessarily shapes, or is resisted by, the female vampire. In "Pixel Parasites: The Virtual Vampire as Enemy, Ally and Self in Video Games," Shawn Edrei considers the wider migration of vampires to virtual space and its adaption to and evolution with the ever-transforming gaming world. Derek Newman-Stille's "Vampire as Doll: Transformations of Meaning Through Play in the *Vampirina* and Draculaura (*Monster High*) Franchises" moves to the merchandising side of franchises, in particular those associated with dolls, connected to popular teenage shows *Monster High* and *Vampirina*. Both franchises have created their respective worlds from untypical starting points and see their ongoing engagement with their audiences taken into areas of play where the original authors no longer have control. The last essay in this section, "'Do Vampires Get Their Periods?': The *Carmilla* Web Series and the Politics of Bleeding Women," by Alexandra Heller-Nicholas, further examines the extended narrative world of franchises where branding and product placement/association collapses the boundaries between real and fictional worlds seeing vampires as ambassadors for female hygiene products.

"Part III: Transnational Transmedia," considers vampire story worlds from cultures outside of the dominant white, Anglo-American one and the ways in which they have managed to resist, incorporate or rewrite dominant Western franchises. The section begins with Lorna Piatti-Farnell's "Vampire Tourism: Transmedia Narratives, Cultural Histories and Locating the Undead," which looks at how seminal vampire narratives migrate from fictional to real spaces. Specifically, Piatti-Farnell shows how Stoker's narrative world subsumes the real history of locations such as Whitby or Transylvania often, as in the case of the latter, rewriting local and national history to fit that of the Transmedia Vampire. "Thinking in Connections: A.A. Carr's *Eye Killers* and F.W. Murnau's *Nosferatu*," by Svetlana Seibel, considers the appropriation and reimagining of the vampire figure by indigenous culture within North America. The section ends with Katarzyna Ancuta's "From Revenants to Vampires: The Transmedia Evolution of the *Jiangshi*," traveling further afield to consider the home grown "vampires" of China that have developed their own narrative world, though one that has increasingly encountered and appropriated features of more Western undead figures, creating curious resonances and dissonances between the two.

The final section, "Part IV: Interventions, Fandom, Ownership" considers more closely ideas around authorship and urtexts, adaptation and fandom and how agency is negotiated within Transmedia worlds. In "Transmedia Interventions and Palimpsestuous Relations: *Carmilla* Meets Carmen Maria Machado," Natalie Wilson looks at a contemporary female author's dialogue with the text of a seminal nineteenth century female vampire narrative, *Carmilla*. More so, Wilson considers this in the light of the palimpsest, the wiping clean and rewriting of a text, but one which inevitably leaves ghosts and gaps in the re-telling. "*The Originals* and Family History Two-Fold: Caught Between Two Worlds," by Verena Bernardi, looks at the resonances and dissonances of an expanding narrative world, where the side characters from one, namely the Mikaelsons from *The Vampire Diaries*, then become the central protagonists of their own spin-off series. This highlights the curious terrain of many franchises—in particular the newest episodes of the *Star Wars* franchise—that expand their narrative worlds backward; creating a past for characters that previously only had a present. Next, in "Transmedia Vampire Stories and Their Consumers in Anne Rice's *The Vampire Chronicles*," Laura Davidel discusses a similar phenomenon in relation to Anne Rice's novels where the author subsequently tries to maintain control of her characters as they move across mediums—though the characters themselves can be resistant to this. The section closes with Evan Hayles Gledhill's "First-Person Gothic: Anne Rice, Vampirism, Authorship and Identity," returning to the seminal figure of Anne Rice and seeing her ongoing attempts at retaining authorial control as resulting in her own transition to being a transmedia vampire author.

This collection begins to sketch out the emerging terrain of the transmedia vampire, one that is only ever getting larger and more interconnected. As new mediums become involved and the ways that readers/users/fans/collaborators become more entangled within the creation and evolution of narratives, who knows where the limits of the transmedia vampire might establish themselves? Or, whether the division between the virtual/imaginary world and the real world will dissolve so completely that we will no longer need to invite the vampire into our lives, for it will already be an intimate part of it.

Works Cited

Auerbach, Nina. 1996. *Our Vampires, Ourselves*. Chicago: University of Chicago.
Gelder, Ken. 2012. *New Vampire Cinema*. London: Palgrave Macmillan.
Jenkins, Henry. 2008. *Convergence Culture: Where Old and New Media Collide*. New York: New York University Press.

_____. 2018. "Foreword: 'I Have a Bad Feeling About This': A Conversation About Star Wars and the History of Transmedia." *Star Wars and the History of Transmedia Storytelling*, edited by Dan Hassler-Forest and Sean Guynes, Amsterdam: Amsterdam University Press, pp. 15–34.
Twitchell, James B. 1981. *The Living Dead: A Study of the Vampire in Romantic Literature*. Durham: Duke University Press.
Wicke, Jennifer. 1992. "Vampiric Typewriting: Dracula and Its Media." *ELH*, vol. 59, no. 2 Summer, pp. 467–493.
Wolf, Mark P. 2012. *Building Imaginary Worlds*. London: Routledge.

Part I
Dracula: Adaptations and Re-Creations

We Are Dracula

Penny Dreadful *and the Dracula Megatext*

JEFFREY ANDREW WEINSTOCK

A Date with Darkness

In "Predators Far and Near," the second episode of the third and final season of the Showtime/Sky Atlantic series *Penny Dreadful* (2014–16), series protagonist Vanessa Ives (Eva Green) has a date with Dracula. Having been instructed by her alienist Dr. Seward (Patti LuPone) to do something she believes will make her happy, "however capricious or unlikely," Vanessa returns to the London Natural History Museum where she had previously crossed paths with charmingly awkward and prim zoologist Dr. Alexander Sweet (Christian Camargo) in what she—and we—had assumed was a chance encounter. She discovers him in the midst of a public lecture to a group of women, transitioning from a consideration of foxes and dogs (*Canis Lupis Familiaris*, says Dr. Sweet, using the Latin, reminding us of the series' werewolf, referred to as *Lupis Dei*) to arachnids, and here we learn that Vanessa knows a good bit about scorpions, including that the smaller varieties are the most dangerous—that looks can be deceiving is a lesson Vanessa knows all too well.

Vanessa lingers following the lecture and, as she and Dr. Sweet perambulate through aisles of taxidermied animals in the museum, Dr. Sweet reveals himself to be only an armchair adventurer. While the museum displays are the result of naturalist expeditions around the globe, Dr. Sweet does not himself participate in such travels and explains that he is "not made for adventuring." Though as a child he had been captivated by Jules Verne, admiring the "swagger and freedom" of Captain Nemo in *Twenty-Thousand Leagues Under the Sea*, "We're not made of such stuff as our heroes, are we?" he laments. "But, if we can't walk with them, we can always follow," he adds. This admission prompts Vanessa (whose own hero, fittingly, she proposes is Joan of Arc) to extend an unusual and rather bold invitation: she invites Dr. Sweet to an evening at the theater—to view a cinematograph adaptation of *Twenty-Thousand Leagues Under the Sea*. Dr. Sweet accepts, although he balks at Vanessa's suggestion, they then go for a coffee afterward. That Dr. Sweet might not particularly relish coffee, however, makes good sense to the viewer because, at the end of the last episode of *Penny Dreadful*, "The Day Tennyson Died" (S3E1), he had revealed himself as Dracula, the master of all vampires; we also learned that Renfield (Samuel Barnett), Dr. Seward's secretary, is in thrall to Dracula and has been ordered to gather information about Vanessa. Despite her familiarity with creatures that bite and sting, it appears that Vanessa has not appreciated the lesson that looks can be deceiving fully enough.

The postmodern pastiche formula of the series is shown when Vanessa Ives, a character specific to *Penny Dreadful*, goes on a date with Dracula, a character originating in Bram Stoker's 1897 novel, but who has been adapted and appropriated countless times in other contexts, to see a cinematic adaptation of a nineteenth-century novel by Jules Verne. Further, it freely intermingles characters appropriated from Victorian novels with its own original inventions, inviting not just Vanessa Ives but the viewer as well along on a date with Dracula—or rather "Dracula" because this Dracula is not Stoker's Dracula, but instead an overdetermined vampiric figure with multiple points of origin. *Penny Dreadful*'s Dracula, as we shall see, certainly gestures in various ways toward Stoker's vampire ur-text, but he is just as much a product of subsequent representations.[24] The cinematograph performance of *Twenty-Thousand Leagues Under the Sea* is a case in point: Dracula in Stoker's novel is never shown going to the movies. In Francis Ford Coppola's 1992 *Bram Stoker's Dracula*, however, Mina Harker (Winona Ryder) dallies with a mysterious stranger calling himself Prince Vlad (Gary Oldman)—who we know to be Dracula—at "the amazing cinematograph." The feature shown in Coppola's adaptation is different than in *Penny Dreadful*—cinematic tricks a la Georges Méliès and a Lumière brothers-esque train rather than an imaginative adaptation of Jules Verne's 1870 novel—but the scenes are otherwise analogous: both Mina and Vanessa have dates with darkness at the cinema. *Penny Dreadful*'s scene involving Dracula thus, intentionally or accidentally, finds its point of reference not in Stoker, but in a late twentieth-century adaptation of Stoker that rescripts Dracula as a Byronic hero seeking to be reunited with his lost love—a plot that corresponds as well with *Penny Dreadful*'s depiction, as we shall see.

24. Stoker did not invent the vampire of course, but his novel is the text against which all subsequent vampiric representations are measured.

22   Part I—*Dracula*: Adaptations and Re-Creations

"Vanessa and Dr. Sweet/Dracula at the Movies," with Christian Camargo as Dr. Sweet and Eva Green as Vanessa. *Penny Dreadful*, created by John Logan (Showtime Networks: 2014–16).

The Dracula Megatext

Scholars have addressed the contemporary practice of detaching characters from their original literary or cinematic contexts and reimagining them in a variety of ways. In her consideration of *Penny Dreadful* as part of her study of contemporary "monster mashups," for example, Megen de Bruin-Molé suggests, citing Dan Hassler-Forest, that each new version of a famous monster such as Dracula further develops the "storyworld" associated with the character. "In a culture where Frankenstein's monster (for instance) has transcended any single text and become a popular myth," she writes, "a work that utilizes the character in a new context can be seen to build onto that tradition, rather than overwriting or even re-writing it" (2020, 43). Dragoș Manea takes things the next step in his discussion of *Penny Dreadful* by suggesting that once famous monsters have storyworlds in which they float freely, detached from a specific source text, they become "archetypal": "Vampires, werewolves, monsters of all shapes and sizes carry with them a media history. The most famous of them—Dracula, the Wolf Man, Frankenstein's Monster—are easily recognizable staples of popular culture, grounded perhaps in an original text, but given shape in our collective memory through countless retellings, remakes, and reimaginings" (40). Benjamin Poore turns to Kamilla Elliott's six categories of adaptation articulated in her 2003 *Rethinking the Novel/Film Debate* to argue that *Penny Dreadful* primarily operates in the "De(Re)composing mode" in which, according to Elliott, "novel and film"—or, in the case of *Penny Dreadful*, novels and television series—"decompose, merge, and form a new composition at 'underground' levels of reading" (157). Adaptations such as these are "composite[s] of textual and filmic signs merging in audience consciousness together with other cultural narratives and often [lead] to confusion as to which is novel and which is film" (157). Such adaptations are often criticized as "unfaithful," although their alleged infidelities, notes Elliott, often do find their basis in the source text in details readers tend to overlook (157).

All three of these approaches—storyworld, archetype, and de(re)composition as a mode of adaptation—seek to address how we come to appreciate fictional characters that not only have become detached from their point of origin in a particular work, but that, as a consequence of multiple subsequent representations in various texts, transcend being specific characters and become more general character types. The Draculas in Bram Stoker's *Dracula*, *Penny Dreadful*, Francis Ford Coppola's *Bram Stoker's Dracula*, Terence Fisher's *Horror of Dracula* (1958), John Badham's 1979 *Dracula*, Daniel S. Goyer's *Blade: Trinity* (2004), and so on differ dramatically and yet they are all Dracula—and, as Elliott suggests, the various representations "merge" in the audience's consciousness until it becomes difficult to disentangle the different aspects of the composite representation.

For my part, I would like to borrow a term generally associated with science fiction studies—the idea of the "megatext"—as a useful way to consider not only how Dracula functions in *Penny Dreadful*, but how he circulates in twenty-first-century culture. In *Science Fiction: A Guide for the Perplexed* (2014), Sherryl Vint devotes an entire chapter to the idea of the megatext, noting that the term was coined by Damien Broderick to refer to the way that science fiction is "generated and received ... within a specialised intertextual encyclopaedia of tropes and enabling devices" (Broderick qtd. in Vint, 57). The megatext, explains Vint, "reveals the way that sf explicitly refers back to earlier instances of itself, each text adding to and playing with the larger body of signs, images, and scenarios that make up sf's shared world" (57). The idea here, continues Vint, is not just that later works of science fiction explicitly reference or allude to earlier ones. Megatext instead:

> describes a context in which writers operate within an understanding of a certain set of established images and motifs, such as cyborgs or hyperspace or FTL [Faster Than Light] travel, that do not belong to any single text or author, but are

shared, each new iteration both relying upon established meanings and associations, and also opening them up to new possibilities, creating a vast and interconnected web of meanings that exceeds what appears in any single text [57].

Coincidentally suggesting a connection with *Penny Dreadful*, a series that includes Victor Frankenstein and his creation, Vint explains that "Certain prominent texts become dense centers of gravity, inevitably pulling the meaning of icons toward their influential formulations. For example, any created being in sf carries a trace of Frankenstein's Creature" (57). Important here is that the "megatextual" understanding of genre "requires a certain kind of apprenticeship of both reader and writer to fully perceive the complex web of meanings evoked by certain words, images, and scenarios.... A large part of the pleasure of reading sf," Vint concludes, "comes from the interplay between familiarity and novelty that is created by interactions between individual texts and sf's larger history" (58).

Appropriating this idea of the megatext from science fiction studies, I wish to propose here something we may call the "Dracula megatext." Congruent in ways with the idea of a Dracula storyworld or a consideration of Dracula as archetype, the idea of the Dracula megatext has the advantage of allowing us to acknowledge not only Stoker's novel as a "dense center of gravity" at the core of the representation, but also the roles that familiarity with vampire narratives in general and Dracula stories in particular play in the pleasure derived from consumption of contributions to the megatext. In the same way that every science fiction narrative involving created beings (robots, AIs, cyborgs, etc.) finds its roots in Shelley's ur-text *Frankenstein*, all twentieth- and twenty-first-century vampire narratives—whether explicitly naming their vampire Dracula or not—unavoidably have as a point of reference Stoker's novel. What is more, creators of new Dracula texts, themselves possessing a general understanding of the "web of meanings" associated with the vampire, can assume, at least to a certain extent, a conversance with the "established meanings and associations" connected to the vampire on the part of their audience. Each new iteration of the vampire in general and Dracula in particular thus charts a path between the poles of repetition and innovation, and, as Vint suggests of science fiction, much of the enjoyment of Dracula narratives is derived from the interplay of comfortable familiarity and surprising novelty.

Indeed, vampire narratives in general often insist on being read as part of a more general vampire megatext through scenes of explicit intertextuality as vampire experts rehearse the history and characteristics of vampires for the benefit of neophyte hunters and the audience, referencing the literary and cinematic tradition in the process. In Stephen King's 1975 novel *Salem's Lot*, for example—a novel inspired by King's pondering about "what would happen if Dracula came back in the twentieth century, to America" (King 2014, n.p.)—preparation for combating vampiric antagonist Kurt Barlow (actor's name) involves author Ben Mears (actor's name) turning to the vampire literary tradition and reviewing Stoker's *Dracula*, as well as other works ranging from James Malcolm Rymer's penny dreadful, *Varney the Vampire* (serialized 1845–47) to the comic book *Vampirella* (introduced in 1969). Along similar lines, in Joel Schumacher's 1987 film *The Lost Boys*, young vampire hunters Edgar (Corey Feldman) and Alan (Jamison Newlander) derive their understanding of vampires from the horror comics they avidly consume. This process of rehearsing the familiar characteristics of vampires for the benefit of both less-knowledgeable characters and the audience then allows for an appreciation of not only the narrative's adherence to tradition, but of its innovations as well. Using King's *Salem's Lot* as an example again, religious icons in the text do not possess the intrinsic prophylactic power against vampires that they do in Stoker; instead, they depend upon the faith of their wielder—while the faith of King's character Father Callahan (actor's name) remains strong, his cross repels the vampire Barlow; when his faith falters, the cross no longer protects him. Viewers conversant with the vampire tradition are well positioned to appreciate this as King's riff on the genre.

These innovations can then be incorporated into the megatext and may be repeated to the point where they become canon. Religious icons as conduits for their bearers' faith as depicted in King then gets reprised in Tom Holland's *Fright Night* (1985) where Peter Vincent's crucifix wards off vampire Jerry Dandrige, but only while his faith remains firm. And then in Robert Rodriguez's *From Dusk till Dawn* (1996), it is not until Jacob recovers his faith that he can finally act as a vessel of God's power and bless his friends' weapons.

An even more striking example of a post–Stoker contribution to the general vampire megatext is the increasing flammability of the vampire. In Stoker's novel, Dracula can and does move about during the day. That this is surprising to many is due to the effect of subsequent adaptations, especially cinematic ones. It is in fact F.W. Murnau's cinematic adaptation of *Dracula*, *Nosferatu*, in 1922 that introduces the notion of sunlight as fatal as our vampire Count Orlock (Max Schrek), held in thrall by protagonist Ellen's (Greta Schröder) willing self-sacrifice, is caught off-guard by the sunrise and disappears in a disappointingly small puff of smoke. Because the dissolution of the vampire presents such a compelling visual image, it not surprisingly then received consistent elaboration over the course of the twentieth century and into the twenty-first with the effects of sunlight becoming increasingly dramatic. In *The Horror of Dracula* (Terence Fisher: 1958), when exposed to sunlight by Van Helsing (Peter Cushing) (who pins the supine Dracula, played by Christopher Lee, in place using two crossed candlesticks!), Dracula graphically dissolves and turns to dust; William Crain's

Blacula (1972) riffs on this by having its melancholic anti-hero (played by William Marshall) commit suicide by walking into the sun—his decomposition is quite graphic and includes maggots squirming on his face. In Tomas Alfredson's *Let the Right One In* (*Låt den rätte komma in*, Alfredson's 2008 adaptation of John Ajvide Lindqvist's 2004 novel of the same name), vampires exposed to sunlight literally burst into flames. The death by sunlight trope has been repeatedly so frequently that it is now assumed to be a central characteristic of the vampire megatext—and, as such, it becomes available for revision as in the *Twilight* franchise (2008–2012) in which sunlight causes vampires to sparkle rather than burn or decay.

The Dracula megatext, which overlaps significantly with the more general vampire megatext, then consists of the constellation of representations of and narratives involving Dracula. Each new contribution to the megatext is by necessity overdetermined, with its origins traceable back to multiple possible sources. Although there are inevitably traces of Stoker— one cannot use the name Dracula without having Stoker's text as a point of reference, exerting its gravitational attraction—new entries into the megatext also draw from and innovate upon all the subsequent adaptations and appropriations of Stoker's character and narrative. Put differently, it is hard to trace blood back to a single source, when it is pouring in from all sides. Nevertheless, turning our attention back to *Penny Dreadful*, the remainder of this essay will do three things: it will first consider the familiar framework of *Penny Dreadful*'s Dracula narrative, showing the ways that the series uses repetition to establish its indebtedness to the literary tradition; it will then explore how *Penny Dreadful* revises the Dracula narrative, aligning it both with broader trends in vampiric representation and with contemporary anxieties related to global destruction; finally, it will consider the convergence of *Penny Dreadful*'s Dracula megatext with others as part of the series' "monster mashup."[25]

What's in a Name?

Interestingly, the word "vampire" is only used once in the first season of *Penny Dreadful*—and, notably, it is in conjunction with the only time the

25. As Bruin-Molé addresses in her 2020 *Gothic Remixed: Monster Mashups and Frankenfictions in 21st-Century Culture*, our current moment is marked by a profusion of narratives that, like *Penny Dreadful*, combine monsters from different sources in the same text. "Films and shows like *Van Helsing* (2004), *Mary Shelley's Frankenhole* (2010–12), *Once Upon a Time* (2011–18), *Hotel Transylvania* (2012), … *Castlevania* (2017–19), and even *Monster High* (2010–15)," writes Bruin-Molé, together with various book series and video games, songs, and other media, have helped popularize what she refers to as the "monster mash" genre, which "builds new stories through the amalgamation of well-known literary texts and monsters" (42).

title phrase, "penny dreadful," is used in the series' entire run. Having been introduced in episode 3 of season 1, "Demimonde," the character Abraham van Helsing (David Warner) serves as a hematologist in the employ of Sir Malcolm Murray (Timothy Dalton). Together with Victor Frankenstein (Harry Treadaway), Van Helsing is tasked with seeking a cure for a blood disease Sir Malcolm believes afflicts his kidnapped daughter Mina. It is in episode 6 of season 1, "What Death Can Join Together," that Van Helsing, playing his traditional role from Stoker as vampire expert, introduces the word "vampire" to the program, and he does so by way of referencing James Malcolm Rymer's nineteenth-century penny dreadful, *Varney the Vampire*. "Do you know the word 'vampire'?" Van Helsing asks Victor. When Victor answers no, Van Helsing explains that it is unfamiliar to many "Aside from a small percentage of the reading public with a taste in a certain kind of literature. A penny dreadful?" "One in particular," he continues, "As literature it is uninspiring, but as folklore from the Balkans popularized, it is not without merit. Mr. Rymer missed the facts, but he caught the truth. There is on this earth a creature that exceeds what is commonly known as the limits of life and death. This creature feeds on the blood of the living and can have transformative effects on those upon which it preys." Rather remarkably, it is not until seventh episode of season 2, "Little Scorpion," that the word vampire is used again—this time, as I shall develop below, with a more expansive understanding of the monster that goes beyond anything suggested in Rymer, or Stoker for that matter.

Used even more sparingly in the series is the name Dracula. In fact, it is not until the end of the first episode of the third season, "The Day Tennyson Died," that the name is uttered—and it is done, as noted above—by the master vampire himself who reveals to Renfield and the viewer the true identity of the story's central protagonist. It is thus a curious feature of the program that, despite having Stoker's *Dracula* as a central point of reference and vampires as primary antagonists, these linguistic markers are seldom used until the third season.

Rather than announce the series' focus on Dracula and vampires at the start then, *Penny Dreadful* instead playfully enlists engagement by drawing upon the viewer's knowledge of the Dracula megatext (intertwining it of course with the Frankenstein megatext, as well as with knowledge of *Dorian Gray* and, later, *Jekyll and Hyde*). This is primarily done through using character names as reference points. At the start of season 1, Sir Malcolm Murray, a character not present in Stoker, is substituted for his daughter Mina, who has been abducted, and Sir Malcolm's search for his daughter becomes the driving force of the first season. As noted above, Abraham van Helsing is introduced as a blood specialist and vampire expert (who is quickly killed off!) and then, in season 3, substituting for Stoker's Dr. John

Seward, Dr. Florence Seward is introduced as an alienist and Mr. Renfield is her secretary. While there are occasional small flourishes taken from Stoker that reward viewer knowledge—Florence, for example, was the name of Bram Stoker's wife, and Dr. Seward in the program records patient consultations on wax cylinders as the character does in the book—the narrative in general departs so extensively from Stoker's text that names function as the primary anchors attaching *Penny Dreadful* to the Dracula megatext. But so deeply entrenched in popular culture is the Dracula megatext that names are all that are needed to initiate a process of reader or viewer comparison.

His Name Is Legion

Having signaled through character names that *Penny Dreadful* will participate in the Dracula megatext, the series then departs in substantial ways from Stoker's narrative and draws instead from other threads of the megatext that have been overlaid on Stoker and are now inextricably associated with Dracula and vampires. I will attend to four of these threads here: the Satanic, the Egyptian, the Immortal Beloved, and the Werewolf Antagonist.

In Stoker's *Dracula*, Dracula's origins are never specified. Dracula himself reveals to Jonathan Harker that he fought against the Turks, and Van Helsing speculates that he is Vlad the Impaler, the "Voivode Dracula who won his name against the Turks, over the great river on the very frontier of Turkey-land" (1993, 309). However, how Dracula became a vampire is never explained. We also know that Dracula is Satanic; not only is he repelled by Christian icons, but Van Helsing makes this abundantly clear when he explains the consequences of failing to stop Dracula:

> It is that we become as him; that we henceforward become foul things of the night like him—without heart or conscience, preying on the bodies and the souls of those we love best. To us for ever are the gates of heaven shut; for who shall open them to us again? We go on for all time abhorred by all; a blot on the face of God's sunshine; an arrow in the side of Him who died for man [305].

However, again, Stoker does not explain how Dracula became a vampire or what he did to deserve the curse of vampirism.

Later contributions to the Dracula megatext have sought to fill in the gaps left by Stoker by explaining what Dracula did to become accursed by God and how he became a vampire. In Coppola's *Bram Stoker's Dracula*, for example, Coppola invents a backstory for Dracula nowhere present in Stoker's text. A sequence at the start of the film shows us Vlad Dracul (Gary Oldman) returning from a successful campaign against the Turks only to discover that his beloved wife, Elisabeta (Winona Ryder), has committed suicide as a consequence of false rumors of her husband's death. The distraught Dracula desecrates his chapel and renounces God, raving that he will rise from the dead to avenge his wife; he then stabs the chapel's stone cross with his sword and drinks the blood that pours from it in a kind of literalized, profane communion. Coppola thus shows us the moment that Dracula, by virtue of turning his back on God, becomes a vampire. Taking things to the next step is the lackluster *Dracula 2000* (Patrick Lussier, 2000) in which Dracula (Gerard Butler) is revealed to be none other than Judas Iscariot himself, cursed to live 2000 years as a vampire for his betrayal of Jesus; that Dracula cannot tolerate silver—a detail also not present in Stoker and that seems to have been imported into the Dracula megatext from werewolf narratives—is thus explained by the fact that Judas betrayed Jesus for thirty pieces of silver. Dracula here has not just renounced God, but literally betrayed Jesus.

Penny Dreadful elaborates on this Satanic thread of the vampire megatext almost as far as it can go by making Dracula "brother" to Satan. The pieces of an eleventh-century manuscript, written in the "devil's language" (the "Verbis Diablo") when deciphered by *Penny Dreadful*'s resident Egyptologist and linguistics expert Ferdinand Lyle (Simon Russell Beale) in the second season, tell the tale of two angelic brothers cast out of heaven for opposing God:

> One brother to earth and the other brother to hell. And thus were we set in eternal enmity. My brother on earth to feed on the blood of the living by night. And myself in hell to feed on the souls of the dead. Both in an eternal quest for the Mother of Evil who will release us from our bondage and allow one of us to reconquer heaven and topple God from his bloody throne ["Memento Mori," season 2, episode 8].

"Apparently Lucifer isn't an only child," quips Mr. Lyle, as the team speculates that the brother cast to earth is the "vampire master" that abducted Mina.

This theory about Dracula's identity is then confirmed in season 3, notably in the stand-out episode "A Blade of Grass" (season 3, episode 4) in which Vanessa, through hypnotic regression, is returned to her period of confinement at an institution called Banning Clinic. During her confinement, she was visited both by Lucifer and his demonic brother, each of whom took the form of the tender orderly assisting her—who, in an inspired detail, is the man who will later become John Clare, Victor Frankenstein's creature (Rory Kinnear). Vanessa is able to recall that both Lucifer and his brother sought her willing submission, which would then usher in the apocalypse. When she asked the latter his name, he responded, "I am the Demon. I am the Dragon. My name is Dracula." Through a century-long process of elaboration, Dracula's antagonism toward God, present without explanation in Stoker's source text, has developed from heresy to betrayal to supernatural opposition.

This Satanic thread of the Dracula megatext in *Penny Dreadful* is then interwoven with what we can call the Egyptian thread of vampire mythology. The Victorian vogue for Egyptology is absent from Stoker's *Dracula* (although central to his later mummy narrative, *The Jewel of the Seven Stars* [1903]). Later vampire narratives, however, have frequently associated Dracula in particular and vampires in general with Egypt and the Middle East more generally. Notable in this respect are Whitley Strieber's novel, *The Hunger* (1981), and Anne Rice's *Vampire Chronicles* series of books. *The Hunger* explains that vampires originated in Egypt as a long-lived species, while Rice in the third entry to the Vampire Chronicles series, *The Queen of the Damned* (1988), explains the existence of vampires as a form of demonic possession originating in ancient Egypt.

Penny Dreadful riffs on this aspect of vampire mythology, incorporating it into the Dracula megatext by not only making Dracula a demon, but associating him with Egyptian mythology. Somewhat confusingly, *Penny*

"I am the Demon. I am the Dragon. My name is Dracula." Rory Kinnear as John Clare and Eva Green as Vanessa Ives. *Penny Dreadful*, created by John Logan (Showtime Networks: 2014–16).

Dreadful connects Dracula and Vanessa Ives with Egyptian gods Amunet and Amun-ra. Mr. Lyle explains in season 2, episode 7 ("Little Scorpion") that "The gods Amunet and Amun-ra were immortal and their love was without end as well. According to the myth, if they were to become conjoined all light would end and the world would live in darkness. The hidden ones would emerge and rule…. In Biblical terms, it's the coming of the beast." In response to Vanessa's query about "the hidden ones," Mr. Lyle explains, "Call them the fallen angels, as our relics do. Or any such name that pleases you. Devil, creature, demon. Vampire? His name is legion, for he is many." The proposition is thus that Vanessa is in some way the human avatar of Amunet. If she reunites with Amun-ra, AKA Dracula, light will fade and eternal darkness will reign.

It is then through the Amunet/Amun-ra Egyptian thread that *Penny Dreadful* introduces what I am calling the "Immortal Beloved" thread of the Dracula megatext. In Stoker's novel, Dracula pursues Lucy, Mina, and the other characters not out of affection but rather as a predator pursuing prey. Increasingly, however, Dracula has been portrayed as a melancholic lover seeking to be reunited with a reincarnated bride. This, of course, is often the central motivation of mummy narratives as in 1932 version directed by Karl Freund and its later remakes in which revived mummified Egyptian prince Imhotep (played by Boris Karloff in the 1932 version) believes his lost love Ankh-es-en-Amon has been reincarnated as the modern woman Helen Grosvenor (Zita Johann in the 1932 film). This same narrative of lost love and reincarnation plays out in the 1972 blaxploitation film *Blacula* and in Coppola's 1992 *Bram Stoker's Dracula*. In *Blacula*, the title character believes that he has found the reincarnation of his lost love Luva (Vonetta McGee). In *Bram Stoker's Dracula*, Dracula believes Mina to be the reincarnation of his lost Elisabeta (a conclusion reinforced for the viewer by having Winona Ryder play both Mina and Elisabeta).

Penny Dreadful then draws inspiration from this mix of reference points, plucking Dracula and other characters from Stoker's novel and infusing the narrative with elements of the Egyptian and Immortal Beloved variants. Dracula, we discover, is the god/demon referred to by the Egyptians as Amun-ra. Vanessa is his lost consort, Amunet. If she gives herself freely to him, the consummation of their love will result in the end of the world as they two will rule over eternal darkness.

What stands in their way, apart from Vanessa's own devotion to Sir Malcolm, her friends, and the world she knows, is one final element that has become central to vampire narratives and the Dracula megatext: the werewolf antagonist. In Stoker's *Dracula*, Dracula feels a kind of kinship with wolves—the "children of the night" (29) as he refers to them. He seems to assume the form of a wolf when he arrives in Whitby aboard the

Demeter and an escaped wolf from the zoo assists his assault upon the Westenra family. The history of cinema however has been one of growing antagonism between Dracula (and vampires in general) and werewolves that often pivots along class lines and associations. While the early monster mashup film *The House of Frankenstein* (Erle C. Kenton, 1944) features both Dracula (John Carradine) and the Wolf Man (Lon Chaney, Jr.) the two do not actually meet. The first film that pits the two against each another is most likely *Abbott and Costello Meet Frankenstein* (Charles Barton, 1948), which has Dracula (Belá Lugosi), the Wolf Man (Lon Chaney, Jr.), and Frankenstein's monster (Glenn Strange) plaguing Abbott and Costello. The deep-seated antagonism between vampires and werewolves in general, however, becomes a central theme in the first part of the twenty-first century in the *Twilight* franchise (novels 2005–2008), the *Underworld* franchise (films 2003–2017), and the *True Blood* novels (*Southern Vampire Mysteries* series 2001–2013) and television series (HBO, 2008–2014). In all three franchises, vampires and werewolves are enemies, with vampires dismissing werewolves as provincial and animalistic. The conceit of vampires turning up their noses at their hairier supernatural cousins is now so firmly entrenched in vampire narrative that it can be played with, as in the reality-TV vampire parody, *What We Do in the Shadows* (Jemaine Clement and Taika Waititi, 2014) in which vampires and werewolves are initially at odds but come together as friends in the end.[26]

Penny Dreadful makes the vampire/werewolf opposition central as Dracula's apocalyptic desires are thwarted by werewolf Ethan Chandler (Josh Hartnett). Ethan—whose real name within the series we learn is Ethan Talbot (a reference to the character Larry Talbot, played by Lon Chaney, Jr., who becomes the Wolf Man in the 1941 film directed by George Waggner)—vies with Dracula for Vanessa's affection. For reasons never adequately explained by the series, werewolves are *Lupus Dei*, "the wolf of God," and, despite their bloody curse, they serve a kind of holy purpose as vampire antagonists. In the series' lackluster finale, "The Blessed Dark" (season 3, episode 9), Ethan has traveled back from America to come to Vanessa's aid. While his companions fend off vampires and give him cover, he discovers Vanessa and, at her request, kills her with a bullet, thus averting the apocalypse. Though Ethan has not used his claws or teeth in the service of God here (and the bullet is not even silver!), he has nevertheless thwarted Dracula's design and presumably helped save mankind.

26. A similar friendship is seen in the series *Being Human* (Whithouse: 2008–13), and its American adaptation *Being Human* (Carver: 2011–14) where a ghost, a vampire, and a werewolf share a house together.

The Megatext Mashup

Penny Dreadful is, in the end, a contribution to the Dracula megatext that plucks Dracula along with other familiar characters from Stoker's text and then stages a conflict that is inflected through the lenses of other specific elements of the megatext: Satanic origins, Egyptian mythology, lost lovers, and werewolf antagonism. One final element that must be remarked here, however, is the way in which *Penny Dreadful* weaves together elements taken from *Dracula* with aspects of other nineteenth-century novels: Shelley's *Frankenstein* (first published 1818), Wilde's *The Picture of Dorian Gray* (1890), and Stevenson's *The Strange Case of Dr. Jekyll and Mr. Hyde* (1886). This tapestry of reference points returns us to our starting point, a cinematograph performance of *Twenty-Thousand Leagues Under the Sea*, because this scene does not just allude to Coppola's *Bram Stoker's Dracula*, but Alan Moore's comic book series, *The League of Extraordinary Gentlemen*.[27] What Moore does in *The League of Extraordinary Gentlemen* (both comic books [1999–present] and film adaptation [Norrington 2003]) is to bring together characters from different Victorian novels, including Mina Harker from *Dracula*—who in this reimagining is a vampire—Dorian Gray from Wilde's novel, Dr. Jekyll and Mr. Hyde from Stevenson's novel, and Captain Nemo from Jules Verne's *Twenty-Thousand Leagues Under the Sea*. These characters are required to join forces to stop various nefarious plots for world domination. So when Vanessa and Dr. Sweet/Dracula attend the showing of *Twenty-Thousand Leagues*, this scene not only parallels the scene of Mina and Dracula at the cinematograph in *Bram Stoker's Dracula*, but also playfully references *The League of Extraordinary Gentlemen*—a comic book series and film to which *Penny Dreadful* has often been compared due to its incorporation of many of the same characters.

What this suggests, finally, is that part of the Dracula megatext is now its inclusion of monsters derived from other novels (and one could reasonably characterize other monster megatexts, such as the Frankenstein one, in the same way). The proliferation of narratives pairing Dracula with other monsters means that the Dracula megatext now ironically exceeds itself, overlapping as it does with other monstrous megatexts. As with superhero narratives, the ubiquity of monster mashups makes it increasingly difficult to consider any monster on its own, apart from the other monsters with which it is routinely paired. We are thus moving toward a megatext mashup in which the histories of individual monsters converge and overlap; as a

27. *The League of Extraordinary Gentlemen* began publication in 1999 (it continues today) and was loosely adapted as a film of the same name in 2003 starring Sean Connery (directed by Stephen Norrington—that both Connery and Timothy Dalton have played James Bond is another connection, but outside the scope of this essay).

consequence, it will become increasingly difficult to just have a date with Dracula without Frankenstein, the Wolf Man, and the rest of the gang coming along for the ride.

Works Cited

De Bruin-Molé, Megen. 2020. *Gothic Remixed: Monster Mashups and Frankenfictions in 21st-Century Culture*. London: Bloomsbury Academic.
Dragoş, Manea. 2016. "A Wolf's Eye View of London: *Dracula*, *Penny Dreadful*, and the Logic of Repetition." *Critical Survey*, vol. 28, no. 1, pp. 40–50.
Elliott, Kamilla. 2003. *Rethinking the Novel/Film Debate*. Cambridge: Cambridge University Press.
King, Stephen. 2014. "'Salem's Lot." StephenKing.com. https://www.stephenking.com/library/novel/_salem_s_lot_inspiration.html.
Poore, Benjamin. 2016. "The Transformed Beast: *Penny Dreadful*, Adaptation, and the Gothic." *Victoriographies*, vol. 6, no. 1, pp. 62–81.
Stoker, Bram. 1993. *Dracula* [1897]. London: Penguin.
Vint, Sherryl. 2014. *Science Fiction: A Guide for the Perplexed*. London: Bloomsbury.

"Better Parts"

Redemptive Portrayals of Count Dracula as Vlad the Impaler in Selected Film Adaptions of Stoker's Dracula

WAYNE DEREK PIGEON-COOTE

This essay will look at the figure of Count Dracula and show how *Dracula* (Curtis, 1974), *Bram Stoker's Dracula* (Coppola, 1992) and *Dracula Untold* (Shore, 2014) redeem Bram Stoker's vampire by affecting the way in which the films' respective audiences are able to identify with the undead aristocrat. This involves a migration across media that sees Count Dracula evolve from a malevolent demonic creature that haunted Stoker's novel and become an increasingly humanized, sympathetic figure on screen primarily by connecting the fictional Dracula to the real historical figure of Vlad Țepeș.

Stoker's Enigmatic Vampire

Stoker introduces Count Dracula to us as almost non-human. When Jonathan Harker meets him, he cannot reconcile the peculiarities of his host with his "remarkable ruddiness" and the "astonishing vitality" of the lips, even though Dracula is supposedly an old man. This sense of otherworldliness is exacerbated when Harker further notices his "peculiarly sharp white teeth," pale ears and "extraordinary pallor" (Stoker 1997, 23–4). As the story continues the supernatural nature of Count Dracula increases. He is shown crawling along the exterior walls of his castle, changing into a bat and casting off the corporeal shape altogether, vanishing into elemental dust, seeing him capable of coming and going undetected, making him metaphorically and literally the stuff of nightmares.

In this sense Dracula does not actually exist and may be just a figment of the beholder's imagination, or even a psychic projection of some kind. This is suggested in the novel when Harker is shaving in front of a mirror and hears the Count behind him. He notes: "no sign of a man in it, except myself" (Stoker 1997, 31). The vampire cannot be seen in the mirror as it only exists in Harker's mind. This does not necessarily discount supernatural causes but does suggest using a psychoanalytic reading, where vampirism can be read as "something already lurking inside," a manifestation of "a second self" (Skal 2004, 59). For Stoker and Late Victorian society this "something" would largely be interpreted as the things they most obviously repress such as transgressive sexuality (see Craft 1984, 107–8). In fact, this is exemplified quite soon after the shaving incident when Harker is confronted by the Count's brides who similarly materialize out of thin air. Once confronted by these three apparitions the betrothed and devotedly chaste Harker experiences a "wicked, burning desire" to be kissed and, by implication, bitten and penetrated, despite his "dreamy" and "deadly" fears of such intimacy (Stoker 1997, 42). Harker admits that to know the sexual nature of his encounter with Dracula's brides would cause his fiancée pain, but remains faithful to Mina only due to Dracula's interruption rather than successful repression of his desire. Interestingly, there is no scene in *Dracula* that describes the Count biting a man. We rather we see him sinking his teeth into Harker's wife, Mina. This is of note as Mina, as his wife, is effectively the property of Harker when she is bitten by the Count and does little to hinder the vampire, despite his "reeking lips" (Stoker 1997, 251). It is almost as if she is acting out her husband's transgressive sexual longings. In this sense Count Dracula is purposely made into an abject and dangerous figure not only manifesting Harker's repressed desires but able to unleash them across the entire population of Britain, starting with the women and turning them into insatiable nymphomaniacs (Dijkstra 1988, 347).

Despite this, though, Stoker does hint that his non-human monster is not totally without a soul and across the pages of the novel drops the crumbs of his former humanity. This is largely centered around his sense of loss and living far longer than the human three score and ten years. We initially hear the Count tell Harker that he is burdened with "a heart not attuned to mirth ... through weary years of mourning over the dead" (Stoker 1997, 29). This is later reinforced by his brides who reproach him for having never loved, which is countered with the Count's "soft whisper" of "Yes, I too can love; you yourselves can tell it from the past. Is it not so?" (Stoker 1997, 43). Indeed, it can be inferred that if he remains at home, Dracula is condemned to be haunted forever by those he is no longer able to love. England then would seem to be a way to escape this, though even there he is drawn to the same memory-laden surroundings as seen in

Carfax Abbey. Once there, however, it is not the Count that expresses his loss, but rather it is recognized and pitied by another, namely Mina herself. Even though she has seen her friend killed and her husband violated by the vampire, Mina still believes that "one ought to pity any thing so hunted as is the Count" (Stoker 1997, 202). She pleads for compassion, successfully tempering her husband's hatred with her conviction that "That poor soul who has wrought all this misery is the saddest case of all. Just think what will be his joy when he [...] is destroyed in his worser part that his better part may have spiritual immortality. You must be pitiful" (Stoker 1997, 269). This finds its culmination at the story's end when the Count, on the point of expiring, dematerializes and Mina expresses gladness that "even in that moment [...] there was in the face a look of peace, such as I never could have imagined might have rested there" (Stoker 1997, 325). This starkly contrasts with Van Helsing's opinion of Count Dracula as one "predestinate to crime" and as an "evil thing ... rooted deep in all good" (Stoker 1997, 213).

Of course, Stoker does not allow his monster to be redeemed or redeemable as to do so would be to accept the darkness within himself and the Late Victorian society. As such, Mina's sympathy is shown as a point of danger not just to her marriage and her husband but the British Empire itself. However, movement across time and media have changed this necessarily negative image of Dracula as a supernatural and existential threat. Curiously, one of the most obvious ways this has happened is through the fictional connection between the literary Dracula and the historical figure of the same name. In fact, although Stoker used the name of Vlad III, Vlad Dracula (1431–1476/7), for his vampire he was not based upon the actual person but rather just the occasional details that suited the author's story. Yet, it was this fictional connection to historical reality that was to provide humanity to Stoker's non-human monster.

Dan Curtis' *Dracula* (1974)

It should be noted that the transition from novel to film did not in itself make Dracula seem more human, or even more real. F.W. Murnau's *Nosferatu* (1922), one of the earliest adaptations of Stoker's story to survive on film, makes the Count seem even more ethereal and a nightmare that literally disintegrates in the light of day. Tod Browning's *Dracula* (1931) fares little better and although the vampire does not evaporate into thin air, he never seems human in a relatable way. Indeed, even the lurid freshness of the Hammer Dracula films from the late 1950s to the early 1970s, while showing the contemporary reality of the Count, never make him a sympathetic character, and certainly not in the way that Dan Curtis' vampire is. *Dracula* (Curtis, 1974) names its vampire Vlad Țepeș, Prince of Wallachia (Warchol 2003, 7), linking him to the real historical person and instantly creating a link to a former human self. Alongside this he is no paler than Harker (Murray Brown), and is presented as distinctly non-vampiric, appearing natural and real, as compared with Stoker's seemingly more supernatural or psychic manifestation discussed above. Establishing the vampire's reality further, Curtis's Dracula (Jack Palance) never transforms into any animal (Silver and Ursini 2011, 94), and does not fade away at the end, providing corporeal proof of his existence even in death. We even see Dracula grimace when he is shot showing that even if he has superhuman abilities he is sufficiently human to feel and show pain.

In fact, pain seems to define Jack Palance's portrayal of Dracula in Curtis' film. Unlike many other portrayals of the Count, Palance is constantly and visibly ill-at-ease with himself, and even his fangs appear to cause him continual discomfort. The vampire is distressed rather than excited at the sight of blood, and when Harker cuts himself, it only serves as a troubling reminder of his baser instincts (Silver and Ursini 2011, 95). The essential mechanics of vampirism thus bring about "a kind of existential anguish" (Silver and Ursini 2011, 95) within him so that, accordingly, Dracula is tired and world-weary, giving physical form to the fleeting moments of anguish felt by Stoker's Count. It is not long, however, before we learn the cause for his pain. In Dracula's castle hangs a painting from 1475 revealing his identity to be that of the historical Vlad, but also featuring a woman, his wife, who is reminiscent of Lucy (Fiona Lewis), the friend of Jonathan Harker's betrothed. When Dracula sees Harker's photograph of his fiancée Mina (Penelope Horner) with her friend Lucy, the vampire is visibly affected, and so much so that he later experiences a traumatic remembrance of his past and the woman he lost. Understandably, Dracula seeks out Lucy as being the reincarnation of his beloved, and turns her into a vampire so they might be together forever—this idea was first used in *Son of Dracula* (Siodmak 1943) when the female vampire plans to turn her human fiancé into a vampire so they can always be together—only for Van Helsing (Nigel Davenport) to stake her, parting the lovers forever. The visceral portrayal of the murder of the Count's "soulmate" necessarily gains our sympathy and frames his subsequent desire for revenge in terms that we can not only understand but even wish for its successful fulfillment. Yet even here Dracula appears to abhor the acts of aggression he is compelled to perpetrate, and he takes little pleasure in them, finding his only solace in memories of his time with his wife. In this sense Dracula is portrayed as both human and monster, a conflicted personality who is constantly at war with himself; his innate monstrous nature versus his desire to be human once again. As noted by Nina Auerbach, Curtis' Count fits in with other 1970s vampires in being "paragons of emotional complexity and discernment ... adding a tenderness and ineffable sorrow human beings have become too monstrous to comprehend" (Nina Auerbach qtd. in Skal 2004, 267–8). More interestingly though, in the same period Dracula becomes a symbol of romantic fidelity, in defiance of his own transgressive nature, and indeed that of the swinging 1960s and the generation of free love. *Blacula, Scream Blacula Scream* (Kelljan 1973), Curtis' *Dracula, Love at First Bite* (Dragoti 1979), and *Dracula* (Badham 1979) all show their respective Dracula figures as being faithful to one woman and, more often, the reincarnation of their former wife.

The 1970s also marked something of a change in the representation of the vampire hunters and more likely seeing them as more non-human than the vampire. Curtis' Van Helsing clearly shows this in the film with a purposeful close-up focusing our attention on his unflinching and impassive gaze as he brutally impales Dracula with a spear, ironically in front of the Impaler painting. This casts Dracula's vanquisher not as the savior of humanity but as a cruel murderer of both the Prince and his beloved. This too humanizes the vampire, garnering it a sympathy that the humans in the story quickly dispel, turning the undead monster from the villain to, almost, the hero.

Francis Ford Coppola's *Bram Stoker's Dracula* (1992)

Coppola's *Dracula* is a cinematic creation. It is a work of cinematic excess that can only be produced on screen, and more than Curtis' film humanizes its vampire through the medium of film itself. The Count (Gary Oldman) in *Bram Stoker's Dracula* is nowhere near as solid or wholly corporeal as Jack Palance was, yet his constant and vivid transformations, his passion for life, nation, and love all graphically shown in lurid technicolor and extravagant CGI create him as completely human in his soul.[28] This excess is seen at the very start of the film as we witness Vlad leading his troops against the invading Ottoman hordes, creating a literal sea of blood as he hacks his way through bodies and impales hundreds of Turks on large wooden spikes. This scene's connection to the actual historical Vlad is confirmed by a dissolve in the movie from the iconic woodcut of the *voivod*

28. The reincarnation of a beloved is a theme that first appeared in Mummy films, starting with Freund's 1932 *The Mummy*, but only made its transition to vampire films in the 1970s with an early example being in *Blacula* (Crain: 1972), though, of course, Curtis himself had used something very similar in his televising series *Dark Shadows* (1966–71). Here the vampire, Barnabas Collins (Johnathan Frid), finds the reincarnation of his former beloved in his family's new nanny, only to be thwarted in his attempts of reunion by a scorned former lover who just happens to be a witch and who made him undead in the first place.

Vlad Drăculea. Colored woodcut print 1500, artist unknown (Wikimedia Commons).

feasting among impaled victims to the film's Prince Vlad, sat in a similar position at a table.

Even though shown as a monster here he is doing so in the name of God and defending Christian Europe from the invading Muslim Ottoman Empire. As such, he feels he is on a holy quest as evinced in the first lines we hear him speak: "God be praised. I am victorious" (Coppola 1992), as he duly kisses the cross. However, rather than being rewarded for his efforts, he is seemingly abandoned by his God. At the moment of Vlad's victory the Turks falsely communicate to his wife, Elisabeta (Winona Ryder), that he had been killed in battle, and in despair she takes her own life to be reunited with her husband in Heaven.[29] Dracula is understandably mortified by this news, but it quickly turns to rage when he is informed by the priests attending the princess that, as a suicide, she is damned and her soul is lost. Dracula then curses God and renounces his faith shouting to Heaven: "Is this my reward for defending God's church? ... I RENOUNCE GOD! I RENOUNCE HIM! I shall rise from my own death, to avenge hers with all the powers of darkness" (Coppola: 1992). As he finishes the large cross in the room begins to bleed, and Dracula sups on the blood which then turns him into a vampire. This is a hugely emotive start to the film, its dramatic sweep picking us up and carrying us along with it, connecting us to Dracula's pain in a way that we will always feel sympathy for him. While none of this is natural in any sense, it explains the vampire's motives in a very human way. As noted by David Glover this reduces "the vampire's pure unmotivated evil to rational proportions from the very beginning" (Glover 1996, 140). So much so that we will even be on his side later in the narrative as he cuckolds the most decent, if dull, character in the story, Jonathan Harker (Keanu Reeves), by making love to his wife in the same bed he is sleeping in—the conceit being of course that Vlad was married first to Mina hundreds of years ago so that Harker has effectively stolen her from him. The vampire then becomes far more seductive and compelling than the plodding but virtuous heroes trying to catch him, particularly his rival for Mina's affections, the insipid Jonathan (Scott 2013, 114). Following on from this, Coppola cleverly focuses on the eternal love motif—the film's tag line was "love never dies"—so that it overshadows the otherwise monstrous nature of Dracula whom we have seen transform into all manner of creatures and even kill Mina's friend Lucy (Sadie Frost). In this respect, the film's screenwriter James Hart confirms that the idea was to portray Dracula as a tragic and charismatic hero, a man who lost his soul, and "not just

---

29. In fact, the film portrays the vampire as something of a Romantic artist in the mold of Byron or Shelley, a connection given physical form in the slightly later film *Immortal Beloved* (Rose: 1994) about Ludwig van Beethoven also played by Oldman. In the run up to the film's release it was literally sold as something of a companion piece to *Bram Stoker's Dracula*.

another blood-sucking monster we have to do away with" (commentary, *Bram Stoker's Dracula*, 2007). Similarly, Gary Oldman, who played Vlad in the film, said he tried to play him as a "fallen angel," and we accordingly see the vampire demanding sympathy as an outcast from Heaven as he cries out, "Look what your God has done to me!" (commentary, *Bram Stoker's Dracula*, 2007).

Love, then, becomes the driving imperative of the film, a point emphasized in the appearance of Dracula himself. While still with his wife at the start of the film, he is strong and virile, but once she is gone, he becomes a shriveled up old man, indeed his own shadow seems to possess more energy that his physical body when Harker visits his castle. However, once he knows of the existence of Mina, he gains new determination, and by the time he reaches England and meets the reincarnation of his wife he is a dapper, youthful, attractive and love-struck tourist (Phillips 2013, 233). Yet even then, not unlike Palance's vampire above, he battles with his innate nature, and a turning point in the film is when Mina catches Vlad, as a werewolf, ravishing Lucy (LeBlanc 1997, 264, and Scott 2013, 122). As Vlad looks over into Mina's shocked face, shame floods his being. Accordingly, we never see him bite anyone else other than Mina for the rest of the film. This somewhat changes the nature of the film into that of a fairytale, joining together themes from both *Beauty and the Beast* and also the Prince Charming figure (LeBlanc 1997, 263) who has come to awaken the sleeping beauty of Elisabeta's soul that lives within Mina. When one also considers the film director's own comments on the movie, exemplifying the idea that everyone has at some point been in love with someone who is bad for them (commentary *Bram Stoker's Dracula*, 2007), *Bram Stoker's Dracula* can be seen to have much in common with later films such as *Let the Right One In* (Alfredson 2008) or even *Twilight* (Hardwicke 2008).

As with many such stories—at least pre- the twenty-first century where all vampires are redeemable—their love is doomed. Unsurprisingly, it is down to Mina to provide the vampire with his final release, and as he becomes human again, she cuts off his head. As observed by Fred Botting, this actually means Dracula is finally dead because, unlike all earlier versions, he has died as a human and not a vampire (Botting 1996, 149). Oddly, it is in his death that Dracula becomes more human than ever before, representing a Romeo that has sacrificed himself so that his Juliet might live.

Gary Shore's *Dracula Untold* (2014)

Gary Shore's *Dracula* uses the idea of connecting the historical Vlad with Stoker's Count Dracula in a different way. Rather than using it as background to a more contemporary tale as the first two films, it views it purely as an origin tale. Even with that, the story begins with Vlad's (Luke Evans) impaling days behind him, and the film opens with his son, Ingeras (Art Parkinson), narrating his father's past as a hostage in the Sultan's household guard (the janissary) as part of a tribute to the Ottoman ruler and his later rise to Prince of his homeland, Wallachia. This was achieved through his legendary, and monstrous, exploits on the battlefield that finally saw peace return to his kingdom, but is equally a period of his life that Vlad prefers to forget. However, such things rarely stay buried for long. When the Sultan demands 1000 Wallachian boys, including Vlad's own son, as tribute, then the Prince is forced to resurrect his monstrous self which he does in suitably psychoanalytical style by awakening the Master Vampire (Charles Dance) who lives in a dark cave on Broken Tooth mountain that has "watched over" the kingdom for years. Before turning him, the Master Vampire asks Vlad why he wants to become one of the undead. Vlad replies, "Because men do not fear swords. They fear monsters.... Sometimes the world no longer needs a hero. Sometimes what it needs … is a monster." The Master Vampire finds this rather a quaint idea and tells his willing victim "And you believe you know what it means to be a monster? Hmm? … You have no idea … but I'm going to show you" (Shore 2014). This point is the defining one of the film, and it is mentioned a few times in it, that sometimes the world needs monsters and the people that are willing to sacrifice all they are to become them. Vlad is just such a person. In relation to this, it is worth briefly noting some political events occurring around the production and release of *Dracula Untold*. America, and indeed the Western world, was still involved in the ongoing War on Terror, and ISIS had gained prominence over Al-Qaeda in the Middle East and its ongoing war with those it saw as outsiders. Alongside this, reports of abusive treatment, torture and suicides at the Guantanamo Detention Camp had become common knowledge. While many were appalled by the treatment of suspected terrorist, others in power thought it a necessary evil in fighting those they described as monsters.[30] It is not coincidental then that Vlad is offering to become a monster to save Western Christianity from the inhuman Muslim horde threatening to overrun it—the film purposely represents them as monsters, pedophiles and unholy, not least in their almost lascivious demand for young boys during the Easter festival. Consequently, Vlad's Faustian deal with the devil (Babilas 2017, 252), is shown to be one undertaken as the only way to save his son, his family and his people. Unlike the two earlier films discussed here Dracula is not humanized by his love for

---

30. This loosely follows folkloric tales of a Turkish spy firing an arrow into Vlad's castle, warning of the impending Ottoman attack, and Vlad's wife, or mistress, panicking over her possible capture throwing herself from the battlements (Trow 2003, 207–8).

a woman and the pain he goes through to be with her, but rather his love for his children and the nation. To establish the primacy of this love for the future of the nation—children being the strongest symbol of this—his wife, Mirena (Sarah Gadon), sacrifices herself and gives her blood so that Vlad will become a vampire forever and vanquish the invading Ottoman Army. Curiously, and again in contrast to the other films looked at here, because of Vlad's willingness to sacrifice everything for his holy cause, literally saving Christendom itself, he is rewarded. In the film's epilogue he meets the reincarnation of his wife Mirena in present day London.[31] *Dracula Untold* then uses its connection to the historical Vlad to place its undead Count in the growing tradition of protective vampires representing sacrifice, redemption and hope (Louis 2017, 249–255), as seen in films such as *Blade* (Norrington 1998) and *Angel* (Greenwalt 1999–2004), casting him as the monster that is always on hand watching out for us.[32]

Conclusion

As the vampire has become increasingly sympathetic and domesticated (Auerbach 1995, 192), its migration to being a tragic and romantic hero is maybe not so surprising. After all Emily Brontë's Heathcliff in *Wuthering Heights* (1847) had fulfilled a very similar role fifty years before *Dracula* was even published. The more we understand a monster's emotions and motivations, the more it is allowed to speak for itself, the more we are able to empathize with it. And this would seem to be one of the functions of connecting the fictional and supernatural monster known as Count Dracula to the real historical figure of Vlad III, Vlad Dracula. Vlad's positioning in European history and as a product of the times in which he lived sees him equally as hero and villain, tragic and self serving and yet maybe all the more human for that. The three films discussed here all chose aspects of the real life of Vlad III to build their stories around: he did apparently lose his wife due to her committing suicide after hearing he had been killed, though Vlad did remarry afterwards; he was also tactically gifted and inflicted many defeats on the Ottoman forces advancing towards the Danube in their attempt to overrun Europe and the Austro-Hungarian Empire, though his eventual demise was more due to internal political machinations than the war with the Turks. What all the films also do

31. The camp was opened in 2002 under George W. Bush' presidency, and although President Obama tried to close it, once he was elected there was much bipartisan opposition to this in the Senate and the House.
32. Originally, the film was meant to be part of an ongoing series, but after disappointing box office figures the planned "Dark Universe" it was meant to be part of was shelved.

is take something of the excess of the real Vlad's life and use it to romanticize the fictional vampire, seeing the jouissance of mass murder and torture transposed into the passion of eternal love. As noted above, the cultural context of each film looked at has rather dictated how Dracula's romantic excess has been expressed: eternal love as sexual fidelity; love as personal redemption; sacrifice for family and nation. All of these are very Christian virtues, and unsurprisingly so if one is humanizing a monster for a Western audience. In relation to this is the idea of the flawed hero who fights their baser instincts but often fails, as seen in Palance's frequent grimacing, Oldman's look of shame and Evans' continual regret over difficult decisions—his past life as a monster, killing those he has turned into vampires, drinking his wife's blood. Seeing such a flawed character aiming for redemption and occasionally relieving it can only encourage identification with our own attempts to be better versions of ourselves, and the hope that one day we will find love and/or redemption. What is of particular note for this essay is how the medium of film helps facilitate this. Curtis' film from the 1970s is obviously low key in this respect, though uses many cuts and fades to indicate the porosity between past and present in Vlad's love-torn mind. Coppola's, as noted before, is much more cinematic, and the dimension of Vlad's inherent monstrosity is shown through the power of CGI with his multiple and high-speed transformations to a human bat, a tower of rats and the wolf-like sex-vampire that rapes Lucy. Shore continues in this vein but the transformations of Vlad into an all-consuming vortex of bats does not reveal his monstrosity, but rather the amazing power he possesses to use against his, and our, enemies. None of this is to say that a similar humanizing of Dracula through his connection to the historical Vlad could not have taken place in other media, or even within the written form that the Count first called home. However, the excessive nature of the life, love and sacrifice of the vampire in these three films means it could only find the true spectacle of its humanity by migrating to arguably the most spectacular of mediums—film.

Works Cited

Auerbach, Nina. 1995. *Our Vampires, Ourselves*. Chicago: University of Chicago Press.
Babilas, Dorota. 2017. "Papa Dracula: Vampires for Family Values?" *Dracula an International Perspective*, edited by Marius-Mircea Crişan, London: Palgrave Macmillan, pp. 243–257
Botting, Fred. 1996. *Gothic*. London: Routledge.
Bram Stoker's Dracula: Collector's Edition [1992]. 2007. Directed by Francis Ford Coppola. London: Sony Pictures Home Entertainment. DVD.
Craft, Christopher. 1984. "'Kiss Me with Those Red Lips': Gender and Inversion in Bram Stoker's *Dracula*." *Representations* vol. 8, Fall, pp. 107–33
Dijkstra, Bram. 1988. *Idols of Perversity: Fantasies of Feminine Evil in Fin de Siècle Culture*. Oxford: Oxford University Press.

46   Part I—*Dracula*: Adaptations and Re-Creations

Dracula [1974]. 2014. Directed by Dan Curtis. United Kingdom: Latglen. DVD.
Dracula Untold. 2014. Directed by Gary Shore. Universal City: Universal Studios. Film.
Duțu, Alexandru. 2018. "Portraits of Vlad the Impaler: Literature, Pictures, and Images of the Ideal Man." *Dracula: Essays on the Life and Times of Vlad the Impaler,* edited by Kurt W. Treptow, and Radu Florescu. Buffalo: Histria Books, pp. 323–331.
Glover, David. 1996. *Vampires, Mummies, and Liberals: Bram Stoker and the Politics of Popular Fiction.* Durham: Duke University Press.
Hindle, Maurice, ed. 1993. *Dracula* [1897]. London: Penguin.
Leatherdale, Clive, editor. 2012. *Bram Stoker's Dracula Unearthed.* Desert Island eBooks. https://www.amazon.co.uk/Dracula-Unearthed-Desert-Island-Library/dp/1905328141.
LeBlanc, Jacqueline. 1997. "'It Is Not Good to Note This Down': *Dracula* and the Erotic Technologies of Censorship." *Bram Stoker's Dracula: Sucking Through the Century, 1897–1997,* edited by Carol Margaret Davison, Oxford: Dundurn Press, pp. 249–268.
Louis, Stella. 2017. "Twenty-First Century Vampires: From the Dracula Myth to New (American) Superheroes." *Journal of Adaptation in Film & Performance* vol. 10, no. 3, pp. 249–262.
Phillips, Ivan. 2013. "The Vampire in the Machine: Exploring the Undead Interface." *Open Graves, Open Minds: Representations of Vampires and the Undead from the Enlightenment to the Present Day,* edited by Sam George and Bill Hughes Manchester: Manchester University Press, pp. 225–44.
Scott, Lindsey. 2013. "Crossing Oceans of Time: Stoker, Coppola, and the 'New Vampire' Film." *Open Graves, Open Minds: Representations of Vampires and the Undead from the Enlightenment to the Present Day,* edited by Sam George and Bill Hughes, Manchester: Manchester University Press, pp. 113–30.
Silver, Alain, and James Ursini. 2011. *The Vampire Film: From Nosferatu to True Blood.* 4th ed. Pompton Plains: Limelight Editions.
Skal, David J. 2004. *Hollywood Gothic: The Tangled Web of Dracula from Novel to Stage to Screen.* New York: Faber & Faber.
Sparks, Tabitha. 2009. *The Doctor in the Victorian Novel: Family Practices.* Farnham: Ashgate.
Stoker, Bram. 1997. *Dracula,* edited by Nina Auerbach and David Skal. London: Norton.
Trow, M. J. 2003. *Vlad the Impaler: In Search of the Real Dracula.* Stroud: Sutton Publishing.
Warchol, Tomasz. 2003. "How Coppola Killed Dracula." *Vampires: Myths & Metaphors of Enduring Evil,* edited by Carla T. Kungl, Oxford: The Inter-Disciplinary Press, pp. 7–10.
Zarieva, Natalija Pop, and Krste Iliev. 2017. "The Contribution of 'Dracula Untold' to the Evolution of Bram Stoker's *Dracula*: A Comparative Analysis of the Protagonists." *Second International Scientific Conference, Philology, Culture and Education, Conference Proceedings.*

"I've crossed oceans of versions to find you"
Remediating Mina from Novel to Screen in Bram Stoker's Dracula (1992)

CATHLEEN ALLYN CONWAY

As the most abject character in *Dracula*—most notably because she is alive but dying, neither dead nor undead—the presentation of Mina via remediation shapes the overall message and meaning of the adapted text. The characters and themes in Bram Stoker's *Dracula* (1897) are so rich they continue to reward interrogation regardless of era, therefore it is worthwhile to examine how subsequent authors and artists reinterpret these characters and story by tracing the adaptation of characters and how they are presented the further from the original source text they go. The purpose of this essay is to demonstrate how the character of Mina is reconfigured and changed as it makes its way through the process of adaptation and particularly across mediums.

This essay focuses on the 1992 Francis Ford Coppola film *Bram Stoker's Dracula*, not only because it has been seen to "respond[s] more authentically to the original *Dracula*" (Reed 2010, 289–90), but also because its merchandising story world include a four-part comic book adaptation (1992)—collected as a graphic novel (2019)—and an ironically meta novelization of the film adapted from the novel, thus providing multiple examples of how the character of Mina journeyed from Stoker's novel to Coppola's film. I also make use of a second draft of the screenplay (1991) by James V. Hart, which, as the first stage of transition, provides a point of orientation for Coppola's end product. While it is a somewhat esoteric source with a limited audience, it provides insight into how each author of the transmediated text views and interprets the characters differently within the scope of the same project.

Adaptations can often miss the mark or be a disservice to the characters and/or story, changing or influencing how we as readers/audience engage and understand the vampire, and Mina provides a good example. Despite being the presumed architect of the dossier presented as the text of *Dracula*, she is often relegated to "victim" or "love interest," and not recognized as the powerful force she is, even though Van Helsing and Dracula themselves recognize her to be one in the novel. It is one thing for readers to approach Stoker's text and form their own opinions of Mina; it is another for vampire genre consumers to approach *Dracula*-related adaptations by other authors, who carry their own interpretations and prejudices into the new texts, and have views of Mina—indeed, all the characters—colored by these interpretations.

Mina is transgressive and contradictory: she both teaches etiquette and disobeys it. As I argue later, she saves herself from her own transition to vampire, and in that liminal state, becomes the scariest thing in the story. Therefore, recognition and engagement of this element in her transmedial presentation changes the story, its meaning, and its message.

"You do not know me": Mina as Intellectual

When the reader of Stoker's novel first encounters Mina's voice, they are told via a letter to Lucy that she has "been simply overwhelmed with work" (Stoker 2003, 62), not only as an assistant schoolmistress but also because she has been keeping "up with Jonathan's studies" and has "been practicing shorthand very assiduously" (62): that is, she has been working full-time as a school administrator as well as studying law and stenography in what spare time she has. Indeed, as the novel itself is a dossier assembled by Mina—"Let me write this all out now" (239)—the reader's first introduction to the character is not Jonathan's note to obtain a recipe but actually the unsigned, unindexed note that prefaces the entire text, which reflects what Mina later describes in her journal: "How these papers have been placed in sequence will be made manifest in the reading of them" (6). We are presented with a character who is ambitious, determined and overachieving from the start, and one who was a vanguardist of the era in which she was created: the New Woman "chose to explore many of the avenues recently opened to her: education, careers, and other alternatives to women's traditional roles" and was "a symbol of all that was most challenging and dangerous in advanced thinking" (Cunningham 1978, 2). Mina may not have self-identified as a New Woman; she even gently mocked them, but she benefited from the movement.

When Mina's voice enters Stoker's narrative via a letter to Lucy, its entire contents are an inventory of all the studies she is currently undertaking: law, stenography, learning to type, and building her cognitive recall, as she says, "I am told that, with a little practice, one can remember all that goes on or that one hears said during a day" (Stoker 2003, 62). When she mentions her fiancé, she does so at the end of her letter, and she expresses no impatience nor suggests there is a delay to the wedding; rather, she expresses a wistfulness at his travels—"It must be so nice to see strange countries" (62)—and a desire to one day experience foreign travel herself.

This is not the Mina audiences eventually meet on screen in Coppola's film. In the screenplay by Hart, this scene eliminates Whitby as a setting, taking place instead at Lucy's estate in London, where Jonathan calls on Mina excited about his promotion. While this interpretation presents Harker as "full of himself" (Hart 1991, 8), Mina appears much more cautious than she does in the film or the graphic novel, which is more true to the novel, and more in line with the description of her in this version of the screenplay as the opposite of Lucy: "spoiled, coquettish, and blonde—everything Mina is not" (4). In Hart's script, Harker claims Mina can "forget typing and teaching and all that forever" (7), neglecting to note that "all that" is in fact of great interest to Mina. In contrast, the penciller and inker of the graphic novel adaptation—Mike Mignola and John Nyberg, respectively—show Mina in her undergarments—anticipating her presentation in Alan Moore's *The League of Extraordinary Gentlemen*, published seven years later. Here she is leaning back while Lucy washes her hair, alongside diary entries that inform us Mina "first tutored [Lucy] at Mrs. Whitehall's school" and that she is "working very hard" at stenography and typewriting to "be useful to" (Roy, Mignola and Nyberg 2019, 9) Jonathan after their marriage. There is no mention in this version of Mina's attempts to "keep up" with Jonathan's law studies, and her range of vocabulary is substantially diminished.

By the time Mina appears onscreen in Coppola's film, her introduction is a coquettish upwards glance and resignation as Jonathan explains he must go abroad for work: "Of course. We've waited this long, haven't we" (Coppola 1992). Instead of the hard-working schoolmistress or the over-achieving New Woman, Coppola introduces this complex character as acquiescent, childish, and passive-aggressive. It also shows her as sexually bold, which will be explored in more detail later on. The sexuality is registered as well in the script draft from April 1991, in which the first sight of Mina is at her typewriter "working very hard," and in which her "schoolmistress attire" is "designed to prevent any sensuality from escaping," despite her peeking at a book filled with "erotic etching[s]" (Hart 1991, 4).

Although dismissed as "a virtuous footstool ready to do man's bidding in the world of scientific accomplishment and intellectual evolution" (Dijkstra 1984, 346), Mina shows a keen interest in technology in the novel. She taught herself how to type, which later becomes a portable skill as Seward informs readers when he collected her from Paddington Station and "got her luggage, which included a typewriter" (Stoker 2003, 234), as well as her excitement for Seward's phonograph, which she "felt quite excited over" (235). Mina's enthusiasm for the new, her ability to embrace change, and her studious nature all mirror the assiduous nature and planning of the Count himself. Mina as a full-on vampire would be a formidable foe indeed. This suggestion is implied in Stoker's text, yet erased from any of the Hart-Thomas-Coppola adaptations, leaving audiences with a Mina that is by turns only interested in marriage and status, and not someone who—even in human form, even as a woman—is a highly persuasive character.

This persuasion is inaccurately presented as manipulation off Stoker's page, as demonstrated with the coquette seen in Coppola's film and the scold in the graphic novel. What we see in Stoker's text is a Mina who has learned how to deftly manage and navigate the emotions of men while preserving her ambition and agency. For example, when she first meets Van Helsing, we see a savvy and sharp character who has already earned the reader's trust, so that by the time she encounters Van Helsing, we are aware of the dramatic irony at play:

> VAN HELSING: "Ah, then you have good memory for facts, for details? It is not always so with young ladies."
> MINA: "No, doctor, but I wrote it all down at the time. I can show it to you if you like" [Stoker 2003, 195].

Mina feigns modesty as she hands Van Helsing Jonathan's shorthand diary instead of the one she transcribed and typed, but it is in fact a power move. By unsettling Van Helsing in presenting him pages that he cannot read—specifically, a language form coded as women's work—Mina earns his respect and favor, particularly when she takes the sting out by immediately presenting him the typeset diary with a flattering apology: "Forgive me.... I know your time must be precious—I have written it out on the typewriter for you" (195). Mina admits this moment is a "little joke" but read in context it is an act of managing masculine fragility, a labor she performs throughout the novel, and one she has taught as part of her work teaching etiquette. Mina earns Van Helsing's respect without damaging his ego.

As a woman, Mina effortlessly manages male egos, even going so far to admit it is a highly gendered thing to do, a "taste of the original apple that remains still in our mouths" (195). If Van Helsing and the others had the self-awareness to recognize how Mina handled them, it could lend new urgency to their cause to destroy Dracula in order to prevent her turn.

An intellect that savvy in human form would, after centuries of practice, become very dangerous indeed, especially in concert with Dracula's other powers. Instead, this aspect of Mina's character is "de-fanged"; she takes on secondary roles as a victim or love interest, is thereby removed as a threat, denied her agency, and erased as the architect of the plan to hunt Dracula: in effect, saving her own soul.

"You are one of the lights": Mina as Love Interest

Another area that requires interrogation is Mina's positioning as a "love interest" for Dracula, or indeed, as a sexualized object. Although it has been suggested that the inclusion of the romantic subplot and its use as a framing device in Coppola's film "evidences the film's engagement with pre-existing vampire narratives that had already tapped into a broader female market" (Lindsey 2016, 121), the decision to include this deviation from Stoker's narrative has unsettling consequences.

In the book, Van Helsing heaps praise on Mina during their first meeting, saying: "There are darknesses in life, and there are lights; you are one of the lights. You will have happy life and good life, and your husband will be blessed in you" (Stoker 2003, 196). This line is delivered as a blessing to a woman who outsmarted an established academic, who is so impressed by her that he instantly awards her his respect and devotion.

However, Hart's screenplay played with this timeline, and this change is retained in the graphic novel and Coppola's film: Mina is with Lucy as her health deteriorates, and when she leaves to join Jonathan abroad, Lucy is still alive. Consequently, when this line appears in the graphic novel, it comes as consolation: "There are darknesses in life, and there are lights. You are one of the lights, dear Mina. Go now, see your friend" (Roy, Mignola and Nyberg 2019, 67). In Hart's screenplay, Van Helsing takes Mina's diary from her and reads without consent, claiming he will "be discreet," for he does "not wish to know your [her] secrets" (Hart 1991, 60).

The film alters further: when the line is delivered, Mina meets Van Helsing for the first time, and he twirls her in a dance, suggesting he knows about her relationship with the Count, which visibly shocks her. His sniffing the air around her implies he is aware of her affair with the Count, as if he can smell the sex—or his prey—on her. When he tells her she is one of the lights, it comes as a warning, read both as concern for her safety as well as policing her indulgence in transgressive sexual behavior.

In these adaptations, Mina is wanton, a term Stoker uses to describe Lucy's sexuality as a vampire. I posit that Stoker makes Mina "vampire" before the Count himself does, and Hart's screenplay follows Stoker's lead by portraying both her and Lucy as preoccupied by sexual desire, furthering Bram Dijkstra's argument that nineteenth century female vampires "represent woman as the personification of everything negative that linked sex, ownership, and money" (Lindsey 2016, 100). Indeed, "four of the five women characters are portrayed as vampires ... aggressive, inhuman, wildly erotic, and motivated only by an insatiable thirst for blood" (Senf 1982, 34), the odd one out being Lucy's mother. Hart presents a Mina curious but uptight about sex; one who, in a scene that did not appear in the graphic novel or Coppola's film, appears bisexual:

> LUCY: We'll dress as whores and surprise Art at his bachelor do. You will make a ravishing tart. All the men will undress you with their eyes—lusting for you.

"She begins to paint Mina's lips, playfully caressing her neck, her breast—Mina backs away, surprised at her arousal" (Hart 1991, 32). Coppola's film retains only a hint of this homoeroticism by including a brief, chaste kiss between Mina and Lucy while playing outside in the storm that accompanies Dracula's arrival to England. There is also a female-focused eroticism in the callback to Sheridan le Fanu's *Carmilla* (1872) by styling Sadie Frost's Lucy with red hair.

Lucy and Mina, who immediately fail the Bechdel-Wallace[33] test from their first conversation, exist in these adaptations for the male gaze and male enjoyment[34]; this is somewhat supplemented by the appearance of the Brides—the only other female characters—performing just that function when they are seen "attacking" Harker. By reducing Mina to a sexual object, one whose friend mocks her by joking that her fiancé "could be *forcing*" (italics mine) her "to perform unspeakable acts of desperate passion on the parlor floor" (Hart 1991, 4), the film validates concepts of rape culture by imposing, or supporting, the policing of women's sexuality and puritanical views of women's purity onto (or currently embedded in) Stoker's narrative. As we see in Stoker's novel, when Mina manages the feelings of the men, we are reminded that these texts are all male-authored, and even as Stoker's surrogate, Mina still falls into the trap of being a woman, even by her creator.

Hart reinforces puritanical archetypes and makes light of male violence most overtly by changing the context of Mina's blood-taking from the Count as one in which she not only consents, but initiates, which deviates

---

33. The "Bechdel-Wallace Test," based on a conversation between author Allison Bechdel and her friend Liz Wallace, is when a text has two women characters in conversation other about a topic that is not a man or relationships with men.

34. See Laura Mulvey, 1999, "Visual Pleasure and Narrative Cinema," *Film Theory and Criticism: Introductory Readings*, edited by Leo Braudy and Marshall Cohen. (New York: Oxford UP), pp. 833–44.

substantially from Stoker's novel. The scene, as narrated by Dr. Seward, describes Dracula holding "both Mrs. Harker's hands, keeping them away with her arms at full tension; his right hand gripped her by the back of the neck, forcing her face down on his bosom," and that "the attitude of the two had a terrible resemblance to a child forcing a kitten's nose into a saucer of milk to compel it to drink" (Stoker 2003, 300). Mina later describes this act in her own words, which do nothing to moderate the violence. This scene is always presented through a male lens: Seward describes his version and records Mina's words. As the violence is evident in this male-authored view, it is difficult to dismiss that the violence happened, or exists: and that it is acknowledged as violence by the men in the novel themselves, as well as its victim.

Further, the scene in the novel violates the Count's rules about invitation, as he is "this inhuman creature [that] is meant to wait for an invitation before crossing a threshold" (Stasiewicz-Bienkowska 2017, 191), and Mina's body language, in which her hands are held away from her body at "full tension," her neck is "gripped," her mouth is being "forced"—Stoker uses the word "force" twice in this description—tell the reader no invitation to enter her body, in any way, was issued.

Despite the attempted softening with the kitten metaphor, which implies that, much like pushing a kitten to drink a saucer of milk is for its own good, Mina being "forced" to drink the blood of the Count is "for her own good." This scene depicts a rape, an act of "patriarchal terrorism," described by Agnieszka Stasiewicz-Bienkowska as: "an uninvited intimacy in the form of blood exchange, unwanted isolation from her family, control of her bearings and conversations, taking essential decisions in her place" (193). Stasiewicz-Bienkowska argues that "as many such incidents ultimately conclude in the victim's 'advantage' and gratitude, the lack of her consent remains unproblematized" (193). This coercive behavior of the vampire entering where it has not been invited—that is, entering Mina physically and mentally—has unintended consequences for Dracula later, and ultimately results in his destruction.

In making *Bram Stoker's Dracula* a love story, Hart *et al* change this scene from a rape to an act of female sexual aggression. Harker is removed from the room and Mina is left alone. Dracula makes the first advance, but her response, in the screenplay, is consensual as she takes the lead (italics mine): "*She* kisses *him*. *She* opens her legs and buries *his* face in her neck—sliding *him* down to her breasts. Her gown slips down her pale shoulders—His mouth meets her flesh. *Her* legs wrap around his waist. *She* arches against him" (Hart 1991, 85, italics mine). In the graphic novel, Thomas *et al* show Mina alone in bed, saying "Oh my love…. Yes…. You found me" (Roy, Mignola and Nyberg 2019, 97), consenting before the Count has even materialized. Onscreen in Coppola's film, Mina says "yes" four times before the Count bites her, and when he tries to stop her from drinking his blood—"I love you too much to condemn you"—she says "please" and "take me away" before she drinks, resulting in his onscreen orgasm (Coppola 1992). Mina's decisions are presumably driven by her libido here, as the screenplay makes clear at her wedding that "there is no passion" for Jonathan (Hart 1991, 56).

Further complicating the issue is the suggestion in Hart's screenplay that Mina's feelings are unreciprocated, and the entire crisis is due to her erotomania. When confronted by Van Helsing, Dracula replies: "My revenge has just begun.... And she that you all love is mine! More will follow. My armies to do my bidding" (89). The audience could now be less sympathetic to Mina's grief, as the Count's admission to the men makes her appear foolish. When she says "unclean" afterwards, is it because she is polluted with vampire blood, or because she made her husband a cuckold?

If Mina is read as a rape victim in-text, the end of the novel becomes a revenge, or a tale of survivor justice against patriarchal terrorism. Erasing Mina's status as rape victim changes the counterbalance from Stoker's text. In the film and graphic novel, the pendulum doesn't swing back to make Dracula the prey and *Mina* the predator; indeed, Jonathan admits she has become their decoy. Instead of being doubles for one another, in the film Mina becomes merely a tool used by men for hunting the Count.

Onscreen, Mina muses that "perhaps, though I try to be good, I am bad. Perhaps I am a bad, inconstant woman" (Coppola 1992). Presented on film as this kind of "bad" woman, she no longer poses a challenge to male dominance, as she may be perceived as doing in the source text. The Mina of the novel continually negotiates male fragility, a labor to protect herself and eventually them all, as she gently assuages male egos while taking charge and guiding the men to success. Coppola's film shows us what happens when male fragility is threatened: Dracula's pain at Mina leaving for the continent to marry Jonathan results in the pathetic fallacy of his calling up a storm, under cover of which he perpetuates the intimate partner violence that results in Lucy's murder (Coppola 1992).

Hart *et al* put Mina back into what is perceived to be a "woman's place," erasing evidence of the abuse she suffered, and potentially implying that the threat to the men, and Lucy, is her fault. As Jude Ellison S. Doyle argues, "When we live in a climate of distrusting women's voices, of viewing women as primarily obliged to service the relationship demands of men, their pain ... is always suspect.... We can say, not that abuse has made them act angrily or strangely, but that they were abused because they were angry or strange" (59–60). In Coppola's film, Mina invites Dracula into her body—arguably pressuring him to do so against his good sense—with full knowledge of what he is, and what she is agreeing to, because she is "a bad, inconstant woman," one who is "strange" (59–60) and sexually predatory, despite it being Dracula himself who is the predator.

"You must remember that I am not as you are": Mina the Un-Dead Undead

Dracula's attempt to turn Mina in Stoker's novel reveals what a danger she poses. Mina as un-dead Undead means she can behave like a vampire, a predator, and hunt Dracula as the prey. She is abject and liminal: she can go where Dracula cannot, she can go where the men cannot, and therefore she is far more dangerous than both.

Mina's careful planning and research mirrors the work Dracula put into his emigration to England; indeed, she follows his route back to his homeland, making the journey—uninvited—in reverse. This is another way Stoker made Mina a "vampire" before Dracula himself did; the characters are foils for one another. Mina makes the passage across the Styx (Bacon 2017, 219) to the land of the undead: in the inverse of the guest and host roles of Dracula and Harker, where Dracula invaded Mina without permission, she invades back with her own entourage of Brides.

The further into the East they go, the more the thresholds between civilization and superstition, life and undeath, blur. The closer to the castle Van Helsing and Mina are, the more vampire Mina becomes. She can no longer be hypnotized during the liminal times of sunset and sunrise, she no longer eats, and she sleeps all day. When Van Helsing draws a protective circle against the Brides, she cannot cross it: "God be thanked she was not, yet, of them…. They could not approach me … nor Madam Mina whilst she remained within the ring, which she could not leave no more than they could enter" (Stoker 2003, 391). At no point in the novel perhaps is Mina more abject than this moment.

Dracula tells Mina that her turning was to "countermine" the men, and as punishment, she will come to his call: "When my brain says 'Come!' to you, you shall cross land or sea to do my bidding" (307). What he does not count on is that the connection between them goes both ways, as Mina says: "I have an idea. I suppose it must have come in the night and matured without my knowing it" (331), which Van Helsing later understands to mean she can read the Count's thoughts. Dracula himself realizes that their connection poses a threat—"He has so used your mind…. He think, too, that as he cut himself off from knowing your mind, there can be no knowledge of him to you; there is where he fail" (364)—he realizes he has invited Mina into his mind, and she entered.

While in the adaptations it is clear Transylvania is Dracula's space, it is unclear as to whether it is Mina's space, also. In the graphic novel she tells Van Helsing "I know this place!" (Roy, Mignola and Nyberg, 2019, 106); in the film, when Van Helsing says, "We must rest here now," Mina forcibly takes the reins of their carriage and drives on: "We must go on. No, we must go! He needs me. We must go!" (Coppola 1992). In the screenplay, she recognizes it because it is "exactly as Jonathan described it in his journal" (Hart 1991, 96), although in the novel it reads more as if Mina is discovering her growing vampire powers. Hart's version of Mina is unconcerned, as she clearly states "I know what I am!" (96) and upon arrival of the Brides says, "I am their kind" (98). Mina's acknowledgment of her own vampire-self does not make it to the final film version or the graphic novel and yet somehow haunts them, just as the memory of Dracula hangs over the end of Stoker's novel.

In the heart of Dracula's space, Mina in Stoker's text shows no concern for the Count's desires; when she speaks of a connection, it is to Jonathan: she "knew Jonathan was coming" (Stoker 2003, 395). When Van Helsing tells her Jonathan is coming, she writes: "I knew at all events neither of them was Jonathan. At the same time, I *knew* Jonathan was not far off" (397); looking around, she spies them coming at "break-neck speed. One of them I knew was Jonathan" (397). Mina admits to "breathlessly" watching Jonathan, who shears off the Count's head. Mina's connection to Jonathan—through love, mutual respect, or marriage—proves stronger than her connection to the Count. Jonathan admits in an earlier diary entry that he will follow her: "if we find out that Mina must be a vampire in the end, then she shall not go into that unknown and terrible land alone" (317). In this respect, Mina has already "turned" her first vampire progeny, so the connection she feels to Jonathan during the novel's climax is in keeping with that shared telepathy of Mina and the Count, and counter-balances the beginning of the novel, when it was Jonathan in this place in crisis thinking of Mina to get him through. Jonathan and Mina save one another, the binary to the mutual destruction of Dracula and Mina.

It is also important to note the contrast between Mina and Dracula's other progeny. She is recognized as a vampire by the Brides, who materialize outside the Holy circle Van Helsing constructs around their camp and address her as "sister" (Hart 1991, 97; Thomas, Mignola, Nyberg 2019, 107; Stoker 2003 391). The Brides stay in the Count's house and grounds and rely on him for food, and when they disobey, as they did with Jonathan, they do only because he entered *their* space: they at no point crossed the threshold into the area Dracula marked as safe for him. That the Brides remain at Dracula's castle long after he abandons them for England suggests they do not outright rebel regardless of how unsatisfied they are.

In contrast, Mina trespasses Dracula's boundaries, as he did with hers, She invades his mind and uses the information she obtains to track all his possible movements by land, water or rail, which she outlines thoroughly in a memorandum (Stoker 2003, 373). And although Mina is confined to the circle when the Brides appear, she makes no motion to join them, and warns Van Helsing to stay within to protect himself: "Do not go without. Here you are safe! ... None safer in all the world from them as I am" (390). As previously mentioned, this was incorporated into initial screenplay adaptations but did not survive the process, as the final film places her at the mercy of the Brides, who use their shared vampire bloodline to torment her, eventually pressuring her into attempted seduction of Van Helsing, despite the fact Mina in the novel ignores them.

Mina's assertion that she is safe from the Brides not only suggests a rejection of the role Dracula proscribes for the women he turns, but also that she recognizes *she* is different from them: she is not under the Count's control; he fears *her*. And indeed, with the mental connection shared with Jonathan, Mina has taken the first step to becoming a vampire-master. The meaning of this scene changes on screen: instead of providing evidence of Mina's agency from Dracula, it becomes about Mina's sexual temptation of Van Helsing, despite the Brides (who earlier tempted Jonathan) being present. In the film, Mina reveals her décolletage, advancing on Van Helsing: "I know that Lucy harbored secret desires for you. She told me. I, too, know what men desire" (Coppola 1992), reiterating movie-Mina's admission of being a "bad, inconstant woman," and changing the nature of Van Helsing's paternal care in-text to one of sexual desire onscreen. Making Mina the temptress is once again making her a sex object or love interest.

This scene is also out of character for the Brides. It was previously established that they are reliant on Dracula for food and that he underfeeds them, therefore it taxes belief that Dracula would delegate the mentoring of Mina through her first kill to anyone else, regardless of their great ancient love, and that the Brides settle for animal blood when faced with an option of attacking Van Helsing, upon whom no restriction or protection was made.

Conclusion

The pitfalls of adaptation and moving across media can have unintended negative consequences. Stoker gives readers a somewhat happy ending when he places a signed note from Jonathan Harker at the end of the dossier with a quote from Van Helsing calling Mina "brave and gallant" (Stoker 2003, 402) and how "some men" risked their lives to save her from becoming a vampire. If the editor of this dossier is Mina, this letter, unedited, placed at the end of the file, is an example of how Mina subtly demonstrates her confidence and acknowledgment of her own self-worth. Indeed, Van Helsing's quote acknowledges the male vampire hunters' respect for Mina and how they are not threatened by her. But this is not the Mina we see in Coppola's film. Within one transition process alone the character of Mina has been stifled and limited, working against the narrative world constructed by Stoker. As further adaptations of *Dracula* are developed, perhaps there will be one that, rather than find new ways to radically reinterpret and recontextualize the text, actually portrays it as written, and recognizes Mina—one of literature's great heroes and investigators, indeed one of its greatest minds—as the rightful hero.

Works Cited

Bacon, Simon. 2017. *Becoming Vampire: Difference and the Vampire in Popular Culture.* Oxford: Peter Lang.
Bram Stoker's Dracula. 1992. Film. Directed by Francis Ford Coppola. Culver City: Columbia Pictures.
Creed, Barbara. *Hospitality, Rape and Consent in Vampire Popular Culture: Letting the Wrong One In,* edited by David Baker, Stephanie Green, and Agnieszka Stasiewicz-Bienkowska. London: Palgrave Gothic, 2017, p. v.
Cunningham, Gail. 1978. *The New Woman and the Victorian Novel.* London: Macmillan.
Dijkstra, Bram. 1986. *Idols of Perversity: Fantasies of Feminine Evil and Fin-de-Siècle Culture.* Oxford: Oxford University Press, 1986.
Doyle, Jude Ellison S. (originally published as Sady Doyle). 2016. *Trainwreck: The Women We Love to Hate, Mock and Fear… and Why.* London: Melville House Printing.
Hart, James V., and Bram Stoker. 1991. "Bram Stoker's Dracula." Scriptslug. Matt Lathrom, April 16. https://www.scriptslug.com/assets/uploads/scripts/bram-stokers-dracula-1992.pdf.
Lindsey, Scott. 2013. "Crossing Oceans of Time: Stoker, Coppola, and the 'New Vampire' Film." *Open Graves, Open Minds: Representations of Vampires and the Undead from the Enlightenment to the Present Day,* edited by Sam George and Bill Hughes Manchester and New York: Manchester University Press, pp. 113–30.
Reed, Thomas L., Jr. 2010. "'Belle et le Vampire': Focus and Fidelity in Bram Stoker's Dracula." *Literature/Film Quarterly,* vol. 38, pp. 289–310.
Thomas, Roy, Mike Mignola and John Nyberg. 2019. *Bram Stoker's Dracula.* San Diego: IDW Publishing.
Senf, Carol A. 1982. "'Dracula': Stoker's Response to the New Woman." *Victorian Studies,* Autumn, 34.
Stasiewicz-Bienkowska, Agnieszka. 2017. "The Lower Dog in the Room: Patriarchal Terrorism and the Question of Consent in Charlene Harris; the Southern Vampire Mysteries." In *Hospitality, Rape and Consent in Vampire Popular Culture: Letting the Wrong One In,* edited by David Baker, Stephanie Green, and Agnieszka Stasiewicz-Bienkowska, London: Palgrave Gothic, 2017, p. 183–200.
Stoker, Bram. 2003. *Dracula* [1897]. London: Penguin.

Part II
Across Mediums, Platforms and Levels of Engagement

Byzantium Stage to Screen
Gina Wisker

"The best vampires are companions."
—Auerbach 1995, vii

Vampires are perfect, ideal, were made for filming, for film scripting and for imagining onto the screen with all the mixture of realism and the fantastic, the all too visceral and tactile richness dissolving into the truly vicious. This is an excess managed with the bounds of film, which is already a fantasy space relying on its insistence that it is both real and a constructed dream or nightmare space, one which invites and enables us to traverse the boundaries of the imagination into that realized action and fantastic embodiment offered by film. It would be more difficult, perhaps, oddly less realistic, more disgusting, less metaphorically about a comment on something else (life/death boundaries, the fragility of the body, the actuality of eternal undead existence, gender and power, queering the seeming everyday and so on) to see the fangs, or in the case of *Byzantium* (Jordan 2012), the long pointed fingernail appear and do the vampire's work, in a play enacted on a small stage in a fairly intimate theater setting as was *A Vampire Story* (Buffini 2008). We do of course have a long history of suspending disbelief with Gothic horror theater (Shakespeare, Jacobean revenge tragedies, Japanese Noh theater, Grand Guignol) (Galluzzo 2016). Perhaps much of the sweep of action, setting, and the bodily dissolution would be more difficult to be shown onstage, more likely to be re-told by a bystander or servant than enacted. These would be some of the decisions made, and some of the opportunities embraced when translating Moira Buffini's drama *A Vampire Story* (2008) into the film *Byzantium*, directed by Neil Jordan.

Vampires inhabit a dangerous and delicious liminality, as does drama and even more specifically film. As boundary crossers of gender, life and death, day and night, they remind audiences of our own vulnerability and mortality while constraining these with the time and space bounds of the stage play and of the film. Producing, directing, taking part in a stage drama means months of rehearsals until it is ready to be shared, followed by variations on the identical performance every night. Angela Carter (1985) observes that Edgar Allen Poe watched his mother die every night while she played Ophelia, and his love of the Gothic, the performativity of death and the normality of revenants emerged from nightly seeing his mother die and rise again the next night. For Poe, the stage drama was the essence of the revenant, the ghost, or the vampire, played out, and the boundaries of life and death were troubled as a result. This is a perfect gap for Gothic horror and most particularly for the ghost or vampire to enter. In addition to the suspension of disbelief required of all drama, film offers the opportunity for further displacement of the real, yet fulfillment of the characteristics of the real—movement in time and space, real places as settings, and a possible eternity of revisiting the film text, the replay of life, death, and life again, which a film offers. For the filmic vampire, that return and replay resembles the need of film goers, displays and enacts a consuming desire, the desires of the consumer and in terms of their every night/everyday activity, their "habitual desires" drive the plots. In *The Instinctive Screenplay* (2017) Sam North, quoting Jonathan Gottschall, comments: "In order to write the poetry of human events it is the human hunger for story, and the story itself that must be the screenwriter's first concern—he or she must reach the human animal in his cave and realize why we are 'the storytelling animal'"[35] (North 2017, 45). North emphasizes how these practices have led to the evolution of dramatic techniques, using the language of the human and of hunger. Building on Wittgenstein's discussion about will, North links desire, explicit or hidden, and morality: "the distinction between what a character wants in the surface and what, under the surface the character needs and unconsciously desires is the model for some of the most rewarding expressions of the desire principle narrative" (2017, 45). He notes "the desire principle is used in conjunction with morality ... in order to engineer the audience's increasing involvement in the desire" (2017, 45) and sees increasing this desire "magically" (46) carries the audience throughout the drama—involves us.

Theater and film are pleasurable because of our immersion: "the pleasure of theatre is having the spectator touch (but from a safe distance) anything he fears, or feared as a child—the threat of death for example" (Ubersfeld 1982, 245). North reminds us what we fear is physical and mental, such as madness, dissolution of self, and also quotes Gumbrecht: "authentic experiences oscillate between a presence-dimension and a meaning-dimension, between experiential and semantic levels"

35. Gottschall 2013.

(Gumbrecht 2003, 156). Vampires are a sound vehicle for discussions about surfaces and inner desires, and North goes on to discuss the fear and the conventions associated with the vampire, focusing on *Let the Right One In* (film: Alfredson, 2009; book: Lindquist, 2004) for its readjusting of conventions, since it has a female vampire and an older male carer. The disruption and difference, desire and fear of the characters and setting, in a contemporary apartment block in Sweden, open up the audience to new responses. This set of responses "require both literary and financial investment," placing audiences in a "transactional economy" (North 2017, 46).

All fictions demand a suspension of disbelief, none more so than fantasy fictions. Drama takes the fiction into a solid world bounded by time and space, the solid real of the stage setting (more so if it is immersive, in the round), a rift we decide to cross recognizing magic and fantasy are trickery but desiring to be fooled, as we do with the work of stage mediums (Hilary Mantel 2005). In the United Kingdom recently, 2020, the revived play *Ghost Stories* returned for a new run at the Ambassadors Theatre in London after the success of the film (Dyson and Nyman 2017), which of course began life in the theater (Dyson and Nyman 2010). The play opens with an academic researcher (a purveyor of facts) enquiring of the audience: who believes in and has seen ghosts? (fiction?) thereby blurring those boundaries. The film offers what seems like lived memories, testimony revived, featuring fantasy figures (ghosts), which you might believe are real, as moving in front of you on screen rather than produced by the management of revolving stage settings, darkness and bangs and crashes on stage.

Though known simultaneously as a mix of the embodiment of the real of both action and of fantasy, a story extended into the extra, more artificial (on screen only) realized medium of film can be seen as convincing and effective beyond drama, even though the drama is being enacted within actual physical grasp.

Adaptation

Discussing adaptations, Ken Gelder (2019) moves on to popular fictions and comments on the singular fascination with and adaptability (beyond the popularity of everything Shakespeare) of fantasy fictions. While he mentions merchandising (*Harry Potter, Game of Thrones*, etc.) he also explores the adaptations between fictions and performance of some sort. Murray (2012, 5) reminds us that adaptation places authors in a transactional position because of the necessary investment to transform the often-small fry fiction into that consumer-oriented performance of film. For Buffini's *A Vampire Story* (2008) the adaptation was between a locally performed, relatively small audience at the Royal Court for a limited run, then some even more local performances in colleges, and a blockbuster film. Since *Byzantium* (2012) uses locations as diverse as a Caribbean island (recognized as one off the Irish coast by Aubrey, 2017) and the rundown British seaside town of Hastings (which was no doubt very pleased with the temporary extra revenue of a film company), there must have been considerable investment involved, as Murray indicates film adaptation requires both creative and financial investments working in "a transactional and cultural economy," where the author becomes one of many players in an "interdependent network of agents" that also involves corporate money, advertising revenue and licensing agreements (Murray 2012, 5). Gelder (2019) mentions J.K. Rowling (*Harry Potter*, 1997–2007)[36] and George R.R. Martin (*A Song of Ice and Fire*, 1996-forthcoming)[37] as "contemporary examples of modern fantasy writers who have developed extensive transmedia portfolios out of their genres" (Gelder 2019, 4), "building on the leading role of J.R.R. Tolkien's *Lord of the Rings* series and its transmedia afterlives" (4), citing Kristin Thompson's recognition of the poor relation status of fantasy revived by such as Tolkien, so that "a previously despised genre"—modern fantasy—went on to become nothing less than a "major international franchise" (Thompson 2007, 18, 175).[38] Gelder argues that fantasy benefits from the longevity of investment in character and story.

Vampires in Film

This, the film medium, is the natural dimension for the vampire, with her embodiment of human desires and fears, her enactment of the most destructive dark behaviors, deliberate death, revenge, and a newly powerful return. Vampires, as life/death, male/female boundary breakers, are in particular a Gothic vehicle for the disruption of complacency and an embodiment of challenge to the everyday, the taken for granted. They can be and are often used to destabilize the seeming fixity of all rules and constraints. Some of this is wicked playfulness, and some of it a vehicle to interrogate and then disrupt the socially restrictive and destructive order.

The vampire in fiction, drama and on screen, is both a figure taking pleasure in disruption and wielding their own power over ordinary, everyday mortals, and in more radical vampire writing (particularly in the 1980s and afterwards) one using the liminality and boundary-crossing of the vampire condition to move between fixed positions—social, gendered, bodily,

36. The associated films were released from 2001 to 2011.
37. The associated HBO series, *Game of Thrones*, ran from 2011 to 2019.
38. Quoted in Gelder 2019, 4.

historically, geographically, mortally/immortally—undermining this fixity, creating a space and form for new liberal, liberated behaviors. Radical vampires do so to expose, disturb, challenge and destroy these inequalities. The vampire figure also represents freedom from gendered constraints and an opportunity to make some changes. Radical women vampires in twentieth and twenty-first century literature often revel in the liberty offered by their undead but everyday-seeming roles to turn the tables on sexual abuse, draining victims of their power as they drain them of their blood. They move beyond a historical and socially constructed revenge to the creation and validation of different forms of behaving, being and of social order. The range of sexually celebratory fictional women vampires and lesbian vampires of the 1980s and 1990s are accompanied by other fictional women vampires in the work of authors who take similar pleasures as those used to break gender binaries and gendered power structures. Radical women vampires deal with economically constrained rules of behavior, with the results of politically motivated othering and constructions of waste, stepping beyond the individualistic freedoms offered by being a liberated woman vampire to expose social ills (Victoria Brownworth, 1996; Poppy Z. Brite, 1992, 1995; Gina Wisker, 2000, 2012).

Moira Buffini and Adaptation

Moira Buffini (1965), born in Cheshire, with Irish parents, studied English and Drama at Goldsmiths College, London University (1983–86) and subsequently trained as an actor at the Welsh College of Music and Drama. She is a prolific dramatist and screenwriter, preferring to write in the fantastic rather than realistic modes, but always situating that fantasy in everyday realistic settings. Her background in English and drama, playwriting and screen writing would have been useful in building on literary vampire lore, writing a play for young people to perform and then working with the production company and Neil Jordan to adapt the play to the screen.

In interview with Aleks Sierz (2003) Moira Buffini argues that she is first and foremost a writer: "Buffini shrugs off the label 'woman writer'—'I'm a writer, I'm a female, get over it. I fight my corner because I'm a writer not because I'm a female'—she's more open than any man about saying how having her two kids affected her work." She has been outspoken about the costs, the problems of breaking even with new plays compared to the lavish amounts spent on re-running mediocre old plays, so these new plays come out on just the equivalent of what is spent on wigs for the older ones: "the wig budget" (Sierz 2003). She and a few other contemporary dramatists used the research and development space at the National Theatre to work out their new drama, labeling themselves the "monsterists" (Eldridge 2005) because they wanted to bring big plays to large audiences rather than be confined by the small stages, which seemed to stage the work of new dramatists but which they could not afford. Her own work has been performed, for example, at the Almeida—a small community theater in Islington, North London. Buffini notes of writing dramas to reach more people:

> It's our job to take people where they don't expect to go. It's our job to provoke, move, unsettle and inspire. It goes without saying that plays that manage to do this are big. It is possible to write them for a cast of two and perform them in a box barely bigger than a lounge but I've got to the point where I want to kick down the walls of these boxes. I'm sick of writing epics for six [Eldridge 2005].

So, what can we say of the transfer from stage to film of fantasy and horror-based, Gothic texts? Ken Gelder (2019), in considering fantasy source texts which become big box office draws, mainly focuses on the franchising of the great films from the great book series, but the comments about the kind of crossovers, changes, echoes of the original texts in the adaptation is of interest here. Anthony Smith in *Storytelling Industries* (2018) notes that "the unique characteristics of traditionally differentiated media are essential to an understanding of contemporary popular narratives and wide media culture in the twenty-first century" (Smith 2018, 1). Gelder argues after Smith that source texts do not disappear in this adaption process since "Adaptations always create relationships to it, to their source text; they both cite it and transform it ... their faithfulness to the source text is open in some ways and closed in others; some adaptations might even make a point of stressing their *fidelity* to a source text, as if an adaptation should at the same time be an act of reverence or homage" (Gelder 2019, 14). Gelder debates the freedom of movement of adaptations and particularly franchises and so differentiates between Clare Parody's view of the free roaming of a franchise through a source text (so it could take some elements and not others) against Simone Murray's views that such fidelity "is in any case often and necessarily a prioritised component of an adaptation, no matter what the media platform might be" (Gelder 2019, 14). Gelder looks in the main at adaptations from fiction to film, rather than from drama to film, with the early exception of his comments on Shakespeare, and usefully identifies the history of the sudden emergence in the mainstream of fantasy from its relative marginality pre 1950s: "something happened to the fantasy genre in the mid 1950s that enabled it to make the shift from a marginal popular literary genre to a creative course for some of the largest entertainment and media franchises in the world" (Gelder 2019,

16). However, some fantasy authors resist the translation of their fictions into film (Stephen Donaldson, for instance, although this has happened and he does not have the right over his own text to refuse) (Gelder 2019, 23). Argument about what is possible to extend and what is lost mainly ranges for fantasy works around the translation from fiction to theater or film, and Babbage (2018, 2)[39] notes that commentators see adaptations to the theater of novels as rather superficial, unnecessary (it is not possible to put in all the back story), "reductive, superficial or a travesty" (2), and the "performative action" of the theater is ignored, in which the source text is over prioritized (Gelder 2019, 31, referring to Babbage 2018, 15, for the short quote).

A Vampire Story (2008) and *Byzantium* (2012)

Commissioned by the National Theatre for New Connections and contemporary with *Twilight* (Meyer 2005–8), *A Vampire Story* (Buffini 2008) was turned into the film *Byzantium* (Jordan 2012). The play has been performed by young actors in schools and colleges and at the Lyric Theatre, Hammersmith. Buffini's tale is set in two time frames, initially the eighteenth, or early nineteenth century, where the women become vampires to escape a life of sexual predation and early diseased death, and the twentieth or twenty-first, where their lives can eventually be more economically stable and agentic. Buffini's vampires comprise both female vampire sisters/mother and daughter Claire/Clara and Eleanor/Ella, and the powerful brotherhood of male vampires who seek them out to punish their deviant grasp at gendered equality. Interestingly, in both film and play Buffini uses Ruthven from Polidori's *A Vampyre* (1819) and Darvell from Byron's unfinished vampire tale "Augustus Darvell" [The Burial: A Fragment] (1819) upon which Polidori based his novella. Lord Ruthven, Polidori's protagonist, captures Clara and forces her into prostitution while his friend Darvell who holds the secret of eternal life through becoming a vampire, is another Polidori character initially chasing the two women in the twenty/twenty-first century and finally siding with them. The women are driven by their poverty, transient state and their desires to right wrongs. They eventually level out the inequalities which led to their becoming vampires in the first place, and are still perpetuated hundreds of years later in the merchandising of women's bodies by pimps and where the only way to survive is to become part of that economic chain. In both *A Vampire Story* (2008) and *Byzantium* (2012) Buffini's Claire/Clara acts as an agent to enable herself

39. In Gelder 2019.

and other marginalized and disempowered women to earn money, food and some power. In her own case, she reverses the victimization of the pimp/punter/prostitute exchange by choosing and draining her victims. The vampire curse or gift for Eleanor/Ella is different, a perpetual teen. In the twentieth century she can release the exhausted aged when they are ready to die (in the care homes in the seaside retirement community) and can also offer eternal life to the dying young (her friend Frank, who has leukemia). Theirs is a gendered revenge tale and a social justice mission with an edge.

The Play: *A Vampire Story*

What would you do if a teenage girl in your school or further education college writing class wrote an assignment based on her life which revealed she was herself a vampire, rescued from a life of certain death in a brothel, by being turned by her mother two hundred years ago? The mixing of the play (Buffini 2008) initially performed at the National Theatre by a group of young people, a realistic-based stage drama produced there and performed by teens—to a film set in a seedy run-down South coast town, splices two hundred years ago and now, and so proves the vampire myth of eternal life (of a sort). The transition of this stage play to the screen is one which tests and extends that suspension of disbelief normal in the theater. It emphasizes the performativity of both modes while moving beyond what would be a stretch to believe in a play performed in F.E. college halls, to something on a par with *Interview with the Vampire*'s (Jordan 1994) fantastic drama.[40] The whores are not allowed to keep their children but Claire/Clara pays for her daughter's keep and visits her and so she survives. Each woman survives through stealing the vampire power intended for a man—and they do so because they are reacting against a patriarchal order much older than the 200 years ago when they were living, where young Claire/Clara was forced into and brought up in the circle of the brothel.

The film places events in a semi-surreal time, with the travelling vampires in their parallel world of seediness and glitz, the need for survival fueling their activities. In the film, the mother and daughter are already illicit. The imaginary and representation elements of the story ironically make more real the different time zones, the oppressive male control and violence, the longevity of the sickness and death, and the vitality of blood which turns from evidence of human rot to eternal undead life. The play and the film are two modes which question versions of reality and fantasy. Each has the

40. Jordan's film being an adaptation of Anne Rice's 1976 novel of the same name.

vampire story and the autobiographical fictional version of it at its core and the tale is essentially similar—but the film, through this tradition, is able to give further credence to the story of the vampire over time, since we see the mother and daughter in two time frames, commenting on coping with endless shifts of home and identity, condemned to be perpetually at the age they were "turned," and we can imagine their struggles for the 200 years in between. For the Brotherhood which seeks them out, the women are an offense against their historical, legitimated codes of power, those of ownership of money, power and of eternal life, which they would forbid women. This film and play resemble *Interview with the Vampire.* Yet the pace in and out of time, parallel time zones, and constant seediness moves beyond time frames, their roles, vulnerabilities and imaginative resilience enabling survival. In Rice's novel and Jordan's film, as in Buffini's work, the making of new vampires is prohibited, and women making women vampires doubly so, so that Madeleine (Domiziana Giordano) and little Claudia (Kirsten Dunst) die in the sun, victims of a monstrous contract, which in its fantasy highlights the cruelty of men, of power, money, physical power and the lie of eternal life. In both the play *A Vampire Story* and the film *Byzantium* the dominance of men is extensive, destructive, controlling. First there is the power of the captain, Ruthven, over the woman Clara, picking clams on the beach in Hastings, abusing and owning her beauty, stealing her into prostitution. Clara is brutally inducted into the brothel, which refuses ironically to let women create new life. Eventually, in this instance, like Claudia "creating" Madeleine, they are also not meant to create new vampires.

Buffini's women, however (written after both Anne Rice's, and Poppy Z. Brite's, and the radical women vampire revolution of the 1990s) are able to destroy one Brotherhood pursuer and change the mind of another. In Buffini's tale, these feisty vampire women, mother and her daughter, eventually do more than just survive but win in the battle against centuries of economic, sexual and gendered oppression and also escape from the constraints of the small town in which they began their lives 200 years previously.

Eleanor, 16, dressed in a costume from 1822, sits on stage through most of the play, focusing on the action of the drama which she is authoring and which plays out before us: "People will always believe the most fabulous tale you can tell," she tells us (scene 1, 225). Claire appears on the train for the first scene. Buffini is using a convention we also see in *The Taming of the Shrew* (Shakespeare 1590–2), where the play is acted out in front of both an audience and someone playing an audience member/narrator. Perhaps, like a ghost or vampire story, this enhances the "truth" and acceptance of the most fantastic, a mix which Eleanor suggests, satisfies people. Claire, 21, talks with Ella, 16, who has told us what her name is. This play begins in transit, with their escape and renaming, and we immediately wonder what they are running from, where to, and why. Eleanor and Claire Wythenshawe, whose identities Claire/Clara and Eleanor/Ella adopt, were killed in a car crash, so newly renamed they can hide in plain sight. Eleanor/Ella has to go to school since, like Claudia in *Interview with the Vampire* (Rice 1976; Jordan 1994), and Edward and his siblings in *Twilight* (Meyer 2005), she never ages, she is always 16. Here she takes Food Technology (although we do not yet realize the irony—she cannot eat the food), and A level Drama. This class is peopled with teens with teen names: Briggs, Point, Debit and Moon, who look like detached, fashionable, effortlessly nonchalant vampires (scene 2, 230), extras for a Poppy Brite novel perhaps, although her vampires perform as vampires in plain sight, believed to be ordinary people pretending, until they start taking out the humans who watch them perform. These late teens in the A level class are familiar to the teacher Mint, who defines them as "same old spoilt rebels and fashion victims as last year" (scene 2, 230). Home-schooled Frank, and Eleanor, as the new students, are of interest to everyone else, and the in-joke is that both Claire's and Frank's parents see drama as "a totally useless subject" (scene 2, 236), and his fantasizing about an imaginary friend, a darker self who had to go, sets the scene for tall stories, when Ella reveals she is Eleanor Wythenshawe. They decide to interview this version of Ella—and she tells of three in a bed at a private orphanage, memories of the rout of Napoleon. Clearly she has done a lot of research and is congratulated for that but when asked why she's still alive, she surprises them by going one step too far: "I freely confess that I have stayed alive for all these years by drinking human blood" (scene 2, 240). Of course, this is true. As it turns out, she is a vampire from the early-nineteenth century, but to everyone else this is revolting and fiction. Ella enters a drama class; her admission that she is a vampire is treated as a psychological and social problem, a kind of acting out because of her other traumatic history, part of her "hilarious sense of fun." Rebellious, Frank is also an outsider. However, Claire/Clara stalls Ella's collusion in his plan to escape to London, living in a tent, doing whatever turns up. Scenes of the school and the play alternate with nineteenth-century scenes of Eleanor/Ella in the orphanage in bed with two other girls, and in the brothel, where Claire/Clara meets Captain Ruthven. Ruthven tells her a tale which saves her but not him and began with his friend Darvell, another character out of Polidori's *A Vampyre* (1819). Clara travels to a lofty mountain where a soucriant lives, dies, and rises from the grave, a vampire, so surviving forever and avoiding STDs and tuberculosis in the human world. In the twentieth/twenty-first century Claire/Clara's revenge on men is selective, a schoolteacher who knows too much, the annoying, sexually harassing teenager Briggs, and abusive pimps. Through these selective removals she remains out of sight but takes eternal revenge on men who manipulate or abuse women. The play ends with Eleanor being congratulated for writing a play. The complex interleaving of two sets of characters and time frames allows parallels and leakage between their past and present. The women are always on the move, outsiders, always vulnerable, but their strength is their vampire curse and the incredulity of others when they suspect or hear that these are real vampires.

Moira Buffini's play *A Vampire Story* and the film *Byzantium* offer an intriguing new take on what it might mean to be a woman vampire in the contemporary world. Claire/Clara and Eleanor are mother and daughter posing as sisters who survive because they stay close and fend for themselves, two women in a male-dominated world negotiating everyday behavior. The film and play concern the need to consume and the transience of relationships; both represent some of the demands on twenty-first century vampires. Clara/Claire and Eleanor's tale of abuse at the hands of violent, legally protected aristocratic men two hundred years earlier indicts hierarchies of gender and class. This new working of the myth does not celebrate vampire sexuality as radical freedom. Instead, it sees these women as survivors, imaginative, learning to change, living as they must according to how society constructs them, becoming agents in a depressingly seedy, continuously abusive cultural society, where Otherising and disempowerment are constant, morphing with time and place. In both play and film, mother and daughter are homeless transients, a product of two centuries of rootlessness based on their gendered vulnerability and resilience.

The Film—*Byzantium*

Byzantium (2012) is set in Hastings, an arty, but run-down seaside town, which has bohemians mixing with refugees and a faded grandeur about its seaside buildings, a kind of less opulent version of its sisters Eastbourne, and further, Brighton. Neil Jordan's earlier work leads naturally to *Byzantium*. He adapted Angela Carter's short story (and related other short stories) "The Company of Wolves" (1979) for his film in 1984, and in so doing shows an insight into the vulnerability and feistiness of Carter's version of Little Red Riding Hood, called Rosaleen in the film, as well as creating luscious color, a mix of the real and fantastic (in *The Company of Wolves* film the toys are threateningly semi-alive though wooden, and the family dog, a domestic comfort, is translated into a horror pack of ravening wolves who chase and devour Rosaleen's sister). These are all clear representations of the excitements and threat of adolescent sexuality in locations which hide danger, then reveal it. Home, domestic spaces, become folk tale villages in the forest, friendly men become werewolves, the safety in living ordinary lives is dissolved: "we keep the wolves outside by living well," says Carter's granny just before she is devoured by the handsome werewolf (who looks forward to eating her granddaughter). Jordan is a perfect match to hype up the fantasy, sexuality, vulnerability and mix of the domestic everyday and the perpetually intruding traces of abuse, of patriarchal dominance, destruction and body decay, the time-limited vulnerabilities of the period in which Clara and Eleanor begin. This plays out in *Byzantium* with the mother Claire/Clara (Gemma Arterton) making a living in her self-managed hotel-brothel, while Eleanor/Ella (Saoirse Ronan) works part time at a restaurant and visits a care home, studying at the F.E. college (school in the play, college in the film). While the play is not set in Hastings and it is possible that although Eleanor writes of being a 200-year-old vampire she might just be an anorexic teenager. Set entirely in the same time sphere as the play, the film utilizes a clever conflation of the orphanage and Further Education College, which Eleanor remembers as North Haven Private Orphanage; it is recognizably the same building that serves in the twenty-first century as the North Haven College of Further Education, and the parallel moments of the cloaked orphanage girls walking on the beach separated by 200 years offers a hauntology of place. There is still abuse, still economic and gendered power relations operating in each time sphere, women still have to fend for themselves, and the force of the patriarchy is further emphasized in the film, with the brotherhood seeking out the deviant successful women much as they do in the *Theatre de vampires* in Anne Rice's novel (1976)/Jordan's film *Interview with the Vampire* (1994). In the novel and film, Claudia, the child vampire, and Madeleine, the mother she adopted and turned, are burned alive in the sun by the revengeful vampire clan, something the powerful male brotherhood in *Byzantium* clearly has in mind for Clara/Claire and Eleanor/Ella.

Byzantium is the name of the run-down hotel owned by bereaved Noel (Daniel Mays) and taken over by Claire/Clara but recalls W.B. Yeats' poems "Byzantium" (1930/1996) and "Sailing to Byzantium" (1926/1996). Yeats' poem constructs an initially idealized aesthetically rich artistic world where one can live eternally, as a metaphor for the alternative longevity and also somewhat blind escapism of art. Since Yeats' art is both rich with the mythic and fantastic yet rooted in "the foul rag and bone shop of the heart" (1939), he suggests eternal life for art but warns against losing engagement with reality, history, politics, and the personal.

While *Byzantium* the film does not engage with the longevity of art there is little noticeable transfer between poem and film, it does mix myth and the everyday, undermines the arrogant, timeless, self-appointed controllers of the male-dominated vampire Brotherhood, fooled, brought down to earth and destroyed or recruited by this couple of socially sensitive vampire women. Making Irish links, James Aubrey (2017) argues that Moira Buffini's family background feeds into the Irishness of location and myth underlying the film.

In the Irish context and reading of the film *Byzantium*, Aubrey (2017) builds on the term "neomyth" used by Celtic scholar Mark Williams (2016) in *Ireland's Immortals* to define novels that "adapt mythic traditions to modern circumstances" (Aubrey 2017, 909). Aubrey argues this term can or should also be transferable to film, as he points out the film does not use any of the staples of established vampire lore and the distant island, soucriant, release of bats or birds, and waterfalls and rivers running red in blood are all new in *Byzantium*. The location in Hastings and the Caribbean souriant on the island are also readable through an Irish-induced lens, as Aubrey notes "the distant, rocky island with its steep cliffs and rock-domed cave entrance is recognizably a visual conflation of two locations: the monastic cemetery on the offshore island of Skellig Michael and the waterfall at the base of Mount Torc, both in the scenic Beara Peninsula of County Cork, in southwest Ireland" (2017, 910). But further argues it is not necessary to recognize the locations, rather appreciate a hit of "folkloric, romantic Ireland, where fairies exist and magical things can happen—as opposed to the drab English town with a run-down amusement park and drug-addled prostitutes" (Aubrey 2017, 910). Eleanor writes her story, rips up the pages and throws them to the wind, but this brings in an old man who recognizes her as able to save him from the pains of his life. The old man who reads Eleanor's scattered writings and invites her home speaks Gaelic to her, linking Irish folklore with the Catholic church and vampires normally found in Europe: "the old man is evidently Irish, for he uses the Gaelic expression *neamh-mhairbh*, explained to mean 'revenants neither dead nor alive,'" as he describes Catholic priests having told stories of such when he was younger, which he opines were "meant to frighten the children" (Jordan 2012). As he translates the Gaelic for Eleanor, he simultaneously prepares the film audience to understand that the Irish know about vampires, and that the Irish Catholic church has invested in Continental European vampire lore, with its apotropaic crucifixes, to supplement scriptural teachings (Barber 1988):

> There are Irish vampire tales preceding Irish Bram Stoker's Transylvania/Whitby/London set *Dracula* (1897) and the main tale is that of a minor Irish chieftain King Abhartach, who died falling out of a window, was buried upright because of his status but rose the next day and the next demanding and taking human blood, he was eventually killed finally by another chieftain Cathán, involving swords in the heart, yew stakes, and heavy stones to keep him buried in Leacht Abatach or Slaughtabartach, meaning "the memorial stone or monument of the dwarf" [Donnelly 2019] [as he was apparently short].

The moral message about patriarchy and a male-dominated secret brotherhood seeking after the wayward independent women two hundred years later, led by Darvell (Sam Riley)—named after the character from Polidori's novel—enables some interesting splicing comments and scenes about predation, employability, gender roles of power and the baselines of the body, and the economic position which enables continuity of life. In modern day Hastings, the women on the streets are housed by Clara, who puts them all to work, but they are earning and making the most of their assets to earn a living. It is not merely a man's world in the updated film version because they enter into an economic relationship by some form of choice, and for Clara running the bawdy/boarding house there's control of money, the independent real owner of the hotel and her own body. A moral message can emerge with the time splices—it's payback for the domination of women by the economic power of men.

In Hastings, Claire/Clara befriends Noel, a bereaved man mourning his mother who ran a hotel, sets up a brothel in this run-down hotel, the "Byzantium" of the title, and offers safety and financial independence to local women, taking them off the streets and the pier. Clad in corsets and black fishnet tights, Claire/Clara enacts the routine predatory vampire, siren figure of men's heated imagination, to provide money for her and Eleanor/Ella so they can pay the rent, buy clothes and look normal. Men prey on her and she preys on them, only killing when abused. On the beach, early morning, as the sun rises, we see her bleeding the violent pimp which reminds us that her version of a new vampire experiences no danger from crosses and sunlight. Clara's draining of the pimp can be mistaken by passersby as a lover's kiss. Meanwhile permanent teenager Eleanor/Ella has a mercy mission visiting hospitals and care homes, releasing into death those who wish to be set free and see her as an angel of mercy. The final sequence has Eleanor/Ella rescuing teenage Frank (Caleb Landry Jones), dying from a disease of the blood, leukemia, through turning him, in the cave on the island, with the help of the souciant. Claire/Clara and Darvell also make peace and two sets of vampire pairs sail into the future together offering conformation of many of the tropes of eternal heteronormative romantic love. Like the play, however this is also a feminist film and interpretation, a modern vampire tale of gender and power.

Conclusion

Jordan's vampire film fixes Buffini's work solidly in vampire lore and film, while in the play this was only hinted. So, there is a major transformation not just of place and time frames but of entrance into the well-established filmic world of vampires, with all the Hammer patriarchal power, special effects of bats, black frock-coated vampires and vampire hunters. However, this feminist film refuses to play by the old rules rather preferring to establish its own. If Clara is dressed like a Hammer courtesan in Dracula's castle, Eleanor dresses like a teenager who buys her clothes from a second-hand shop, hides her face in a hood and has an underlying streak of caring—helping the old out of their longevity, helping Frank out of his death sentence of leukemia. We know of the whore with the heart of gold, and Clara is not that as she drains an annoying teenage Briggs, and makes the most of Noel, the lonely man who owns the seaside hotel, but as a vampire with a heart of gold, Eleanor is a new development.

WORKS CITED

Aubrey, James. 2017. "Celtic Vampires: Neil Jordan's Film *Byzantium* as Irish Neomyth." *Journal of Literature and Art Studies*, vol. 7, no. 7: 909–915.
Auerbach, Nina. 1995. *Our Vampires, Ourselves*. Chicago: University of Chicago Press.
Babbage, Frances. 2018. *Adaptation in Contemporary Theatre: Performing Literature*. London: Bloomsbury Publishing.
Barber, Paul. 1988. *Vampires, Burial and Death: Folklore and Reality*. New Haven: Yale University Press.
Baring-Gould, Sabine. 1865. *The Book of Werewolves*. Guernsey: Studio Editions, 1995.
Brite, Poppy Z. 1992. *Lost Souls*. New York: Dell.
Brite, Poppy Z. 1995. *Wormwood* (formally published as *Swamp Foetus*, 1993). New York: Bantam Doubleday Dell Publishing Group.
Brownworth, Victoria A. 1996. *Nite Bites*, edited by Victoria A. Brownworth. Washington: Seal Press.
Buffini, Moira. 2008. *A Vampire Story*. Written and directed by Moira Buffini.
Buffini, Moira, and Neil Jordan. 2012. *Byzantium* movie script. Scripts. https://www.scripts.com/script.php?id=byzantium_4899&p=5)
Byzantium. Film. Directed by Neil Jordan. StudioCanal/IFC, 2012.
Carter, Angela. 1979. "The Company of Wolves." *The Bloody Chamber and Other Stories*. London: Gollancz.
Carter, Angela. 1985. "The Cabinet of Edgar Allan Poe." *Black Venus*. London: Chatto and Windus.
Company of Wolves. 1984. Film. Directed by Neil Jordan. London: Palace Pictures.
Donnelly, Dave. 2019. "Abhartach the Irish Vampire." https://www.yourirish.com/folklore/abhartach-irish-vampire.
Eldridge, David. 2005. "Massive Attack." *The Guardian*, June 27. https://www.theguardian.com/stage/2005/jun/27/theatre.
Galluzzo, Rob. 2016. "Horror in the Flesh: A History of Horror Theatre." *The 13th Floor*, March 16. http://www.the13thfloor.tv/2016/03/16/horror-in-the-flesh-a-history-of-horror-theatre/.
Gelder, Ken. 2019. *Adapting Bestsellers: Fantasy, Franchise and the Afterlife of Storyworlds*. Cambridge: Cambridge University Press.
Ghost Stories. 2017. Film. Directed by Jeremy Dyson and Andy Nyman. Santa Monica: Lionsgate Films.
Gottlieb, Sherry. 1994. *Love Bite*. New York: Warner.
Gottschall, Jonathan. 2013. *The Storytelling Animal: How Stories Make Us Human*. Boston: Houghton Mifflin Harcourt.

Gumbrecht, Hans Ulrich. 2003. "Epiphany/ Presentification/ Deixis: Futures for the Humanities and Arts." *Id., Production of Presence: What Meaning Cannot Convey*. Stanford: Stanford University Press.
Interview with the Vampire. 1994. Film. Directed by Neil Jordan. Burbank: Warner Bros.
Mantel, Hilary. 2005. *Beyond Black*. London: HarperCollins.
Murray, Simone. 2012. *The Adaptation Industry: The Cultural Economy of Literary Adaptation*. Abingdon: Routledge.
North, Sam. 2017. *The Instinctive Screenplay: Watching and Writing Screen Drama*. London: Palgrave Macmillan.
Oliver, H.J., editor. 1982. *The Taming of the Shrew: The Oxford Shakespeare*. Oxford: Oxford University Press.
Polidori, John. 1819. *A Vampyre: A Tale*. London: Henry Colburn.
Sierz, Alek. 2003. "Interview with Moira Buffini." *In-Yer-Face Theatre*. http://www.inyerface theatre.com/archive9.html#h.
Skal, David. 2016. "Something in the Blood: The Untold Story of Bram Stoker, the Man Who Wrote 'Dracula.'" https://www.theparisreview.org/blog/2016/10/27/something-blood-part-1/.
Smith, Anthony. 2018. *Storytelling Industries: Narrative Production in the 21st Century*. Basingstoke: Palgrave.
Stoker, Bram. 1979. *Dracula* [1897]. London: Penguin.
Thompson, Kristin. 2007. *The Frodo Franchise: The Lord of the Rings and Modern Hollywood*. Berkeley: University of California Press.
Ubersfeld, Ann. 1982. "The Pleasure of the Spectator," translated by Pierre Bouillaguet and Charles Jose. *Modern Drama*, vol. 25, no. 1, pp. 127–139.
Williams, Mark. 2016. *Ireland's Immortals: A History the Gods of Irish Myth*. Princeton: Princeton University Press.
Yeats, W. B. 1996. "Byzantium" 1930; "Sailing to Byzantium" 1926; "The Circus Animals' Desertion" 1939. *The Collected Poems of W.B. Yeats*, revised 2d ed., edited by Richard J. Finneran. New York: Scribner.

Pixel Parasites

The Virtual Vampire as Enemy, Ally and Self in Video Games

SHAWN EDREI

One of the most fascinating aspects of the vampire's global, transcultural presence is the swiftness and ease with which that ubiquitous presence adapts to new media, as Bob Curran observes: "arguably no monster has imbedded itself so deeply in the human psyche than the vampire" (Curran 2006, 15). The emergence of cinema at the turn of the previous century included one of the first vampire films, *Nosferatu* (Murnau 1922)—and while the image of Orlok is not the most dominant in contemporary vampiric depictions, neither has it receded entirely from the canonical corpus (as evidenced by 2014 film *What We Do in the Shadows* [Clement and Waititi] and 2015 film *Hotel Transylvania 2* [Tartakovsky]). *Nosferatu* was followed by iconic depictions of Dracula produced first by Universal Studios (1931–) and subsequently by Hammer Films (1958–74), and to this day the vampire is a frequent feature in modern horror (e.g., *Stake Land*, 2010), Gothic romance (e.g., *Only Lovers Left Alive*, 2013) and even comedy films (e.g., *Vamps*, 2012). The history of television is marked by a similar obsession with the archetype, with *The Munsters* (Burns 1964–66) and *Dark Shadows* (Curtis 1966–71) occupying early footholds in popular imagination, followed by *Forever Knight* (Cohen and Parriot 1992–96), *Port Charles* (Kanelos 1997–2003) and the genre-redefining *Buffy the Vampire Slayer* (Whedon 1997–2003) in the final years of the twentieth century. As with cinema, vampires have not receded from modern television, appearing in teen dramas (*The Vampire Diaries* [Plec and Williamson 2009–17], Japanese anime *Hellsing* [Hirano 2001–2], *Diabolik Lovers* [Tagashira 2013–]) and camp horror (*American Horror Story* [Falchuk 2011–], *True Blood* [Ball 2008–14]). These examples all lend further credence to Curran's affirmation that "vampires have continued to exercise a hold on the human imagination. Apart from the films, countless books, magazines, and television programs on the subject have been produced through the years, right up until the present day" (Curran 2006, 65).

Video games, having coalesced as one of the newest narrative media, have followed suit with their own process of adaptation and incorporation. Vampires began appearing in some of the earliest, technologically-primitive games; however, the inherently-interactive nature of the medium—which requires active participation as opposed to simple spectatorship—has caused a particularly curious development in vampiric canon. Where other media have occasionally repositioned the vampire in different roles (from antagonist to supporting character, and at times a protagonist), video games complicate this paradigm due to the player's immersion and embodiment within diegetic space. For the first time, a mode of storytelling exists in which the audience may actively perform the role of a vampire, even as more conventional depictions (as allies and/or opponents to be overcome) persist. This essay will explore several classic and contemporary video games in terms of how these deploy the archetype of the vampire along familiar and innovative configurations.

The earliest—and, broadly speaking, most common—depiction of vampires in video games casts them in the comfortable, traditional role of enemies to be defeated. As with any virtual monster, their purpose is to impede the player's progress until the player successfully destroys them. The 1990 dungeon crawler *Angband*, for example, describes vampires as generic enemies, defining them purely through their programmed gameplay mechanics:

> This evil undead creature moves normally. It is cold blooded. It regenerates quickly. It is always created sluggish. It is magical, casting spells which cause mind blasting, cause amnesia, teleport to, create darkness, cause serious wounds, paralyze, or terrify; 1 time in 9. It can bash down doors and open doors. It is hurt by bright light. It resists poison and cold. It cannot be slept or confused. It is fairly observant of intruders, which it may notice from 200 feet [*Angband* 1990].

The one exception is Thuringwethil, a character drawn from the Tolkien canon, who receives additional descriptors so as to individuate her: "Chief messenger between Sauron and Morgoth, she is surely the deadliest of her vampire race. At first, she is charming to meet, but her wings and eyes give away her true form" (*Angband* 1990). The emphasis on strategic information rather than characterization confirms Bruce A. McClelland's analysis of classical protagonists faced with vampiric enemies:

> The lack of any ambiguity about the righteousness of the destroyers of evil is a feature not only of the cinematic *Dracula,* in all its incarnations, but of other

so-called horror movies at least through the first half of the twentieth century. The emphasis of such stories was less on the process of identification than on the process of eliminating the threat [McClelland 2006, 169].

In other words, Thuringwethil is not invested with any agency or narrative history, so as not to distract from the player's heroism in destroying her through physical combat or magic; insofar as the player is concerned, the sole purpose of any descriptors for vampires in the game is merely to emphasize their resistance to specific tools in the player's arsenal (e.g., poison, cold-based weapons), per McClelland's claim that "the vampire cannot exist without some sort of prescription for identifying or eliminating him. ...there nevertheless must be a prescribed pattern for handling the vampire so that his destructive actions cease and he never returns" (McClelland 2006, 6).

While vampires continue to appear as enemies and obstacles to the player in many contemporary games, the complexity and depth of their portrayals have increased over time. BioWare's 2000 role-playing game *Baldur's Gate II*, based on the ubiquitous *Dungeons & Dragons* (first released in 1974), features the seductive and deadly Bodhi as a secondary antagonist with whom the player can develop a complicated and dynamic relationship. Initially, Bodhi is presented as the leader of a criminal organization contesting the power of the local thieves' guild; though her headquarters, located in a graveyard, bears the obvious hallmarks of vampiric habitation (pools of blood, empty sarcophagi and so on), the player is nevertheless given an opportunity to ally with Bodhi rather than oppose her. That this is a valid narrative option in *Baldur's Gate II* as opposed to *Angband* is indicative of both the technological advances of the medium and the growing acknowledgment that player agency serves to set video game narratives apart from any other medium, as Sebastian Domsch points out:

What most clearly distinguishes video games from other medial realizations of FNs [future narratives] is the range of agency that they allow their readers. This is why we will refer to the user of a video game in the following as a player, even though this player in many cases will also have to be understood as a reader of fictional meaning, a reader of signs and implied or explicit narratives. But it is a core feature of video games that the player almost never (and never completely) stops to be an agent, and is therefore "playing" the story to a much larger extent than in any other medium [Domsch 2013, 3].

Should the player choose to accept Bodhi's offer, the in-game journal is updated accordingly, summarizing and retroactively justifying the protagonist's decision:

Throughout my time in Athkatla and my adventures in and around the city, I have seen hints of some great struggle between the Shadow Thieves and some other source. This other source approached me in the form of Bodhi ... a woman of great power and evil rivaling her ambition. She revealed the nature of my benefactors under Gaelan Bayle to be none other than the Shadow Thieves themselves and offered to give me the same help that they did ... but at a far lesser price.

I have accepted Bodhi's offer, and she has taken me into her confidence for now. The true nature of her motivations has yet to be revealed, but it is obvious that Bodhi is on the winning side of this citywide conflict. As to the gold I have given her for her aid.... I have the feeling that it is just the beginning of the final price I will eventually have to pay [*Baldur's Gate II* 2000].

Of course, as a vampire antagonist, Bodhi's betrayal is a practical inevitability, as is her subsequent annihilation at the hands of the player; but the fascination with vampires in the world of *Baldur's Gate II* would persist for years to come, first manifesting in a player-created modification which added vampire lieutenant Valen as a possible recruit, and later formalized with the introduction of the vampire Hexxat as an official companion in 2013's updated re-release *Baldur's Gate II: Enhanced Edition* (Overhaul Games).

Both mechanically and narratively, the adversarial role performed by Thuringwethil and Bodhi is functionally identical to conventional depictions of vampires in other media, and recurs in many other games: 1993's *Veil of Darkness* (DreamForge Entertainment) strands the player in a remote Romanian valley and pits them against despotic vampire lord Kairn; vampiric "ekimma" and "bruxa" are among the many supernatural creatures hunted by Geralt of Rivia in the popular 2007–2016 *The Witcher* (CD Projekt Red) trilogy; and Japanese game studio Konami found significant success throughout the late 1980s and early '90s with the *Castlevania* franchise, in which players embody various members of the Belmont family throughout history, all of whom oppose the infamous Count Dracula. These antagonistic depictions follow the same broad parameters as literary vampires seen in Sheridan Le Fanu's *Carmilla* (1872), Stoker's *Dracula* (1897), Richard Matheson's Ruth from *I Am Legend* (1954) and others: they are a distant Other for protagonists to confront, with abilities that mark them as supernatural predators incapable of co-existing with humanity. Regardless of suggested psychological complexity, or points of sympathy and identification on the part of the audience, these vampires are an existential threat that cannot be tolerated. However, the rising trend in literature and film of vampires as protagonists and romantic antiheroes during the latter half of the twentieth century had a pronounced effect on video game depictions as well. The archetype of the vampire became, in some instances, an ally to the player, assisting progress rather than hindering it. For example, 2013's *Paper Sorcerer* (Ultra Runaway Games) allows the player to summon an unnamed vampire as a party member who specializes in draining health from the enemy, while 2015's *Shadowrun: Hong Kong* (Harebrained Schemes) features Ku Feng, a self-styled vampire queen who can assist the player in the final stages of the game, provided her life was spared in an earlier encounter. Two characters serve as particularly interesting examples of this "vampiric ally" archetype: Katrina, from 1993's *Quest for Glory IV: Shadows of Darkness* (Sierra Entertainment), and Veles, from 2017's *Hand of Fate 2* (Defiant Development)—specifically the downloadable content titled "The Servant and the Beast."

Quest for Glory IV (an RPG/adventure hybrid with puzzle elements alongside standard character development and combat sequences) deposits the player character—an experienced hero at this point in the series—in Mordavia, a Romanian stand-in constructed almost entirely of classic horror film tropes: werewolves, ghosts, superstitious villagers, an underground cult dedicated to worshipping a Cthulhu-like deity, and more. The first person the Hero meets in the game is Katrina, a mysterious young woman who claims to live in the nearby castle as a servant: "The castle was once home to the Borgov family. My family once served them and so I am allowed to live there.... I mostly just work in the castle. That's why I can't see you during the day. Someone might notice I'm gone" (*Quest for Glory IV* 1993). Katrina's elusive nature prevents the player from fully investigating her, but with each appearance she reveals details about herself: she finds the misshapen, corrupted landscape of Mordavia strangely beautiful; she has some knowledge of magic (though she claims to possess none herself); and she seems to develop some affection for the Hero, assisting him with healing potions. Though she takes no direct action to aid the player in the many challenges contained in the game, the Hero still considers her an ally: "She's one of your few friends in this hostile country.... [I]n fact, you feel very relaxed and comfortable around her" (*Quest for Glory IV* 1993). Katrina is ultimately revealed to be the Dark Master, the game's primary antagonist and a direct threat to all life in the realm—yet unlike Dracula or Bodhi, this vampire's fondness for the Hero persists even after the battle lines are drawn, and she ultimately sacrifices herself to save his life. Though the player has the option to resurrect her in the final game, *Dragon Fire*, she returns as a human ally—still formidable, but stripped of any vampiric characteristics. This transformation makes Katrina stand out among her peers in the medium: any attempt to complete the romantic subplot begun in *Shadows of Darkness* removes the supernatural context of said romance altogether.

A more contemporary example of the vampiric ally appears in 2017's *Hand of Fate*. One of the narrative modules, "The Servant and the Beast," begins with the player captured by goblins and imprisoned with Lord Veles, an aristocratic Shadow betrayed by his family. Veles joins the player as a companion, assisting in both combat and navigation of the world map; upon completion of his introductory quest, he becomes permanently available for use in other parts of the story. At first glance, Shadows may not seem to fit the general profile of the vampire: they have no aversion to holy relics or garlic, are not bound by restrictions in their movement (e.g., needing invitations to enter homes, crossing running water), and they resemble grotesque, diminutive goblins, rather than the otherworldly beauty so prevalent in contemporary depictions. However, the Shadows' most prominent feature—one shared by Veles himself—is a bloodlust that manifests both diegetically and mechanically. The vampire's thirst, so often a source of dread for the audience, becomes a valuable tool in the player's arsenal: Veles will knock down stunned enemies and bite into their throats, instantly killing them and increasing his own power. Sating his thirst repeatedly will endow him with extraordinary strength, a condition referred to as "blood madness" in which his visage becomes even more twisted and monstrous. As a way of hastening the arrival of this berserker state, the player can allow Veles to feast on their own character, though this is an inherently risky prospect: life is drained directly from the player's avatar, and death is eminently possible. The Dealer, who serves as narrator of the game, warns the player of this danger: "Feed your companion however you please, yet you may find the blood of others more efficient ... why give your own blood, when the blood of others is so abundant?" (*Hand of Fate 2* 2017). Unlike Katrina, the threat Veles poses to the player never fully disappears, as emphasized by his frequent disdain for the main character: "Your blood is as fine as any, but as a servant you are a disappointment" (*Hand of Fate 2* 2017). This depiction lines up with other games such as *Vampire: The Masquerade—Bloodlines* (Troika Games, 2004), *Darkest Dungeon* (Red Hook Studios, 2015) and *The Elder Scrolls* series (Bethesda, 1994–present) in that they reaffirm the archetype of the vampire as not strictly defined by its outward appearance, but primarily through its need to sustain itself by feeding on the living.

Katrina and Veles demonstrate one pseudo-evolutionary track of the vampire's transition into new narrative functions in video games: as allies to the player, their parasitic nature is never brushed aside or disregarded, lending a dangerous and unreliable undertone to any assistance they may provide. But in a medium that distinguishes itself through its ability to embody the player within fictional worlds, it was inevitable that vampires would eventually become avatars themselves. This practice is not in any way a modern development: Ubisoft's 1988 game *Night Hunter* is considered one of the first games to cast the player as an evil vampire, stalking moonlit streets and feeding on countless civilians while avoiding hunters styled after Abraham Van Helsing. The main character of *Night Hunter* is explicitly styled after Bela Lugosi's portrayal of Dracula, with slicked-back hair, a black cloak, and a gaunt visage; the player can also shapeshift into a bat in order to fly over obstacles, and assume a werewolf form to more easily dispatch enemies. Though the game has no explicit narrative to speak of, *Night Hunter* does provide a template for mapping traits associated with the vampiric archetype onto ludological and narrative systems unique to video games. The aforementioned *Castlevania* series has, on occasion, allowed the player to control Adrian Tepes/Alucard, estranged son of Dracula; the *Elder Scrolls* series depicts vampirism as a communicable disease the player can contract, receiving powerful abilities in exchange for sustaining continual damage when exposed to daylight; and 2015 stealth game *Invisible Inc.* posits a cyberpunk dystopian iteration in Matei "Draco" Cernat, a novelist-turned-spy with a rare allergy to light who grows stronger with every use of lethal force. This gradual evolution of the archetype as a playable protagonist can be exemplified through Kain, the main character of Silicon Knights' 1996 action-adventure game *Blood Omen: Legacy of Kain*, and Jonathan Reid, the player's avatar in Dontnod Entertainment's 2018 action/role-playing game *Vampyr*.

Set in the medieval fantasy world of Nosgoth, *Blood Omen* begins with the murder of naïve aristocrat Kain, who is then offered an opportunity to avenge himself: "I didn't care if I was in Heaven or Hell—all I wanted was to kill my assassins. Sometimes you get what you wish for. The Necromancer Mortanius offered me a chance for vengeance. And like a fool, I jumped at his offer without considering the cost. Nothing is free. Not even revenge" (*Blood Omen* 1996). Kain's thirst for revenge becomes literalized, as he returns in the form of a vampire. The player's first objective—slaughtering the aforementioned murderers—is quickly achieved, yet Kain is driven to investigate the circumstances and causes of his death, uncovering a more widespread conspiracy. Interestingly, though the game was developed and released at a point where the vampire's literary canon leaned towards sympathetic portrayals and paranormal romance (e.g., the *Barnabas Collins* and *Vampire Chronicles* series), Kain is distinctly an asexual and antiheroic figure, repeatedly denying any interest in engaging with the dominant stereotype of the tragic/poetic vampire. Josiah Lebowitz and Chris Klug draw attention to this facet of the central figure in their case study of the game: "Unlike most game heroes of the time, Kain has little interest in what happens to the world and goes after the guardians in order to complete his revenge" (Lebowitz and Klug 2011, 150). His positioning within the narrative is that of a disinterested protagonist—while his actions are having a cumulative positive effect on the corrupted world around him, Kain is singularly focused on violent pleasures and self-glorification: "I make no pretense to justify my killing. Yet these vampire hunters would cloak their bloodlust beneath a veil of righteousness. Hypocrites! They would make themselves judge and jury. Very well, then. Let us see how they take to my role as executioner" (*Blood Omen* 1996). The narrative concludes with a binary choice offered to the player: if Kain destroys himself, the realm of Nosgoth will be fully restored, whereas he may alternatively condemn the world and seize power as a dark vampiric sovereign. According to Lebowitz and Klug, the ambiguity of Kain's final decision impacts the player's perception of this particular vampiric figure:

> Although the choice changes nothing but the ending movies, it allows the player to think about what he or she would choose to do if facing a similar dilemma, or perhaps how Kain himself would respond based on his character and personality. As neither choice leads to an "ideal" ending, it makes for an interesting decision between the noble and selfish. The later games in the series assume that Kain chose the latter option and doomed the world to save himself, though it's eventually revealed that his intentions weren't entirely self-serving and that there were deeper reasons behind his decision [Lebowitz and Klug 2011, 151].

Interestingly, subsequent games in the *Legacy of Kain* series canonize the latter ending, positioning Kain as an antagonistic ruler of a future Nosgoth overrun by vampires. For the next two installments, *Soul Reaver* (1999) and *Soul Reaver 2* (2001), the player pursues Kain in the role of his "son" Raziel; series finale *Defiance* (date) finds the player alternating between the two as the story progresses.

The ludological mechanics of *Blood Omen* further reinforce the narrative's ambivalence towards Kain as a vampiric protagonist. He suffers all the traditional weaknesses of the creature he has become: water burns like acid, and his strength is diminished during daytime. Injuries sustained during combat may only be healed by consuming blood—and while stunned enemies can be fed upon, this is an unreliable method of replenishing Kain's health (as combat is rarely a one-on-one affair). Rather, he receives the most benefit by feeding on prisoners and otherwise helpless individuals. Kain's most unique attribute—one that serves the player's interests directly—is his ability to telekinetically draw blood from his victims at a distance. In fact, Kain is never shown biting his enemies at all, and the iconic image of the "vampire's embrace" is strikingly absent here. This likely correlates with the pronounced narrative impetus to avoid associating the protagonist with romantic tropes, yet the end result is that since Kain's vampirism is magically induced, the player is unable to perform one of the vampire's most quintessential functions by infecting others. The only other vampire Kain encounters, the elder Vorador, is similarly disinclined to increase their ranks, even as he venerates that same condition: "Vorador thought my curse a blessing. That we were gods, and that mortals offered their blood as sacrifice so that we could enjoy our supernatural powers. And somewhere deep inside my new self, I knew he was right. That mortal dreams *were* prayers. Prayers to us—begging us for power" (*Blood Omen* 1996). This creates a curious and atypical portrait of the vampire protagonist: Kain remains an object of supernatural terror by virtue of his extreme violence and magical abilities, yet these are overt qualities which double as gameplay elements, tools the player can use to overcome enemies. The subtler aspects of vampirism as a source of anxiety—a transformative communicable disease to which anyone might succumb—are entirely absent. This is perhaps an expression of the necessity to maintain a balanced gameplay experience, preventing the player from converting dozens (if not hundreds) of enemies into allies/servants by propagating vampirism. As with the protagonist of *Night Hunter*, Kain must stand alone against a significantly larger number of enemies in order to complete his story.

Vampyr (2018), published over two decades later by Dontnod Entertainment, conditionally restores this discarded tool to the protagonist's arsenal. Cast in the role of Dr. Jonathan Reid, a veteran of the Great War, the player begins the game with their character attacked by a vampire on the streets of post–Victorian London. As with Kain, Reid's transformation is not voluntary—but where Kain's antiheroic personality causes the player to treat victims as disposable sources of health, *Vampyr* places a much greater emphasis on the moral and ethical implications of vampiric activity. Initially, Reid appears to fit the mold of the sympathetic, self-tormented victim, as after unwittingly committing his first kill while feeding he states: "What have I done? This horror, it's a nightmare" (*Vampyr* 2018). However, Reid's moral configuration is wholly dependent upon the player's active pseudo-authorial agency throughout the game: where Kain canonically views human life as disposable, Reid's attitude towards his would-be prey is subject to a branching-path structure. The virtual population of London in *Vampyr* exists as a network of potential victims for Reid to feed upon—in fact, one of the game's central innovations involves unseen causal links between characters. The game's official website offers players a quick glimpse at how this network operates: "Choose a sacrifice and see who will live the consequences (this is just a small sample of the citizens you will encounter in *Vampyr*'s London)" (vampyr-game.com). For example, should the player choose to have Reid feed upon (and kill) waitress Sabrina Cavendish, the storyline of her employer Tom Watts will be affected accordingly. The opposite holds true as well: killing Tom changes the trajectory of Sabrina's personal narrative. Where Kain's human adversaries are anonymous and exist primarily to impede the player's progress, *Vampyr* posits that the taking of any life—even at the hands of a vampire—is an act that reverberates throughout the fictional world. The game reinforces Reid's position on the moral spectrum by gradually altering his appearance towards inhumanity the more people he chooses to kill, developing red eyes, pale and vein-marked skin, claws and more. Reid will also inevitably infect other characters and transform them into vampires (though how many victims suffer this fate is similarly subject to player choice).

In addition to the narrative agency granted to the player, *Vampyr* also mechanically expresses Reid's ambiguous position on the human/monster binary. The avatar's internal progression and development is dependent not on time spent and challenges overcome, but on whether Reid is actively preying upon the people of London. The game refers to this as "Blood Temptation," and explicitly suggests the player indulge Reid's hunger by pointing out both the gameplay benefits and the consequences: "Press x to **embrace** Clay Cox or O to **release** him. Embracing Clay will provide a massive XP boost but be aware there will be consequences. Learning more about Citizens and collecting their **hints** will increase the experience gained" (*Vampyr* 2018). The XP in question allows players to enhance Reid's abilities, granting them more power within the diegetic space, but some of these abilities are explicitly monstrous: "As natural predators, Vampires have received some gifts from Mother Nature, like claws instead of fingernails. These natural weapons can easily cut through tissue, and are very useful for piercing a prey's arteries. 'If you use your claws, you will see humans differently … like soft and tender meat'" (*Vampyr* 2018). Ultimate skills, useful in defeating groups of powerful enemies, are described in even more dramatic terms:

> Some abilities are so powerful that even Vampires fear them. Rage is one of them. The Vampire loses control, and unleashes the beast within to do their dirty work. The Beast teleports itself on targets around them, striking with an unfettered fury. Because of its dark nature, it cannot be used too often. "Just release the beast, my friend, it's more satisfying than you think" [*Vampyr* 2018].

Thus, the internal systems of *Vampyr* are designed to position Reid—as an extension of the player's will—in a state of existential uncertainty. The player can perform the protagonist's role as that of the modern romantic vampire, tortured and nobly suffering due to the loss of his humanity; or he can be regressed into the bestial predator of antiquity, carving a bloody path through a largely defenseless London. Greg Costikyan argues that this existential uncertainty is, in fact, a critical component of the gaming experience: "Certainly these games contain uncertainty; if they were entirely predictable, people would long ago have stopped playing them. The uncertainty is not in the *outcome*, however, because there *is* no outcome. The uncertainty is in the path the game follows, in how players manage problems, in the surprises they hold" (Costikyan 2013, 13).

Naturally, the examples discussed in this essay represent only a sliver of the vampiric oeuvre in video games. However, it is clear that the interactive nature of the medium has had a profound influence on the myriad contemporary depictions of these supernatural predators. The shift from anonymous enemy to ambiguous ally to embodied protagonist carries with it an increasing amount of complexity and depth, in tandem with the varying amounts of control the player can exert over the virtual vampire. Brendan Keogh's assertion that games "blend narratives and fictions with virtual bodies and objects that are physically *felt* through hands wrapped around plastic controllers or tapping away at keyboards or smearing touchscreens" (Keogh 2018, 21) takes on additional significance when the virtual bodies in question are undead. And the medium continues to experiment with new forms and possibilities of depicting vampires—as of the time of writing, 2019 has seen the release of post-apocalyptic action game *Code Vein* (Bandai Namco Studios), in which vampiric fashion and physical appearance are distinctly modeled after Japanese anime; upcoming sequel *Vampire: The Masquerade—Bloodlines 2* constitutes a return to the popular titular franchise, set in a world rife with vampire politics and "clans" with diverse appearances and abilities; and Owlcat Games' *Pathfinder: Wrath of the Righteous* (2021) introduces playable dhampirs, half-vampires born of human women. As with every other narrative platform, vampires have found a permanent home in virtual media, and continue to demonstrate the same kind of amorphous, mutable plasticity that, according to McClelland, maintains their "immortal" presence in fiction:

> If the popular image of the vampire can metamorphose from a prematurely deceased Balkan villager, to a vicious nobleman from Transylvania, to a sympathetic narrator in old New Orleans, to a parasite of adipose tissue or the half-breed paramilitary hero of a futuristic postapocalypse, there is beneath all these shifts of the popular vampire's shape an idea that is not merely politically metaphoric and tendentious (or even specifically cultural) and a meaning that goes beyond whatever one might be inclined to attach to the idea of returning from the dead [McClelland 2006, 17].

As gaming technology continues to improve along teleological trajectories, the iconic monster is likely to undergo new—yet strikingly familiar—permutations.

Works Cited

Angband. 1990. Game. Developed by Angband Development Team. rephial.org.
Baldur's Gate II. 2000. Game. Developed by BioWare. Los Angeles, CA: Interplay Entertainment.
Blood Omen: Legacy of Kain. 1996. Game. Developed by Silicon Knights. Redwood City, CA: Crystal Dynamics.

Costikyan, Greg. 2013. *Uncertainty in Games*. Cambridge, MA: MIT Press.
Curran, Bob. 2006. *Encyclopedia of the Undead*. Franklin Lakes, NJ: Career Press.
Domsch, Sebastian. 2013. *Storyplaying: Agency and Narrative in Video Games*. Berlin: De Gruyter.
Hand of Fate 2: The Servant and the Beast. 2017. Game. Developed by Defiant Development. Brisbane, Australia.
Keogh, Brendan. 2018. *A Play of Bodies: How We Perceive Video Games*. Cambridge, MA: MIT Press.
Lebowitz, Josiah, and Chris Klug. 2011. *Interactive Storytelling for Video Games: A Player-Centered Approach to Creating Memorable Characters and Stories*. Burlington, MA: Focal Press.
Quest For Glory IV: Shadows of Darkness. 1993. Game. Developed by Sierra On-Line. Los Angeles, Sierra On-Line.
Vampyr. 2018. Game. Developed by Dontnod Entertainment. Paris, France: Focus Home Interactive.

Vampire as Doll

Transformations of Meaning Through Play in the Vampirina and Draculaura (Monster High) Franchises

DEREK NEWMAN-STILLE

In his "Thesis II: The Monster Always Escapes," Jeffrey Jerome Cohen expresses the idea that monsters are never erased from our cultural imagination, they simply transform and take on new shapes (1996, 4–5). Cohen point out that "the monster's body is both corporal and incorporeal; its threat is its propensity to shift" (5). Monsters are never stable figures. They shift and change to match the fears, anxieties, and desires of the people who create and re-create the monster. He observes that "monsters must be examined within the intricate matrix of relations (social, cultural, and literary-historical) that generate them" (5), and that the vampire itself keeps transforming to fit the cultural apparatus of contemporary cultures in which it is reformed. He observes that Bram Stoker had shaped the vampire into a figure of foreignness and transgression (5), which reflected the xenophobia of the time which subsequently saw the vampire shift in Murnau's *Nosferatu* (1922) to reflect the fascism of the time, highlighting the self-loathing expressed through the vampire's imagery of plague and bodily corruption, especially illustrated by the vampire's rat-like appearance in the film (5). He further comments that Anne Rice's vampires combine homosexuality and vampire and that Rice created a pop culture phenomenon with her sexualization of the vampire and its construction as a figure of taboo sexuality of the time period (5). Francis Ford Coppola's film *Bram Stoker's Dracula* further advances the homosexuality subtext of the vampire, but allies it with the prevalent fears of the film's contemporaneity by using images of red corpuscles and splashes of blood to embody the fear of the AIDS epidemic, creating a vampire with its own epidemiology and the transmission of vampirism through sex or as a blood-based pathogen. It is no coincidence then that, as Cohen mentions, "Coppola was putting together a documentary on AIDS at the same time he was working on Dracula" (5).

The vampires in these examples reflect the anxieties and alterity of the times in which they were created, shifting to encompass cultural questions of their respective time periods, but also reflecting social ideas of Otherness. The vampire keeps hold of some of its previous cultural baggage while having new meanings written onto it and transforming to meet the issues of its time period reflecting social preoccupations of the time periods in which it is resurrected.

Nina Auerbach reflects on this in a more personal way "they may look marginal, feeding on human history from some limbo of their own, but for me, they have always been central: what vampires are in a given generation is part of what I am and what my times have become" (1995, 1) and she describes vampires as "personifications of their age" (3). Vampires come to constitute a mirror for humanity, reflecting what is pertinent in particular periods of time. They represent "otherness," but in doing so, they reflect the normate.

Yet through these shifts in the imagery of the vampire, the material culture surrounding the vampire has also been shifting and modifying. It shifts from being a figure of oral culture and folklore to one embodied in a codex or book, and then into film. Each of these materials also shapes the type of vampire stories that can be told and the messages they can embody. The blood of Coppola's film would not be captured as strongly in a book, nor incite the kind of panic that was structured around blood in the 1990s. At the height of AIDS panic posters frequently used red as a sign of caution and also as an embodiment of the blood that carried the epidemic. As McLuhan (1964) suggests "the medium is the message" intimating how material culture shapes the sort of messages that can be told using them.

Subsequently characters like Draculaura and Vampirina respectively from the multimedia franchises *Monster High* (Mattel, 2010–present) and *Vampirina* (Disney, 2017–present), not only illustrate the entrenched meanings of their time periods, but are also shaped by the multiplicity of media in which they are embodied. Both franchises use a combination of books, film, television, dolls, playsets of multiple sizes, coloring books, DVDs, clothing, music, stickers, and temporary tattoos to encompass their messages. This wide range of media allows for a shifting, changing set of messages and possibilities that are presented to its predominantly young audience in relation to friendships, school, and other real-world situations.

Monster High

While *Vampirina*'s *urtext* was the book *Vampirina Ballerina* (2012) by Anne Marie Pace, which has been retconned into the Disney media empire with a sticker that now states "Watch it on Disney Junior" even though the television show and Disney media has little to do with the original story. *Monster High* presents a much more complicated engagement of different media. In its production of *Monster High*, Mattel took a different approach than the current trend of producing toys to fit existing media. Mattel decided to "create a toy craze from scratch, with the movies and TV shows coming on its heels" (Zimmerman 2010, n.p.). They wanted to create an "entertainment juggernaut" that would challenge Disney and decided not to use existing book or movie characters as Disney normally would (n.p.). Ann Zimmerman observes that "consumers are willing to pay 50% more for toys based on entertainment properties ... and sales of such toys have grown 40% over the last four years, while sales of other kinds of toys have dropped" (n.p.). Indeed, instead of creating texts for the characters first, Mattel sent dolls to author Lisi Harrison, who was well known for producing stories about teens for young adult consumption (including *The Clique* [2004–11] and *Alphas* [2009]). Harrison was asked by Mattel to use the dolls for inspiration in creating a narrative about these characters. The dolls became an *urtext* for the story text rather than the reverse as had been the case with *Vampirina*. Harrison notes that "Mattel came up with the dolls and the world of *Monster High* before I even came into the picture, and then they approached my publisher and me to see if I wanted to write the series" (Larsen 2011). Unlike her other series, *Monster High* did not develop exclusively from Harrison's imagination, but was already partially shaped by the material items of the dolls. Indeed, Harrison states "Mattel had already created the dolls for the characters so I drew a lot of inspiration from them. Have you seen those things? They're incredible. So sassy and full of attitude. I would stare at them and wonder what their personalities would be like. What would they do when they were nervous, happy, embarrassed, in love..." (*Seventeen* 2010, n.p.). This development of story and character from the materiality of the dolls marked a shift in most existing vampire narratives, which had generally begun with a story that was then modified to fit other media. The open signifier of the doll presents possibilities for interpretation through play both by Harrison as she developed her narrative, and also by the children who played with the dolls. I should also note here that Harrison's narrative was repeatedly retconned by Mattel in order to provide new origin stories for *Monster High* that fit with new branding of the dolls and market research.

Dolls represent new media possibilities for the vampire and new ways of imagining this figure, particularly through *Monster High's* Draculaura. Dolls, like any material culture, carry with them embedded meanings acquired through past use and assumed current use. They are media that already come with a set of expectations. As Mitchell and Reid-Walsh observe, dolls are more than just plastic and should not be trivialized solely because they are objects of girls' play (2012, 1). Forman-Brunell observes that there is a tendency to devalue the role of dolls within scholarship, yet dolls are extremely important in Western notions of girlhood. Dolls have educational roles in constructing ideas of femininity and maternity and have a role in the social relationships of girls (2012, 3).

As such, dolls are not figures with singular meanings, but, rather, their meanings are constantly changeable and multiple. Forman-Brunell observes that "businessmen, women doll makers, and girls [are] frequently at odds over the meaning of dolls" and all of these groups struggle "to define the place and purpose of dolls in girlhood" (2012, 4). Corinne Mason points out the shifting medium of the Barbie doll within multiple cultural contexts, pointing out that although the Barbie doll has been thought to be a conveyer of cultural ideas in a unidirectional way, the doll's context in India illustrates that consumption is not passive, but, instead, active and shifting. In India, Barbie is dressed in a sari, while Ken's clothes are American, illustrating a complex engagement with the dolls that is multidirectional and gendered (2016, 62–73).

Although doll play has traditionally been assumed to encourage normate feminine socialization and essentialization of girlhood, "dolls and the girls who play with them negotiate, revise, and disrupt the cultural categories of girlhood" (Forman-Brunell 2012, 4). Dolls are not stationary signifiers, but, rather, are constantly subject to revision through the act of play, their meanings constantly being constituted and reconstituted through the narratives of the girls who play with them. Dolls are "dynamic texts that represent layered versions of realities that are mediated by often contradictory ideologies, values, or worldviews of doll creators, producers, consumers, and players" (4–5). Girls have agency in their play and reconstruct the cultural texts of dolls (5).

Dolls, however, do represent the body, and the confines of the body that is represented can shape the meaning of the doll. *Monster High* dolls are ubiquitously thin and adhere to normate ideas of gender and conventional ideas of beauty. Although these dolls are supposed to represent monsters, their bodies represent human ideals. Indeed, the narratives surrounding the dolls reinforce these ideas of normativity and conventions of gendered beauty. Lindsey Hanlon observes that:

> The *Monster High* products, rather than embracing flaws and expanding notions of beauty, instead acts as an attempt to tame what Barbara Creed calls the "monstrous-feminine." By reimagining female monsters within the sphere of

conventional teenage femininity, the *Monster High* products rob female monsters of their power to scare. They expand the controlling power of social gender norms to encompass what was once considered abject: The monstrous female body [2016, 152].

Indeed, the character bios provided by Mattel promote these ideas of traditional body norms and Draculaura's "monster quirk" further reinforces this: "I can't see my reflection in the mirror, so I always risk looking a little batty. But thanks to centuries of practice, I'm scary good at applying lip gloss" (Mattel, *Draculaura*). A characteristic of the vampire is tamed into normate ideas of teen femininity, transforming the mirror into an obstacle for the application of makeup and beauty products. To further distance Draculaura from the figure of the vampire, she is also given a vegetarian diet and actually faints at the sight of blood. Her subjectivity is transformed from monstrous to normatively feminine. Hanlon suggests that the characters "adhere to traditional norms of boy-obsessed, body-obsessed femininity" (2016 152).[41]

Despite the body normativity of the dolls, *Monster High* markets itself as a product based on ideas of inclusion. Indeed, the brand catchphrase is "Be yourself. Be unique. Be a monster" and the brand website has the phrase "everyone is welcome" under the *Monster High* title, indicating that Mattel sees inclusion as an integral part of the brand, or at least that it could be a marketable feature (Mattel, *Monster High*). The song for the *Monster High* television show ("Monster High Fright Song") reinforces this idea of acceptance with lines like "Everybody turns to look at you/it's not because you're different/it's just because you're scary cool" (Trilling 2010), yet it also reinforces ideas of normate beauty and conformity with lines like "Frankie's got me fallin' apart/Oh Draculaura's stealin' my heart" reducing the monsters to their perceived connection to relationships. The focus of these lyrics is on the romantic gaze of the male singer (Hanlon 2016, 157). Yet, as further noted by Hanlon "the admonition to 'be yourself. Be unique. Be a monster' is never actually tested against something that is truly different … their uniqueness as monsters becomes a type of uniformity" (155).

The notion of difference was something that Mattel intended to bring out in the characters and Tim Kilpin, Mattel general manager asks, "Who doesn't feel like a freak in high school?" (Zimmerman 2010). Adolescence is intrinsically connected to ideas of freakishness, the outsider, and thus the monster in this articulation. Lisi Harrison further reinforces this notion when describing she adapted the dolls to the idea of being in a high school:

41. See also Jacquelyn E. Bent, 2018, "Under her Batwings: Jung's Shadow Aspect as Depicted in Monster High and My Little Pony Vampires," in *Growing Up with Vampires! Essays on the Undead in Children's Media*, edited by Simon Bacon and Katarzyna Bronk (Jefferson: McFarland), pp. 82–94.

I loved using their monster traits as a metaphor for adolescence. For example, Clawdeen the werewolf is super hairy and is embarrassed about that. I completely remember the horror I felt when my pits started getting hairy. I would walk with my arms pressed against my sides.... Lala [Draculaura] won't smile because she's hiding her fangs. I had braces for four years. And the list goes on and on.... So in a sense I relate to all of the characters. Anyone who went through puberty or is going through it will be able to identify with these characters [*Seventeen*, 2010].

Harrison observes the potential of the monster as a perfect embodiment of the alienation of adolescence, but she also reinforces normate ideas of femininity that encourage compliance defy ideas of alienation. The characters are still obsessed with normate ideas of beauty, sexualization, fashion, and roles in cliques, and are "dominated by identical, and stereotypical concerns: their appearance, their belongings, and boys" (Hanlon 2016, 155). The *Monster High* dolls embody the conflictory nature of the high school experience itself, one that invites students to be unique, but also reinforces the idea that one should conform to normative ideals. Harrison has drawn the *Monster High* dolls into the world that she understands as high school as portrayed in young adult novels, integrating the monstrous into the types of worlds she created for *The Clique* and *Alphas*.

Alongside this *Monster High* is also connected to anti-bullying narratives through their marketing of the Kind Campaign. This campaign, founded by Molly Thompson and Lauren Parsekian, is focused on bringing awareness about "girl-against-girl bullying" (https://www.kindcampaign.com). As part of the partnership between the campaign and the franchise, *Monster High* posted a video in May 2011 about their partnership and began to share links to the Kind Campaign's website (*Monster High Wiki: Kind Campaign*, n.d.). In October 2011, *Monster High* created "monsterfied" versions of Thompson and Parsekian teaching about bullying in a webisode called "Kind: The Shockumentary" (*Monster High Wiki: Kind the Shockumentary*, n.d.). The notion of bullying was also something that Harrison highlighted as central to her ideas about *Monster High* as early as 2010: "The awkwardness and alienation the monsters face in *Monster High* is horrible. My goal is to teach readers how to treat and respect themselves and each other in an entertaining way" (*Seventeen*, 2010).

Lisi Harrison situated her version of the *Monster High* universe in the "real" world despite Mattel asking her to create a school entirely for monsters. For her, this is connected to the need for teens to make a connection between the monster and the metaphor of difference in teen lives: "Mattel thought of one school called Monster High, and it was just filled with monsters. And I had a problem with that. I wanted to put them in a normal world and have normal characters, too, so we could see them not fitting in.

If they were all equals, it didn't seem as dramatic to me" (Larsen 2011, n.p.). Her use of "normies" and monsters reinforced ideas of difference and reified the image of the monster as a figure who was different, but wanted to fit in. She intended this to be a lesson for youth about finding acceptance: "It's an amazing metaphor for puberty and high school, and growing and changing, and how (teens) feel like monsters. I felt you couldn't really show that without putting them in a context where they seem abnormal. I wanted to show how unequal everybody was, and hopefully through struggling and learning and growing, you end up in a place of more acceptance" (n.p.).

Yet Harrison's situation of monsters alongside "normal" teen life reified ideas of normalcy and assumptions about what is normal for teens. Her own description connects these monsters to ideas of "normal" teen novels: "So I decided to say, 'OK, I'm going to make monsters for "The Clique" girls.' Nobody had done it in a fun, glamorous way before. The drama by nature is brooding and dark. They're not functioning in a normal pop culture world" (n.p.). She describes the creation of these stories as ones that do not conform to traditional monster stories: "I just saw this as monster books for girls like me who wouldn't normally read monster books" (n.p.).

Vampirina

Vampirina similarly expresses the image of the vampire as a figure of diversity. In Disney's *Vampirina*, "Vee" and her family move from Transylvania to Pennsylvania and find themselves in a world that is very different from home. In the theme song for the series, the viewer is told "We were normal vampires in Transylvania/like the other monsters on every block/till we packed our things/and we flapped our wings/and we got a case of human race culture shock" (Disney Junior, 2017b). The song expresses the idea that the show will be an exploration of difference and belonging. It presents the image of the outsider moving into a space where they are culturally different and experiencing culture shock. The song further reinforces Vampirina's sameness by saying "I may be blue with pointy teeth/but I'm not so different underneath" (2017b). It presents the idea that difference is only surface deep, making connections between skin color and race and presenting the notion that differences are arbitrary. Yet, the song also reinforces notions of a normate culture, in this case the normate culture of the United States and reifies the idea that cultural others should adapt to fit into the American cultural paradigm. The expectation shaped by the song is that Vampirina and her family need to adapt to life in the U.S. and become more like the Americans around them. In expressing sameness, it erases the importance of cultural difference and in maintaining one's differences in a melting pot culture. Real difference is ignored and obliterated through the message of "fitting in." The song reifies cultural difference as a matter of "taste" stating "It's true that our taste may be a little offbeat" (2017b).

The show expresses a constant dual message of telling the audience that they need to accept others, while also reinforcing the idea that anyone who is "other" needs to work to fit in. For example, Vampirina's father, Boris, tells his family "Just act like the perfectly normal family that we are" in season 1, episode 5 (Disney Junior, 2017a). Indeed, the family gargoyle, Gregoria, reminds the family that any display of difference is likely to prevent them from being accepted: "If they get a picture of you, we won't be able to live a quiet, normal life here in Pennsylvania" (2017a). The characters have to "de-spookify" their house for human visitors. Vampirina's own need for acceptance and conformity is illustrated when she states, "We just want to fit in here" (2017a). Minority status is something that needs to be performed in secret and any cultural difference should only occur when away from normate American culture. Boris states "we're used to keeping hidden from humans" (2017a). Difference is obliterated for the promise of conformity.

Both the *Monster High* and *Vampirina* media articulate ideas of acceptance of difference while reifying sameness. The vampire appears in these narratives as a placeholder for real diversity, instead emphasizing normate notions of the body, femininity, and identity. It is significant that *Vampirina* is situated in suburbia, a place that is often symbolic of American ideological conformity. Vampirina is included in her society only as long as she is able to hide her own culture or only share it with a few open-minded people, reifying the idea of tamed diversity and cultural erasure. Subsequently, *Vampirina* is a "passing" narrative and her cultural difference is only allowed as long as she is able to mask her difference and thus gain social acceptance. In order to reinforce her "passing" she is required to constantly be vigilant of any difference and hide it. Similarly, Draculaura has to hide her vampirisim in order to fit into American suburbia in Lisi Harrison's novels, only able to be herself later in the narrative. Yet, in the *Monster High* television show and webisodes, she is allowed to express herself within a monster-only space of the high school. Despite this ability to be her vampiric self, as illustrated above, she still conforms to traditional standards of feminine beauty and identity and is distanced from the more monstrous characteristics of the vampire like blood-drinking. She is allowed to be "diverse" as long as she is still thin, pretty, and interested in the same things as other teen girls. The abject characteristics of these vampires are removed in their corporate production and consumption by its young audience.

There is an essential contradiction and multiplicity of meaning embedded in the official media for both *Vampirina* and *Monster High*, and that ambiguity and uncertainty allows for a space for challenging the overt normative meanings they superficially encourage and constructing new narratives around identity and sexuality. That narrative multiplicity and uncertainty is expanded upon by the nature of dolls as objects of play and where the potential for play allows for a plurality of meanings. Even within the central onscreen texts of *Vampirina* and *Monster High* there is a narrative disconnect, with multiple different stories. In *Monster High*, this is partially constructed through the use of multiple writers across the franchise, and in *Vampirina* the disconnect can be illustrated between Anne Marie Pace's original *Vampirina Ballerina* and the new Vampirina constructed by Disney.

Yet, the *Monster High* media illustrates a disconnect based on age as well, with one message directed toward parents and one toward children. With other media culture, the relationship between the consumer and the producer of that culture, when it comes to materials directed at children, there is the mediator of the parent involved in that process as well. Materials are not solely marketed at children, but, rather, at children and their parents. However, on *Monster High's* website, there are two possible "about" pages one can click on: "Kids" and "Parents," illustrating a bifurcated marketing strategy. Where audience always effects the message, in the case of children, that message is mediated through parents. Parents hold incredible power over children and their perceptions of "childness" and their beliefs about children's needs affect children's interactions with media. As Bohlmann and Moreland suggest "adulthood is predicated on the abjection of the child one used to be, albeit in an imagined, idealized state" (2015, 15). Childhood is perceived of as a blank slate and children as empty receptacles waiting to be filled with knowledge.[42] Childhood in Western culture is also perceived to be a protected category and children are subject to adult control "for their own good."[43] As observed by Marcus P.J. Bohlmann and Sean Moreland childhood's "discursive and narrative construction seems to have been indelibly colored by the Edenic myth, as a paradoxical paradise we can look back upon longingly, but can never re-enter once we've partaken of the knowledge that inaugurates us into adulthood" (2015, 19). Childhood is viewed as a state of innocence that is differentiated from adulthood and has become a protected category in modernity because "the child has served as both repository and emblem of our aspirations and our fears, our dreams and our nightmares" (19). As Bruhm notes, children are continually

---

42. See James R. Kincaid, 1992, *Child-Loving: The Erotic Child and Victorian Culture*. London: Routledge.
43. See Perry Nodelman. 2008, *The Hidden Adult: Defining Children's Literature*. Baltimore: Johns Hopkins University Press.

subject to greater degrees of control over their behavior in order that they conform to notions of normalcy (2015, 4). Children are invested with a society's anxieties and fears about the future and thus subject to controls around their behavior, directed toward what a society considers morally "good." The addition of material about bullying and acceptance of alterity in the *Monster High* and *Vampirina* franchises is partially connected to the notion that children *should* learn techniques to cope with bullying and to strive toward acceptance.

Despite these levels of control over the meaning embodied in dolls and acts of play and the narratives provided by adults, the figure of the doll opens up possibilities for new meaning creation and adaptation. Rebecca Hains conducted a study of girlhood play and interaction with dolls, noting that many of the scholars, activists, and parents interpreting dolls had not included the voices of girls or the observations of girls engaged in play (2012, 121). Hains concentrated her research on Bratz dolls, which had attracted attention from parent groups because of their perceived sexualization (122–124), and observed that the people commenting on the Bratz dolls had assumed a passive audience and that girls would be mindless receivers of the message of the dolls rather than active agents in creating their own meaning (125). The research that Hains conducted was with 30 preadolescent girls aged between 8–10 years old and the girls demonstrated how they played with their dolls for her. During the course of her research, Hains noted that "girls created productive avenues for Bratz play, actively making meanings that conflicted with the producers' intentions for the dolls" (125). Instead of being passive receivers of producer messaging contained within the look of the dolls, girls constructed their own narratives. Hains further noted racial differences in which dolls were favored, which showed white girls primarily favoring American Girl dolls and black girls primarily favoring Bratz dolls. She suggests that this could be partially attributed to the cost of the dolls, with American Girl dolls being upwards of 4 times more expensive, however, she noted that black girls tended to use the Bratz dolls to negotiate issues around race in the United States (127–128). Hains' results were interesting as the girls "appeared to ignore the dolls sexy clothing, focusing instead on skin tone variations as they wove an array of stories" (127–128) seeing the dolls become a site for negotiating identity and oppression. She observed that they focused primarily on the fact that the dolls had non-white skin tones (128). The majority of dolls produced for Western audiences tend to be white, presenting this to children as the norm and this does not allow for BIPOC (Black, Indigenous, People of Color) girls to see themselves represented. The girls who Haines worked with noted that black Barbie dolls did not represent them, where they saw the variability of skin tones expressed in Bratz dolls as being more representative (129).

During play, the girls Hains (2012) conducted her research with "began using the dolls to act out race relations at their predominantly black schools, and then to explore their understandings of the U.S. history of slavery and the Underground Railroad" (131). Rather than the dolls being passively accepted with the messages intended by the producers, girls reinterpreted dolls to explore their own lives and the issues that were important to them, exploring issues as complex as the American history of slavery and oppression of BIPOC people. Hains observed that the girls did not mimic television narratives, but instead made their dolls relevant to their own lives and the stories they wanted to tell (131). As such, the research illustrates that in the act of play, girls create their own scripts, using the dolls to encode their perceptions of their own experiences and to navigate them. These dolls are not constrained by the narrative shaping intended by the companies that created them, but, rather, illustrate the potential of girls to use play to come up with their own stories and allowing them to negotiate around their own social environments (135–136). Hains concludes that "children's use of pop culture—as evidenced by the African American girls' play with Bratz dolls— is probably more complex than we, as adults, might conclude from simplistic impressions of popular media texts and products" (138). Doll play provides a site for observing the way that children can subvert the cultural messages projected at them and Hains reminds readers that children are "active agents with resilience and the ability to empower themselves" (138).

A similar critique as made by Forman-Brunell about the assumed passivity of girls when engaging in doll play, pointing out that "dolls were not uniform, static artifacts of a single dominant culture" and observing that "dolls and the girls who play with them negotiate, revise, and disrupt" canonical messages (2012, 4). She suggests that dolls are "dynamic texts that represent layered versions of realities that are mediated by the often-contradictory ideologies, values, or worldviews of the doll creators, producers, consumers, and players" (4–5) seeing them as figures that express the agency of girls.

The meaning of dolls is not static, rather they are constantly subject to reinterpretation in the act of play. Acts of play and the adaptability of the doll evokes notions of fan practices and the potential of fan practices to reshape canonical texts. Similar to the work of Hains (2012) and Forman-Brunell (2012), Henry Jenkins has sought to represent fans as actively engaged, critical viewers of materials rather than just passive consumers (2006, 1). Jenkins perceived fans as participants in their media, questioning, debating, and critiquing the messages they were presented with, observing how fans often engage in counterhegemonic messages, challenging the normativity and narrow scope of the media they encounter (186–188). Further, Jenkins explores the way that fan activism that be a means for promoting change, observing that fandom itself represents a form of participatory culture and that this active engagement allows for fans to engage in other active circles (2014, 65). Although *Vampirina* has not attracted a large amount of fan participation, *Monster High*, in contrast, even has its own fandom site (monsterhigh.fandom.com). Fans create their own stories with the characters, debate issues in the fan community, and even upload their own videos of the dolls in play, allowing for them to create new narratives through play and share those via video media. This engagement is encouraged by the Mattel corporation, with the creation of their own doll videos. Mattel further engaged fandom by creating "doll elections," which allowed fans to vote for the dolls they wanted to see in the coming year. In the 2014 doll election, fans were able to encourage the creation of the first disabled doll in the *Monster High* fandom—Finnegan Wake, a wheelchair user, illustrating fan interest in diversity.[44] *Monster High* actively encouraged fan participation and fans connected the dolls to other diversity programs such as the previously mentioned Kind Campaign, and the creation of the Zomby Gaga doll, connecting the doll and *Monster High* to pop singer Lady Gaga and to her foundation "Born This Way." In Mattel's press release about the doll, they suggest that "Today, *Monster High* and Born This Way Foundation revealed Zomby Gaga, a doll inspired by Lady Gaga to champion kindness, instill bravery, and build a world where young people celebrate their differences" (Mattel 2016) connecting the doll to Gaga's campaign and also bringing the pop star into the world of *Monster High*. Born This Way's mission is to create "a kinder and braver world," to "support the mental and emotional wellness of young people by putting their needs, ideas, and voices first" (Born This Way Foundation, n.d.) and presents itself as a collaborative project with youth. *Monster High* cultivates its fandom and reinforces the connection of fan practices to activism through campaigns like those mentioned above, engaging fans in the creation of participatory culture.

Monster High's engagement with and of its fans has been called, by Karen Wohlwend (2017), a "virtual dollhouse," that explores the transmedia potential of the franchise. She observes that "children play in transmedia franchises that bring together media characters, toys, and everyday consumer goods with fames, apps, and websites in complex mergers of childhood cultures, digital literacies, consumer practices, and corporate agendas" (1). She describes these transmedia contexts as virtual dollhouses because they are "assemblages of toys, stories, and imagination that converge digital media, popular media, and social media" (1–2). For Wohlwend, "transmedia websites are not texts to be read but contexts to inhabit" (1–2). There is an active engagement of girls rather than a simple recitation of texts. Through observing children's YouTube videos, she observes that youth are not just

---

44. Finnegan Wake is a wheelchair dependent Mer-man who enjoys extreme sports.

engaging with the expective social practices of the dolls, but, rather rupturing and opening "opportunities for player agency and redesign" (1–2).

Dolls already embody the potential to be read and reread in different and often contradictory ways by the girls who engage with them, but Wohlwend opens up the possibility that digital play can be a form of dollhouse in which children reimagine and challenge canonical texts from their media franchise. The websites that *Monster High* provides are not static, but rather interactive, allowing children to engage with the characters through fan affiliation (2). She observes that there are "multiple sites of engagement" that complicate notions of play, creating a "mesh of interactions among players, materials, actions, and across transmedia" (3). Play is not one-sided, but, rather, dynamic, involving not just the material from *Monster High*'s franchise, but also from the child's imagination, and from the imaginations of other fan creators who the child may engage with. She observes that franchise, fandom, and the person engaged in play are engaged in a mutual web of transformation (4). The efficacy of this web can be illustrated by *Monster High*'s engagement of fan practices and shifts in canonical texts in response to fan desires (such as the creation of new characters).

Within these transmedia franchises, the vampire is subject to constant shifts and re-evaluations, its meaning engaged in re-evaluation even as it is constructed. Fan practices and active engagement through play create a potential for the vampire to shift and change rapidly, acquiring new meanings and associations.

Closing Thoughts

Draculaura and Vampirina represent a praxis of the changing representation of the vampire, perceptions of high school as a space of difference and conformity, adult ideas about childhood, and the adaptability of the medium of the doll within girl culture. These dolls have been embodied with ideas of resistance to bullying, questions around normalcy, and accessing the vampire as a symbol of alterity—an abject form that has been ultimately robbed of its abjection through the vegetarianism or ignoring of blood-drinking of Draculaura and Vampirina respectively.

Before *Monster High*'s Draculaura and Disney's Vampirina, the vampire had already shifted from a threatening figure of abjection toward a symbol of the ultimate outsider, coming to represent the alterous. In writing by figures like Anne Rice[45] and Stephenie Meyer,[46] the vampire was divorced from its overt threat, and was presented instead as an attractive "other." It

---

45. *The Vampire Chronicles* (Rice, 1976–2018)
46. *The Twilight Saga* (Meyer, 2005–20)—including the recent addition of *Midnight Son*.

began to stand as a codified symbol of embodied difference, which children's programs and toy companies latched onto as a way of discussing inclusion and diversity. While the vampire represented otherness in Vampirina and Draculaura, it also came to obscure actual otherness and difference. Instead of dealing with ideas like homophobia, fatphobia, racism, and ableism, instead the narrative of bullying and difference was attached to the vampire who became a figure that could be *included* through acceptance of difference. Consequently it has codified American ideas of the melting pot and put the onus on the figure of the outsider to make itself acceptable to an American public, suggesting that the pedagogical responsibility is on the outsider to both adapt to an American norm and also to teach that norm how to accept difference.

Works Cited

Auerbach, Nina. 1995. *Our Vampires, Ourselves*. Chicago: University of Chicago Press.
Bohlmann, Markus P.J., and Sean Moreland. 2015. "Introduction: Holy Terrors and Other Musings on Monstrous-Childness." *Monstrous Children and Childish Monsters: Essays on Cinema's Holy Terrors*, edited by Markus P.J. Bohlmann and Sean Moreland. Jefferson, NC: McFarland, pp. 9–25.
Born This Way Foundation. N.d. "Our Mission." https://bornthisway.foundation/our-mission/.
Bruhm, Steven. 2015. "Foreword." *Monstrous Children and Childish Monsters: Essays on Cinema's Holy Terrors*, edited by Markus P.J. Bohlmann and Sean Moreland. Jefferson, NC: McFarland, pp. 1–6.
Cohen, Jeffrey Jerome. 1996. "Monster Culture (Seven Theses)." *Monster Theory: Reading Culture*, edited by Jeffrey Jerome Cohen. Minneapolis: University of Minnesota Press, pp. 3–25.
Forman-Brunell, Miriam. 2012. "Interrogating the Meanings of Dolls: New Directions in Doll Studies." *Girlhood Studies*, vol. 5, no. 1, pp. 3–13.
Hains, Rebecca C. 2012. "An Afternoon of Productive Play with Problematic Dolls: The Importance of Foregrounding Children's Voices in Research." *Girlhood Studies*, vol. 5, no. 1, pp. 121–40.
Hanlon, Lindsey. 2016. "Pretty Little Monsters: The Reification of Beauty and Gender Norms in *Monster High*." *Children's and Young Adult Literature and Culture: A Mosaic of Criticism*, edited by Amie A. Doughty, Newcastle-upon-Tyne: Cambridge Scholars Publishing, pp. 152–67
Jenkins, Henry. 1992. *Textual Poachers: Television Fans & Participatory Culture*. New York: Routledge.
_____. 2006. *Fans, Bloggers, and Gamers: Exploring Participatory Culture*. New York: New York University Press.
_____. 2014. "Fan Activism as Participatory Politics: The Case of the Harry Potter Alliance." *DIY Citizenship: Critical Making and Social Media*, edited by Matt Ratto and Megan Boler, Cambridge: MIT Press, pp. 65–74.
Larsen, Peter. 2011. "Author Lisi Harrison to Sign 'Monster High' in H.B." *The Orange County Register*. https://www.ocregister.com/2011/04/02/author-lisi-harrison-to-sign-monster-high-in-hb/.
Mattel. N.d. "Draculaura." *Monster High Characters*. http://play.monsterhigh.com/en-ca/characters/draculaura.
_____. N.d. *Monster High: Everyone Is Welcome*. http://play.monsterhigh.com/en-ca/index.html?mh.

———. 2016. "Monster High Launches Lady Gaga Doll to Inspire Kindness with Born This Way Foundation." *Mattel Newsroom.* https://news.mattel.com/news/monster-high-launches-lady-gaga-doll-to-inspire-kindness-with-born-this-way-foundation.

Mason, Corinne. 2016. "Transnational Feminism." *Feminist Issues: Race, Class, and Sexuality,* 6th ed., edited by Nancy Mandell and Jennifer Johnson, Toronto: Pearson, pp. 62–73.

McLuhan, Marshall. 1964. *Understanding Media: The Extensions of Man.* New York: McGraw-Hill.

Mitchell, Claudia, and Jacqueline Reid-Walsh. 2012. "Girls and Dolls." *Girlhood Studies,* vol. 5, no. 1, pp. 1–2. https://doi.org/10.3167/ghs.2012.050101.

Monster High Fright Song. 2010. Music Video. Written by Wendy Trilling. Segundo: Mattel Rhapsody.

Monster High Wiki: Kind Campaign. N.d. https://monsterhigh.fandom.com/wiki/Kind_Campaign.

Monster High Wiki: Kind: The Shockumentary. N.d. https://monsterhigh.fandom.com/wiki/Kind:_The_Shockumentary.

Seventeen. 2010. "*The Clique's* Lisi Harrison Heads to *Monster High!*" *Seventeen.* https://www.seventeen.com/celebrity/a12277/lisi-harrison-monster-high/.

Vampirina. "Little Terror/Super Natural." 2017a. Television. Created by Chriss Nee. Burbank: Disney Junior.

Vampirina. "Theme Song, Music Video." 2017b. Television. Created by Chriss Nee. Burbank: Disney Junior, Available at: https://youtu.be/SckCTDIvAgM.

Wohlwend, Karen E. 2017. "*Monster High* as a Virtual Dollhouse: Tracking Play Practices Across Converging Transmedia and Social Media." *Teachers College Record,* vol. 119.

Zimmerman, Ann. 2010. "Mattel's New Playbook: Toy First, Franchise Next." *Wall Street Journal.* June 3. https://www.wsj.com/articles/SB10001424052748704515704575282682475749528.

"Do Vampires Get Their Periods?"

The Carmilla *Web Series and the Politics of Bleeding Women*

ALEXANDRA HELLER-NICHOLAS

The vlog-style web series *Carmilla* first screened on Canadian teenage magazine's Vervegirl YouTube channel in August 2014. It was almost two months after this that the first explicit reference to the series' executive producer U by Kotex and their menstrual products were mentioned in a satellite video separate to the core narrative series itself. The video, which linked to various social media accounts ostensibly owned and written by key characters, declared "Do Vampires Get Their Periods?" was a mock PSA that— while the fantastic question of the video's title granted it a fun aspect in tune with the broader supernatural rom-com tone of the series itself—also provided a space to both speak about menstruation and, perhaps from U by Kotex's position, promote their products.

Using the question "do vampires get their periods?" as the basis for the first branded *Carmilla* video was no accident. As CEO Kaaren Whitney-Vernon from *Carmilla* co-producer Shift2[47]—a "youth-focused digi agency" focused specifically on YouTube content—noted in 2016:

> When Shift2 was pitching this idea of a vampire series to U by Kotex, we searched the internet to see if there were any conversations around periods and vampires. Well, there were over 1 million results on Google! People were in heavy debate about whether this is possible! I love the idea that a brand, who already had an Internet success with their cheeky "Reality Check," could come out with a definitive statement: "Yes—Vampires get their periods. They should know—They've had over 400 year's [sic] worth!" [Sauer 2016, n.p.]

---

47. Shift2 was launched in mid-2014 by Canadian production company Shaftesbury Films and research and media company Youth Culture (Haynes 2014).

In this same interview Jay Bennett—SVP of Creative and Innovation for Shaftesbury's digital wing, Smokebomb Entertainment—the idea was not to try and construct an interested demographic themselves, but rather to mine what he called "an already existing audience base" (n.p.). For Bennett, there was already demonstrated interest in Joseph Sheridan Le Fanu's 1872 novella among the demographic they wanted to appeal to; "We didn't make *Carmilla* and then go looking for an audience to watch and love it. We researched social media and found different existing social groups already talking about *Carmilla*" (n.p.).

By the time U by Kotex joined the *Carmilla* project, writer Jordan Hall's script for Series 1 was already finished but both sides felt the brand was a good tonal fit; Kimberly-Clark brand manager Denise Darroch said the idea was never to brand the series as such, but rather to integrate five promotional videos that would appear alongside it, (Martin 2014, n.p.) beginning with "Do Vampires Get Their Periods?" Hall was inspired to write a web series based on Le Fanu's 1872 novella *Carmilla* long before U by Kotex were involved. While the idea was given to her by producer Stephanie Ouaknine, the novella appealed to Hall for a number of reasons. When I interviewed Hall in 2018 about her work, she said "*Carmilla* had so many of the qualities I look for in something that I want to adapt: gorgeous prose and dialogue, fascinating characters, and for myself, personally, several deep dissatisfactions." She continues, "It's a haunting book, and I love it, but I also found myself deeply annoyed by Laura's lack of agency and insight, by the casual disregard for the lives of Carmilla's working class victims, and by the depiction of lesbian desire as unnatural and monstrous." For Hall, "That mixture of qualities I love and things I want to 'fix' makes for compelling source material" (Heller-Nicholas, 2020).[48]

The success of the series cannot be understated; three seasons and a theatrically released feature film *The Carmilla Movie* (Spencer Maybee, 2017). Half-way through the first series, it had already received over 1.2 million views (Martin, 2014, n.p.), was nominated for a Lion award at the 2016 Cannes Lions International Festival of Creativity (Laird 2016, n.p.), was nominated for both Shorty and Streamy Awards, and won multiple AfterEllen Visibility Awards because of its focus on queer women.[49] Perhaps more representative of its success from U by Kotex's position, however, is how well it achieved its intended goals of attracting a specific demographic to their products. Of its viewership, 91 percent were women, three-quarters

---

48. For critical interrogations between the original text and the web series, see Lorna Jowett 2019, and Rahel Sixta Schmitz 2020.

49. For a full list of awards and nominations, see: "Awards: *Carmilla* (web series)," Wikipedia https://en.wikipedia.org/wiki/Carmilla_(web_series)#Awards.

of who were in the 18–34 age bracket; of these, "a full third … reported that they bought the U by Kotex brand because they watched *Carmilla*" (Sauer, 2016, n.p.).

This essay will examine the relationship of Kotex's core role as a producer of commercial menstrual products and how advertising has—and as *Carmilla*'s success demonstrates—continues to be central to their business model. Adapting over time to social norms and mores, I will argue that while *Carmilla* (as a queer YouTube narrative series based on a famous work of classic vampire fiction) both adheres to Kotex's branding model, it also utilizes its very transmedia nature across different social media and streaming video platforms to branch beyond it. At the heart of this lies Sharra Louise Vostra's focus in her 2008 book *Under Wraps: A History of Menstrual Hygiene Technology* on "menstrual politics about women's bodies and technologies of passing with menstrual hygiene products" which, as I argue in the case of *Carmilla*'s transmedia success story in particular, links directly to "both political ideas and technologies [that] are mutually constitutive and co-produced" (2).

A Brief Cultural History of Commercial Menstrual Products

For all the hushed whispers and pastel hues that we may associate with the history of menstrual products,[50] one of the most notable earliest mentions of an object used to assist in controlling the flow of menstrual fluid stems back to a report by Damascius (c. 458–c. 538) about fellow Alexandrine philosopher Hypatia. In his biography of Hypatia (c. 350–c. 415), Edward Jay Watts recalls that the anecdote concerns an overly amorous student of the "extremely beautiful" woman philosopher. Says Watts, "since he was now overcome with bodily passions, Hypatia had to resort to a display that used physical objects to make an impression on him. Her display of the menstrual rag shocked this student and enabled him to remember that body love was ephemeral" (Watts 2017, 75). In more vernacular terms; Hypatia was being sexually harassed and to get the aggressor to back off, she pulled out her used Ancient Greek precursor to the menstrual pad. The young man's poetic delusions were instantly shattered in the face of evidence of this, a ubiquitous bodily function.

Something about the contrast of this famous tale with those oh-so-discreet tiny floral boxes we still see on supermarket shelves today finds a

---

50. This essay will refer to menstrual products without the use of euphemism. As Chella Quint notes of terms such as "Sanitary, Feminine Hygiene, Femcare … and sanpro … constantly reinforcing the taboos we're trying so hard to break" (2017, n.p.).

more contemporary parallel with the twentieth century advent of menstrual products as a marketable consumer item. While menstrual products appeared in Sears and Roebuck catalogues as early as the 1890s, it was not until 1921 that the first ones were successfully advertised and sold in North America (Vostra 2008, 5). Far from the typical terrain of women's private self-care rituals such as bathrooms or bedrooms, the first commercially viable menstrual products found their origins on the battlefields of the First World War. Faced with a surplus of bandages, Kimberly-Clarke—then a paper manufacturer—had an excess of bandages, and nothing to do with them (Ayers 2011, 55), and as Laura (Elise Bauman) perkily summarizes alongside Carmilla (Natasha Negovanlis) in the "Do Vampires Get Their Periods?" faux PSA, it was the discovery by "utterly rad" nurses on the battlefield who realized these bandages also doubled as extremely useful makeshift menstrual pads. Kimberly-Clarke took notice, and as Adriana Ayers has noted, "absorbent and inexpensive, the new product made from these bandages would revolutionize the way women responded to their menstruation," transformed as they were into the very first Kotex-branded menstrual napkins (Ayers 2011, 55).

As Ayers notes, the original marketing of the very first Kotex menstrual products were almost entirely illegible in terms of what they were in fact meant to be selling, but it started a trend that continues today that "these products promised to make women's bodies more hygienic, more feminine and thus, more socially acceptable" (55). The first Kotex ad appeared in *Ladies Home Journal* in 1921 and showed two women with a nurse and an injured war veteran, Ayers underscoring "the idea of menstruation as a debilitating illness, associating it with returning soldiers from the bloody European front" (56). The advertisement was created by Wallace Meyer who understood that ambiguity was key so as to not upset public sensibilities regarding menstruation taboos. An alternate, unused ad was even vaguer, directed on the surface at least explicitly towards men rather than women by emphasizing the original intention of the bandages that resulted in the Kotex menstrual pad's invention; reading "To Save Men's Lives Science Discovered Kotex." Says Ayers, "There was no mention of the product's use or necessity, only a description of its material and where one could purchase it. Furthermore, the ad reinforced how it benefited men and that, with the end of the war, they passed on the same 'comfort' and 'safety' onto women" (56).

The anxieties that accompanied the first commercially successful menstrual products—which, through Kotex's central role, are direct ancestors of the *Carmilla* web series—hinge on anxieties that long pre-dated the twentieth century. The nineteenth century is notable in this essay not for just being when Le Fanu wrote *Carmilla*, but that it occurred simultaneously during a period where there were immense cultural, social and medical shifts in terms of women's bodies more broadly. This resulted in first wave feminism that really began solidifying as an international political movement around the same period that Le Fanu's story was published. As Sharra Louise Vostra writes. "a by now familiar story is the reading of women's bodies as pathological and inferior to men's during the nineteenth century" (2008, 22), which effectively factionalized into two different schools of thought during the decades following Carmilla's publication: "on one side were ideas about women's biological weakness due to menstrual incapacity, and the other side held that menstruation was perfectly normal" (4).

Situated within this history, social, cultural and political changes occurred both earlier in the nineteenth century and more recently at the beginning of the twenty-first century that provide a curious overlap in terms of the *Carmilla* web series as a transmedia marketing success story. As Vostra notes, there is a theory that at the turn of the nineteenth century in the United States, "Revolutionary-era fertility rates began to decline. Ideas of personal autonomy, as promoted by the rhetoric of liberty and freedom during the Revolution, influenced women's actions in limiting family size" (24). Consequently, "pregnancy shifted from a natural and constant state of being to an exception in the life of a rational individual" (24). Compare this to Elissa Stein and Susan Kim's observation that "women in the twenty-first century menstruate a whole lot more in our lifetimes than we ever did before, since the beginning of recorded history. We eat better and weigh more, so we hit puberty younger." Not only that, but "our life expectancy has gone up, so we no longer routinely drop dead at forty [and] … chances are you are not bearing and breast-feeding babies every second of your entire reproductive life, thus suppressing menstrual flow" (2009, xi–xii).

Stein and Kim estimate that today the average American woman will have approximately 500 periods (Stein and Kim 2009, xii). In market terms, in 2017 that was a $31.23 (U.S.) billion industry, estimated to grow to $62.84 billion by 2026 (BusinessWire 2019). Despite only existing as a viable industry as such since 1921, for Stein and Kim it has "meant big money from the word go" (xi). Describing it succinctly as "a very profitable taboo" Camilla Mørk Røstvik, in her examination of the history of the advertising of menstrual products, further notes that while "early ads featured medical authorities and soothing older women," with the explosion of second-wave feminism the menstrual product industry had a dramatic change of tune, shifting their attention instead to "feminists with the language of freedom" (2018, n.p.). Certainly, in terms of the plot and character focus of Kotex's *Carmilla* web series, the latter at least appears to still be more than true.

Carmilla is by no means Kotex's first efforts at utilizing a pop cultural phenomenon to sell their products. The most famous case study in this pre-history is the Kotex-sponsored 1946 Disney 10-minute short film, *The Story of Menstruation*. According to Susan K. Freeman, this collaboration was distributed across American schools free of charge and "had a tremendous impact on menstrual education" at the time (2008, 86). Screenings

Kotex advertising, illustrated by Tom Hall, in *Ladies' Home Journal* (1948).

"*Do Vampires Get Their Periods?*" (Heller-Nicholas) 109

were accompanied by a promotional Kotex pamphlet called "Very Personally Yours" and was said to be seen by 105 million young women (Freeman 2008, 86).

Not everyone is impressed by the Disney/Kotex collaboration, however, and Joan Jacobs Brunburg writing in 1997 observes that "in the Disney world, the menstrual flow is not blood red but snow white. The vaginal

Kotex advertising, illustrated by Tom Hall, in *Ladies' Home Journal* (1948).

drawings look more like a cross section of a kitchen sink than the outside of a woman's body" (1997, 47). Over a decade later, however, Freeman speaks highly in its defense and progressive gender politics: "it was," she notes, "unusual in its use of a woman narrator" and—more notably—its "filmmakers explicitly intended the movie to supplant old-fashioned views and practices related to menstruation, particularly the use of homemade protection" (2008, 86). She celebrates it for "trying to inform girls about the physiology of menstruation" and attempting "to shape attitudes about menstruation" (Freeman 86).

Kotex thus have a central and inescapably complex role in the cultural history of commercial menstrual products that have in the recent century played a central role in the formation of attitudes to menstruation more broadly. Like their collaboration with Disney, as a transmedia marketing artifact designed explicitly to aim at a market demographic of young women, *Carmilla* plays a central role in this continuing history. Looking back at some of the critical discourse that has surrounded Kotex's advertising historically, it is intriguing to see how *Carmilla* both adheres and simultaneously deviates from these earlier marketing strategies in its very successful attempt to attract a new generation of market consumers through the web series. On one hand, Stein and Kim note that "Kotex ads from the very beginning featured women who represented this ideal market: exquisite, exclusively white, fabulously wealthy ladies of fashion and leisure," a Kotex ad from 1926 even stating that "eight in every ten women in the better walks of life have adopted this new way" (2009, 120). While the makers of *Carmilla* are to be commended for remedying the glaring issue of racial diversity in seasons 2 and 3 and *The Carmilla Movie* (with the addition of Sophia Walker's Matska and Nicole Stamp's Mel), season 1 is—except Lisa Truong's small role as Natalie—dominated by an all-white cast. Less overt is the question of wealth, but Silus University, which is the central location, is, after all, in Austria: as all the student characters speak with North American accents, it is to be assumed therefore that they are able to afford the privilege of international study.

And yet—as will now be expanded more fully in the following section—where the *Carmilla* both deviates from past Kotex advertising traditions and marks important new movement in menstrual politics is through its utilization of vampire mythology itself and associated notions of abjection. Referring back to that original Kotex menstrual pad so successfully launched in 1921, Ayers notes that in the advertising then and in that which followed "women's bodily functions were described as defective and unnatural [and that] only by using Kotex products could one be considered socially acceptable" (2011, 55). The utilization of La

Fanu's *Carmilla*—not only the first English-language lesbian vampire story (Park 2017, 399) but also arguably the most famous (Melton 2011, 421)—marks a conscious effort to turn *towards* the idea of "unnatural" bodies in menstrual product marketing in a positive manner. More so, in terms of how notions of abjection and deviance apply to La Fanu's famous character specifically[51] and Barbara Creed's observation that "the female vampire is abject because she disrupts identity and order … [and] does not respect the dictates of the law which let down the rules of proper sexual conduct" (1993, 61). But *Carmilla* is not just about a woman vampire, but a *lesbian* vampire, which for Creed is "doubly abject because woman, already more abject than man, releases the blood of another woman" (61). As I will now discuss, the question of sexuality and sexual identity intersect in the *Carmilla* web series with a fundamental aspect of menstrual product marketing that has yet to be discussed: the concept of "passing."

The Tampon Fandom: *Carmilla* and "Passing"

The timing of the *Carmilla* web series from 19 August 2014 to 13 October 2016 (with the feature film released on 26 October 2017) both reflects and can be seen to be a participant in broader changing cultural attitudes towards menstruation in the West. On November 2015 *Cosmopolitan* magazine announced that 2015 was "The Year the Period Went Public" (Maltby 2015, n.p,), *NPR* declaring a few months later that "this year has been epic for menstruation, with news and social media catapulting the once hush-hush topic into the open" (Gharib 2015, n.p.). As Mørk Røstvik noted, this meant that "the challenge for advertisers today is connecting with millennial women who are critical readers of advertising and back campaigns to ban the tampon tax and end period poverty" (2018, n.p.). Beating "The Year the Period Went Public" by many months, *Carmilla* and U by Kotex's YouTube video "Do Vampires Get Their Periods?" put them well on top of the trend.

As Stein and Kim note, the influence of advertising on broader cultural attitudes on menstruation more generally cannot be underplayed where advertisers "have profoundly influenced what we know and how we think and feel not just about our periods, but our very bodies" (2009, 114). They continue, "one could say our collective menstrual mind-set is the result of effective advertising campaigns" (114). But it is, in many

---

51. See: Hung-Jung Lee, 2006, "'One for Ever': Desire, Subjectivity, and the Treat of the Abject in Sheridan Le Fanu's *Carmilla*," *Vampires: Myths and Metaphors of Enduring Evil*, edited by Peter Day, Amsterdam: Rodopi, pp. 21–38.

ways, a two-way street; advertisers and marketing executives, who opt for informal parlance, need to read the room: they have to know not just who they are selling to, but also to understand what matters to them. Mørk Røstvik detects this in a recent pattern of progressive shifts with a strong social justice tone in menstrual product advertising: the shift from ambiguous blue liquids representing menstrual fluid to red, the eco-friendly Mooncup brand and—of particular relevance to the strong queer core of *Carmilla*—to so-called "period-proof" underwear brand THINX who also included a transgender man in its advertising campaign (2018, n.p.).

The latter shift in both the THINX campaign and in Kotex's *Carmilla* web series to amplify the queer-friendliness of their products to appeal to this younger demographic manifests at the intersection of the important concept of 'passing' in both queer culture and in regards to menstrual taboos. Kelby Harrison offers the following basic definition; "Passing is something we do with identity. 'Passing' designates a successful self-presentation in line with a socially favored identity at the expense of an 'authentic' one—e.g., passing for white when black, heterosexual when BGB/Q, cisgender when transgender etc" (2013, 1). Although written in 2008 (six years before *Carmilla* was launched), Vostra's book *Under Wraps: A History of Menstrual Hygiene Technology* homes in on the intersection of "passing" in regards to both gender identity and menstruation taboos in ways that have direct relevance to the web series.[52] She notes that as "the phenomenon of passing ... is traditionally associated with a person moving from one identity to another, often across lines of race, gender, or sexual orientation," it therefore "offers a means to obtain a new political identity" (3). Crucially, Vostra suggests that "menstrual hygiene products can be interpreted as technologies of passing" because they "hide female bodies viewed as dysfunctional, thus assisting women in passing as healthy. They allow women to present themselves as non-menstruants" (3).[53]

As a rhetorical exercise it is useful perhaps to reflect further on the politics of "passing" in regard to *Carmilla*'s overlapping focus on queer identities and relationships, all housed under the umbrella of a transmedia marketing campaign for U by Kotex's menstrual products aimed at a young consumer demographer. In terms of sexuality and gender identity, *Carmilla* is to be celebrated for the way that the queerness of a number of its main characters is a given and not a point of narrative explication. In Laura's case, it is stated clearly both in the social media accounts linked to

52. A third mode of "passing" is also core to the first season of the *Carmilla* web series in particular; that of the vampire Carmilla herself "passing" as human.
53. Itself a problematic stance as it suggests that menstruation should be hidden.

Natasha Negovanlis (Carmilla, left) and Elise Baman (Laura) on a panel for the webseries *Carmilla* at Fan Expo Canada in Toronto, September 4, 2015 (Jeff Hitchcock from Vancouver, BC, Canada/Wikimedia Commons).

the series and in Season 3, Episode 9, itself in a conversation between Laura and her father (Enrico Colantoni[54]) that her sexual orientation was well-established long before the actions at Silus University had begun; on her Tumblr account, for instance, an anonymous question posted on 26 July 2016 asked "Does your dad know that you are into girls? Or have you not had the chance to talk to him about it?" Her answer was simple and caused a flurry of supportive responses; "He knows." Similarly, while LaFontaine (Kaitlyn Alexander) is non-binary, the issue comes up as a point of conversation rarely; in season 1 they demonstrate visible disappointment when their best friend Perry (Annie M. Briggs)[55] keeps calling them by their dead (previous) name ("I don't want to be Susan anymore," they say in episode 26, "The Standard Issue"), while in Season 3, Episode 9 Laura explains what

54. In one of the many broad pop cultural references across the series, the casting of Colantoni is a sly reference to his previous role as Veronica Mars' likewise supportive single-father in the series of the same name, a television show that Laura namedrops in *Carmilla* alongside a variety of other references, most notably her omnipresent Doctor Who "Tardis" mug.

55. In many of the series' references to Le Fanu's novella, both Perry and LaFontaine's names are a homage to the characters Madame Perrodon and De Lafontaine, Laura's governesses and share the role as her primary women carers; certainly both LaFontaine and Perry (the latter at least to begin with) in the web series can be at times considered to fulfill a similar although perhaps not identical role, being Laura's primary support network both personally and in her investigation endeavors.

non-binary means to Sherman, and is embarrassed to see him struggle using the correct pronouns when talking to LaFontaine.

More centrally, the ups and downs of Laura and Carmilla's romantic relationship are marked by their differences as human and vampire, rather than their status as a same-sex couple. And yet it is the latter's taste for blood (weakly hidden by Carmilla in opaque soymilk boxes in the first series) that raises a more contradictory engagement by *Carmilla* with menstruation. While Denise Darroch stated in 2014 that in relation to the U by Kotex branded videos at least that they are "a brand that talks about the truth. We're pretty blunt about it" (Martin 2014, n.p.), Laura's reference in her introduction to the "Do Vampires Get Their Periods?" to "the ladytimes of yesteryear" instead of "menstruation in the past" hardly evokes the descriptor "pretty blunt." And yet, in this same video Carmilla *does* make explicit reference to "ruined underwear," while—in relation to the controversies surrounding the use of a red liquid instead of a blue one in menstrual pad advertisements for the Bodyform brand in the United Kingdom in 2017 (BBC 2017), for example—Laura opts to demonstrate the (highly visible) U by Kotex pad absorbency by using a pale, pinkish soda.

Perhaps key here is that while a number of supplementary videos to *Carmilla* from 2014 (as well as the narratively non-essential prequel Series Zero that appeared between season 1 and 2)[56] make explicit the overlap between the series' core vampire mythology and the U by Kotex–centric focus on menstruation, none are an actual episode of the main series proper (and as such not essential to following the storyline). The three seasons themselves are comparatively much lighter on the menstruation references, and these supplementary videos also received significantly *fewer* views than the main series. "Do Vampires Get Their Periods?" and "A Period PSA from Perry & LaFontaine" both posted on 16 October 2014 garnered 397,557 and 89,196 views respectively as of October 2019, while the later "Menstruation Mythbusting with Perry & LaFontaine" from 10 February 2015 has received only 51,980 views to date. While the U by Kotex heavier Season Zero fared much better (at the time of writing, it has had 1,515,849 views), this stands in notable contrast to the three core series themselves; at the time of writing, season 1 has received 28,392,398 views, season 2 has received 12,064,054 views, while the third and final season received 10,861,775 views.

56. As Harmeet Singh describes it, "for season two, U by Kotex moved away from the separate integration videos, instead creating another mini-series, dubbed 'season zero,' a 12-part prequel all about a mysterious lack of periods on the university campus where *Carmilla* takes place. Unlike the primary series, season zero (which premiered in late October) more prominently integrates U by Kotex into the setting and storyline" (2015).

Significantly, on the official Twitter accounts for Laura, Carmilla, LaFontaine and Silus University,[57] the only mentions of periods or menstruation are in links or retweets directing followers to the aforementioned supplementary videos. It can be easy then to reduce this to an uncomplicated attack on U by Kotex for merely propelling the previous history of menstrual product advertising summarized above. However, I argue that the very success of *Carmilla* in moving cultural discourse in a progressive direction stems not from the content, but—predicated explicitly on its status as an interactive transmedia phenomenon—has much more importantly granted its fans a space to speak openly about traditional menstruation taboos. There are many examples, including Twitter user @sapphictrash tweeting on 17 October 2014 "@HeyCarmilla has had 4000 periods, and we thought we had it bad! Girl appreciates her @ubykotex #carmillapocalypse." Many responses on social media replicated this sense of a shared in-joke; on 4 September 2015, in response to a line in a recent episode, user @queenvague tweeted to Laura's account "'There's blood everywhere. This is so beyond not good.' When girls wake up on their period lol," while on 13 June 2015, user @aksentnetharia tweeted at Laf "It's a PERIOD of mystery for you guys, isn't it?"

Aside from referring to themselves as "Creampuffs" (a semi-snide nickname Carmilla uses for Laura especially), *Carmilla* fans also self-identify—quite remarkably—as "The Tampon Fandom" (Sauer 2016, n.p.). U by Kotex—recognizing the opportunity this afforded them—even released "Carmilla" branded tampons in a limited-edition box, the manufacturer description reading "Creampuffs can now get full-sized period protection in Hollistein packaging designed by fellow Creampuff, Trixie Mahayag" (Timely Tampon, n.d.). In terms of attracting consumers in their intended demographic to the U by Kotex product—31 percent, of a 2015 survey said they bought the brand specifically because of *Carmilla*, for example (Sauer 2016, n.p.)—this direct correlation between The Tampon Fandom and consumption patterns cannot be undervalued. From a marketing perspective, this is what makes *Carmilla* a transmedia marketing success story; as Smokebomb's Jay Bennett noted in 2016, "The female Millennial demographic is the most sophisticated media group in history. They smell a commercial in 2 seconds and are inundated with ads in every form of media every day. They are blind to ads and the moment they feel they are being sold to." He continues, "Make a commercial and you're just another commercial. Make great content and the audience will become your brand ambassadors" (n.p.).

57. At the time of writing, Twitter handles are as follows: Laura (@Laura2theLetter), Carmilla (@HeyCarmilla), S. LaFontaine (@LaFilphormes), and Silas University (@SilasUniversity).

Works Cited

"Awards: *Carmilla* (web Series)." Wikipedia (no date) https://en.wikipedia.org/wiki/Carmilla_(web_series)#Awards.
Ayers, Adriana. 2011. "The Evolution of Kotex Advertising and the Introduction of the 'Negro Market.'" *Constellations*, vol. 2, no. 2, Winter, pp. 52–65.
"Bodyform Advert Replaces Blue Liquid with Red 'Blood.'" *BBC News*, 18 October 2017 https://www.bbc.com/news/uk-41666280.
Creed, Barbara. 1993. *The Monstrous-Feminine: Film, Feminism, Psychoanalysis*. London: Routledge.
Freeman, Susan K. 2008. *Sex Goes to School: Girls and Sex Education Before the 1960s*. Urbana: University of Illinois Press.
Gharib, Malaka. 2015. "Why 2015 Was the Year of the Period, and We Don't Mean Punctuation." *NPR*, 31 December. https://www.npr.org/sections/health-shots/2015/12/31/460726461/why-2015-was-the-year-of-the-period-and-we-dont-mean-punctuation.
Harrison, Kelby, 2013. *Sexual Deceit: The Ethics of Passing*. Lanham, MD: Lexington Books.
Haynes, Megan. 2014. "Shaftesbury Launches a Youth-Focused Digi Agency." *Strategy*, 2 June. strategyonline.ca/2014/06/02/shaftesbury-launches-a-youth-focused-digi-agency/.
Heller-Nicholas, Alexandra. 2020. *1000 Women in Horror: 1895–2018*. Orlando: BearManor.
Hollis, Laura. 2015. "Anonymous Asked: Does Your Dad Know That You Are Into Girls? or Have You Not Had the Chance to Talk to Him About It." Tumblr, 26 July. https://laura2theletter.tumblr.com/post/125075053601/does-your-dad-know-that-you-are-into-girls-or.
Jacobs Brunberg, Joan. 1997. *The Body Project: An Intimate History of American Girls*. New York: Vintage Books.
KindaTV. N.d. "Carmilla | Seasons One, Two and Three + Extra Content." YouTube, https://www.youtube.com/user/VervegirlMagazine/playlists?view=50&sort=dd&shelf_id=25
KindaTV. 2014a. "Do Vampires Get Their Periods? | Carmilla | U by Kotex." YouTube, 16 October, https://www.youtube.com/watch?v=TAwtIyPvvQI&list=PLbvYWjKFvS5omAzO0IjYlnkNHqAILzzzF&index=1.
KindaTV. 2014b. "A Period PSA from Perry & LaFontaine." YouTube, 16 October, https://www.youtube.com/watch?list=PLbvYWjKFvS5omAzO0IjYlnkNHqAILzzzF&v=jl7vqEvYoXk.
KindaTV. 2015. "Menstruation Mythbusting with Perry & LaFontaine | Carmilla | U by Kotex." YouTube, 10 February, https://www.youtube.com/watch?v=8V2kNWSIIEI&list=PLbvYWjKFvS5omAzO0IjYlnkNHqAILzzzF&index=5.
Jaki'o-Lantern (@aksentnetheria). 2015. "Jaki'o-Lantern Twitter Post." Twitter, 13 June, 11:36 a.m., https://twitter.com/aksentnetharia/status/609549849206218752.
Jowett, Lorna. 2019. "'Most of You Are Wondering Who the Heck I Am': Carmilla (2014–2016, Online) as Digital Reimagining of Le Fanu's 'Carmilla.'" *Gothic Afterlives: Reincarnations of Horror in Film and Popular Media*, edited by Lorna Piatti-Farnell, Lanham, MD: Lexington Books, pp. 79–97.
Laird, Kristin. 2016. "Cannes 2016: Dancing Cookies and Vampires Earn Lions Nod." *Marketing*, 23 June, marketingmag.ca/cannes/cannes-2016-dancing-cookies-and-vampires-earn-lions-nod-177898/.
Maltby, Anna. 2015. "The 8 Greatest Menstrual Moments of 2015." *Cosmopolitan*, 13 October, https://www.cosmopolitan.com/health-fitness/news/a47609/2015-the-year-the-period-went-public/.
Martin, Russ. 2014. "U by Kotex Sinks Its Teeth Into Vampire Web Series." *Marketing*, 22 October, http://marketingmag.ca/brands/u-by-kotex-executive-produced-a-vampire-web-series-128136/.
Melton, J. Gordon. 2011. *The Vampire Book: The Encyclopedia of the Undead*. Canton: Visible Ink Press.
Mørk Røstvik, Camilla. 2018. "Adventures in Menstruation: How Period Product Ads Have Changed to Reflect a More Realistic Experience for Women." *The Conversation*, 9 March, https://theconversation.com/adventures-in-menstruation-how-period-product-ads-have-changed-to-reflect-a-more-realistic-experience-for-women-91417.

Park, Hyungji. 2017. "Gendering the K-Vampire." *Gendering the Trans-Pacific World*, edited by Catherine Ceniza Cho and Judy Tzu-Chun Wu. Leiden: Koninkijke Brill, pp. 396–406.

Quint, Chella. 2017. "I've Stopped Saying 'Feminine Hygiene Products.' Here's Why You Should Too." *The Independent*, 14 October, https://www.independent.co.uk/voices/periods-period-poverty-tampons-menstruation-empowerment-language-sanitary-a8000641.html.

Riley Rae (@sapphictrash). 2014. "Riley Rae Twitter Post." Twitter, 17 October, 2:55am https://twitter.com/sapphictrash/status/522793018529959936.

Sauer, Abe. 2016. "Tampon Fandom: 5 Questions with the Co-Creators of 'Carmilla.'" *Brand Channel*, 13 July, https://www.brandchannel.com/2016/07/13/5-questions-carmilla-071316/.

Simone, Nichole (@queenvague). 2015. "Nichole Simone Twitter Post." Twitter, 4 September, 10:49 p.m., https://twitter.com/queenvague/status/639797468360667140.

Singh, Harmeet. 2015. "Marketers of the Year: Queen of the Creampuffs." *Strategy*, 18 December, strategyonline.ca/2015/12/18/marketers-of-the-year-queen-of-the-creampuffs/.

Sixta Schmitz, Rahel. 2020. "A Tale of Two Carmillas: The Representation of Styria in Le Fanu's 'Carmilla' and Its Web Series Adaptation." *Haunted Europe: Continental Connections in English-Language Gothic Writing, Film and New Media*, edited by Michael Newton and Evert Jan van Leeuwen, New York: Routledge, 2020.

"$62.84 Billion Global Feminine Hygiene Products Market by 2026." *BusinessWire*, 21 February 2019. https://www.businesswire.com/news/home/20190221005810/en/62.84-Billion-Global-Feminine-Hygiene-Products-Market.

Stein, Elissa, and Susan Kim, 2009. *Flow: The Cultural Story of Menstruation*. New York City: St Martin's Press.

Timely Tampon. N.d. "U by Kotex Click Tampon, Regular Absorbency, Carmilla Limited Edition, Unscented, 34 Count (Pack of 6)." Webstore, https://timelytampon.com/u-by-kotex-click-tampon-regular-absorbency-carmilla-limited-edition/.

Vostra, Sharra Louise. 2008. *Under Wraps: A History of Menstrual Hygiene Technology*. Lanham, MD: Lexington.

Watts, Edward Jay. 2017. *Hypatia: The Life and Legend of an Ancient Philosopher*. New York: Oxford University Press.

Part III
Transnational Transmedia

Vampire Tourism

Transmedia Narratives, Cultural Histories and Locating the Undead

Lorna Piatti-Farnell

The connection between Gothic narratives and tourism has recently received growing scholarly attention. The appeal of the Gothic framework—with its recurring tropes and motifs—has found fertile associations with aspects of the cultural industries that rely on visitor experience and, to some extent, a certain fandom appeal. This has been the focus of important examples of research in the intersecting fields of Gothic and tourism studies, such as Emma McAvoy's aptly titled *Gothic Tourism* book (2016). Here, McAvoy suggests that Gothic tourism is a "substantial," but often "unacknowledged part of the tourist scene" (6). This type of tourism relies on the cultural exploitation of Gothic narratives, purposefully understood as an often-forceful mixture of literature, history, and popular culture influences. Gothic tourism ranges from the success of ghost tours—taking place in reputedly haunted locations, often embodied in castles and mansions—to visiting specific geographical places associated with Gothic novels. This type of tourism also extends to the exploration of particular locations that played witnesses to horrible crimes; an example of this includes the "haunted" tours of the Whitechapel area of London (United Kingdom), as the scene of the infamous Jack the Ripper murders. Undoubtedly, Gothic tourism speaks loudly to the importance and appeal of "particular places and locality," and is profoundly "bound up with the way in which we think about our past and our surroundings," as well as "our identities" (McAvoy 2016, 7). It is clear that Gothic tourism relies on a dynamic blend of transmedia and transcultural narratives to ensure its success, as different tastes and knowledge need to be catered for in one sellable package.

Within the broader context of Gothic tourism, one can find a very specific incarnation of the brand: vampire tourism. As the name suggests, this offers the exploration of certain locations culturally or textually associated with vampires. In response to this, this essay provides a critical overview of vampire tourism, by exploring the impact of salient locations commonly associated with vampires in the popular imagination—namely, New Orleans and Transylvania. Specifically, vampire tourism focuses on blending geography and narratives to present tourists with a multifaceted experience in their search for evidence of the immortal undead. This essay does not specifically address the commercial imperatives that fuel the vampire tourism industry; instead, it provides an evaluation of the impact of transmedia vampire narratives—from literature to film and beyond—on the creation of perceived authentic cultural histories, and their influence on the representation of the vampire myth as a whole. The ways in which vampires and their cultural constructions are represented via the tourism industry are a crucial means by which the tension between reality and fiction is articulated.

The Vampires of New Orleans

Many cultural observers might be tempted to deem New Orleans as a city widely populated by vampires. For sure, vampire myths and legends fill the cultural landscape of this particular location. Visitors to New Orleans will quickly encounter the variety of "vampire tours" that are on offer to willing and excited tourists, who can happily pay to be told the stories of how many of the city's landmark buildings hide enticing vampire histories. The tales of vampires exist concomitantly with the plethora of narratives about the supernatural that are often associated with New Orleans and have contributed to building an image for the city as a spooky and ethereal place. Kenneth Holditch contends that "New Orleans is a city in love with its myths, mysteries and fantasies" (quoted in McKinney 2006, 8). As a result, vampire tourism occupies a significant place in New Orleans' cultural fabric, so much so that it is easy to believe the connection to be historically cemented, ranging back to the first settlements, when the population of the city was confined to the limits of the *Vieux Carré*—known as the French Quarter in more contemporary times—and folklore from the Old Continent proved to have an important cultural significance.

There is no denying that New Orleans has certainly been successful in producing a very sellable image of itself, which lies at the heart of its tourism industry. The place of vampires within this is so established that tales of the undead appear to be a long-standing part of the city's cultural and tourism narratives. In reality, however, the connection between vampires and New Orleans is a rather recent one and finds its origins and success in the folds of literature and popular culture. At the heart of this lies the work of Anne Rice, whose well-known novels—starting with, first and foremost, *Interview with the Vampire* (1976)—made a virtue of the fictional connection between New Orleans and vampires. By the time the eponymous film adaptation of the novel—directed by Neil Jordan in 1994—made its debut and found success with audiences, the reputation of New Orleans as a city populated by vampires became irrefutable. As far as the popular imagination is concerned, New Orleans is one of the favored places, at least in North America, for vampires to reside. The impact of Rice's works, and its adaptations, in building this image was instrumental, and her tales of vampires have "actively contributed to the cultivation of vampire tourism in New Orleans" (Ní Fhlainn 2019, 134). The connection has been widely reinforced in recent decades by a variety of examples from popular culture. Charlaine Harris' popular book series, the *Southern Vampire Mysteries*, openly acknowledges Rice's hand in establishing the vision of New Orleans as a "vampire city": "New Orleans had been the place to go for vampires and those who wanted to be around them ever since Anne Rice had been proven right about their existence" (2007, 2).

The status of New Orleans as a vampire mecca has been continuously reinforced by television shows such as *True Blood* (Ball 2008–14)—an adaptation of Harris' novels—and *The Originals* (Plec 2013–18).[58] The latter was extremely successful in continuing to paint New Orleans as the ideal tourism destination for (allegedly) encountering vampires. *The Originals* fully capitalized on the appeal of the visual and cultural connection between the city's landmarks and vampires, often indulging in suggestive cinematographic shots of the city and feeding the urban vampire myth. The series most certainly brings into the foreground the city's reputation for having "opalescent hints" (see McKinney 2006, 1) and a constant layer of mist that bestows upon it an otherworldly glow. This pictorial connection plays testament to how vampire narratives are often generated by a mixture of historical perceptions, transmedia influences, and cultural structures. *The Originals* also openly acknowledges the importance of the vampire narrative in the city's tourism framework. The vampires of New Orleans are known to host regular vampire-themed events, in order to "keep the tourists happy." The vampires also commonly joke that "something's gotta draw in the out-of-towners," otherwise they'd "all go hungry" (Season 1, Episode 1).[59] The comment seems both satirical and sardonic, and it is difficult to discern where it is simply evaluating the vampires' constant hunger

---

58. *The Originals* is a spin-off from the series *The Vampire Diaries* (Plec and Williamson: 2009–17). *American Horror Story: Coven* (Murphy: 2013–14) is set in New Orleans and also features the historical figure of Madam LaLaurie (Kathy Bates).

59. A similar reasoning is used in regard to Fangtasia, the vampire bar in *True Blood*.

for blood within the show's narrative, or whether a broader critique of New Orleans' commercial reliance on the vampire tourism industry is being discussed. While the vampiric image of New Orleans may be based on an unavoidable sense of inauthenticity, this does little to tarnish its reputation as a hot spot for the undead and the cultural identity that goes with it (Piatti-Farnell 2017, 4).

The tourism of New Orleans has provided a source of balm and vexation for the city (Piatti-Farnell 2014, 176). The thriving tourism industry of New Orleans has certainly been a solid source of financial revenue; tourism has been in the forefront of the city's image for centuries, as hedonistic echoes of *Mardi Gras*, drinking, delicious foods, and jazz have dominated its reputation both in the United States and abroad. There is no doubt that New Orleans has capitalized upon "the production of local difference, local cultures, and different local histories that appeal to visitors tastes for the exotic and the unique" (Gotham 2005, 1100). The recently developed opportunities for "Gothic tourism" have added a further layer of complication for New Orleans. Vampires co-exist with tales of voodoo and hoodoo; while the latter may in fact be a widely documented presence in the annals of Louisiana history, what is presented to the tourists is, arguably, a version of people, events, and magic that is as fictional as the undead themselves. The Gothic imagery that is forcefully associated with New Orleans by the tourism industry is, one might want to suggest, only peripherally tied to the city's social and political history, but, in an unexpected twist, has now become indivisible from the city's evolving cultural fabric. This creation is profoundly tied to the fictional narratives that have romanticized New Orleans as a city of vampires and Gothic occurrences over the decades. In spite of the fact that literature and popular culture, rather than true historical evidence, account for New Orleans' relationship with vampires, it is clear that the very figure of the vampire—existing as a mixture of old European folklore and fiction—represents an important and influential part of New Orleans' tourism narrative, highlighting the relationship between media iconography, storytelling, and consumerism.

Where Vampires Come From

When vampires are mentioned, it is virtually impossible not to think about Eastern Europe. Romania, and its well-known region Transylvania, continue to hold their standing as the place where vampires come from. In the common vision of many Western observers, Transylvania maintains a reputation as a land filled with tales of magic, folklore, and sinister occurrences. Remote and seemingly separate from the everyday working of the outside world, Transylvania is often envisaged as a place of mystery and difference, where logic and rationality will inevitably clash with the workings of the supernatural. Transylvania, as far as the popular imagination is concerned, is a land of monsters, and the most famous of all is, of course, Dracula. Since its publication, Bram Stoker's eponymous novel (1897) has gained global and long-standing fame. As a result, it has come to be "almost synonymous" with Transylvania: as far as Western ideas go, Transylvania is "the land of Dracula" (Light 2006, 1). The impact of both Stoker's novel and its vampiric character have been unprecedented. The popularity of *Dracula* has forcefully contributed to the establishment of a textual and cultural narrative for Transylvania, which, within the global scope, is indivisible from its fictional connections. Indeed, it is virtually impossible to mention Transylvania and not think of the Count himself. Whether Romania likes it or not, "Count Dracula is the best-known Romanian" (Light 2016, 1; see also Boia, 2001). Generally speaking, it would be too outlandish to claim that many around the world would know little of Transylvania—or Romania overall, for that matter—except from an indelible certainty that this is where the famous vampire comes from. The land and its people—as physical, social, and cultural entities—are powerfully entangled with the narrative of Dracula, so much so that a powerful "place myth" (Light 2016, 1) has developed about Transylvania as a shadowy place where vampires roam freely.

The relationship between Dracula and Transylvania was forcefully cemented by Stoker's novel, which depicted the figure of the predatory and undead vampire, and to some extent, completely revolutionized the ways in which vampires have been perceived ever since. At the time of Stoker's writing, Transylvania had begun to make an appearance as a tourist destination, firmly placing itself within the bounds of the British nineteenth-century imagination. Tales of Transylvania were being documented in a variety of sources. Political interests were likely at the center of this, as the British colonial eye turned its fascination towards Eastern Europe. Regardless of the political interest that may have inspired the move, however, a distinct effort was made to attract the traveller's attention towards Transylvania. In Britain, perceptions of the region were primarily made available through "travel narratives" (Gelder 1994, 2), which were profoundly mingled with often-summary information from folklore studies. Vampire fiction, as such, was only in its nascent years during this, but there is no doubt that, whatever stories were produced, were heavily indebted to the tales of Transylvania that were widely circulated by the tourism industry.

There is evidence to suggest that Stoker himself was an avid reader of Victoria travelogues; having never visited Transylvania himself, Stoker relied heavily on the descriptions provided by these popular travel narratives. As a result, *Dracula* seemingly provides unavoidable tourism-inspired representations of Transylvania (Gelder 1994, 2). The novel was, undoubtedly, one of the most influential vampire texts, and while establishing some of the tropes and conventions that many commonly associate with vampires, it also created an unshakable geo-cultural link with Transylvania that continues to survive and thrive. The narrative of Stoker's book was instrumental in establishing a Western vision of Transylvania that lies somewhere between text, imagination, and myth. It would not be too ambitious to claim that, even in our hyper-technological twenty-first century, in the popular imagination the very word Transylvania still "conjures up images of howling wolves, midnight thunderstorms, [and] evil looking peasants" (Kaplan 1993, 149).

When Stoker published *Dracula*, Transylvania as a region was still part of the Austro-Hungarian Empire, a political entity that was dissolved after the First World War. As a result of this, the Empire's territories were divided up among surrounding countries, both pre-existing and newly established. As part of this process, Transylvania became part of Romania. The latter, however, had perhaps not quite realized the international cultural importance of this. Indeed, in acquiring Transylvania, Romania did not only inherit the land, but also "unconsciously acquired the Dracula myth" (Light 2016, 1; see also Boia 2001). The connection between Dracula and Transylvania continues to thrive on the back of both textual connections and cultural iconicity. For sure, a lot of the vampire folklore that is commonly recognized by the Western imagination does originate in Eastern Europe, with many tales of the *vampyr* being told over centuries. And even though folkloristic tales of vampires are largely unknown in Romania, the Western association continues to remain strong.

In the popular imagination, the connection between Transylvania and Dracula was further cemented by the release of the 1931 *Dracula* film (directed by Tod Browning), with Bela Lugosi famously taking up the title role. Transylvania was also still part of the Austro-Hungarian Empire when Bela Lugosi was born in 1882. His birth town of Lugoj belonged to the Hungarian side of the Empire, and only became part of modern-day Romania in 1919. The actor, who openly identified as Hungarian clearly felt a close sense of attachment to his place of origin, choosing the stage name "Lugosi," precisely in honor of his hometown. In spite of the fact that Lugoj was part of the political transitions that were a final outcome of the First World War, its Hungarian cultural heritage remained closely felt by its residents. As the years passed, however, its status as a Romanian town became acknowledged by the international community. By the time Lugosi donned the iconic Dracula cape in 1931, his "thick courtly accent" (Kaplan 1994, 149) became quickly associated in the popular imagination with both Transylvania—now part of Romania—and a common depiction of Dracula himself. The connection is enduring, and many would openly suggest that the Transylvanian accent is simply what vampires sound like. Indeed, a similar accent was performatively displayed by Gary Oldman in Francis Ford Coppola's *Dracula* adaptation (1992). This fact was not only an open nod to Lugosi's iconic performance, but also continuously reinforced the idea that the Transylvanian accent is as part of the Dracula myth as much as his need and desire to drink human blood.

Many stories and beliefs surrounding the supernatural exist in Transylvania (Costin 2018). These are, to some extent, not too dissimilar to those claimed to be associated with the region in fiction, even if their cultural significance is inevitably lost, once they become part of the popular culture industries. A belief in undead souls returning to either haunt or "feed" on the living is certainly a significant part of the cultural narrative of the region, establishing the figure of the vampire—in it various forms—as an indelible part of the folkloric make up of Transylvania. This vision of Eastern Europe, and Transylvania in particular, as a land of monsters and difference was certainly already recognized at the time of Bram Stoker. As a novel, *Dracula* openly acknowledged the folkloristic and mystical connections of the land. One might even suggest that the novel relies solidly on this depiction, which is further established by Stoker, as the contrast between Transylvania and England—as an embodiment of the West—are called out. One would be hard-pressed to forget the Count's own ominous warning to Jonathan Harker, which employs the mere mention of Transylvania as a signifier for strangeness and difference: "We are in Transylvania, and Transylvania is not England. Our ways are not your ways, and there shall be to you many strange things. It is a strange world, a sad world, a world full of miseries, and woes, and troubles" (Stoker 2004 [1897], 20).

Within the bounds of the narrative perpetrated by Stoker, and which continues to survive today, Transylvania is a region imagined as being a place of not only "magic and enchantment," but, thanks to the vampiric connection, also as a place of "uncertainty, menace and danger" (Light 2016, 1). It is a land of buried secrets and dangerous pasts. Its name alone is able to evoke the feeling of something both enthralling and treacherous, luring unsuspecting visitors to an unknown and likely perilous fate. In a certain sense, Transylvania is the embodiment of the geographical uncanny: "a place somewhere on the very edge of Europe, close enough to be sufficiently unfamiliar to be threatening" (Light 2016, 1). In its difference and mystery, Transylvania is the ideal place for the vampire to thrive, and continue to be inseparable from it. As a result of a number of transmedia narratives, from literature to film and beyond, Transylvania has come to exit in the Western imagination as somewhat more of a fantasy than a real place. The name Transylvania has been "more or less completely appropriated by vampire fiction and vampire films," and it is now impossible "to hear the name without thinking of vampires" (Gelder 1994, 1). One might want to argue that Transylvania operates in a similar manner to the vampire itself, which is familiar enough to almost look human, but not quite. Its points of difference are overwhelming, and mark it as inevitably strange, remote, and Other.

Vampire Tourism in Transylvania

Vampire tourism is a prominent feature of the Romanian socio-economic, and to some extent, cultural landscape. Transylvania, in particular, is at the center of the business. Just as Dracula has become synonymous with Transylvania, so has the network of vampire tourism. For sure, the tourism industry is booming in the region. Many tourists flock to the region from around the world, interested in exploring "its medieval towns, ancient villages, and vast unspoiled mountains and forests" (Cohen 2011, 5). The great majority of tourists, however, travel to Transylvania with one specific aim in mind: to visit the sites associated with Dracula, the most infamous of all vampires. It is often rumored that Transylvanians themselves are commonly "surprised" to learn that many people think that "their homeland is a fictional creation filled with monsters" (Cohen 2011, 5). The consternation may indeed be a true occurrence, but this does very little to stop the stream of vampire tourism from successfully enacting its trade.

Transylvania is a very large region, and its history has been a tumultuous one. Often at the center of conflicts and battles, it has been the seat of multiple cultural exchanges over the centuries and has maintained its reputation as a land ruled by many different traditions and beliefs. Robert Z. Cohen suggests that, because of its turbulent history, Transylvania is home "to a rich mix of ethnicities, each contributing their history and folklore to a fascinating cultural tapestry" (2011, 4). Many of the stories that provide the cultural background for Transylvania and its people are indeed connected to notions of the supernatural and offer various perspectives on matters of life and death, including the suggestive existence of monstrous and various creatures of darkness. It is perhaps because of its cultural and historical make up, and its continuous entanglement with frightening tales of folklore, that Transylvania has maintained a reputation as a liminal place, where the intangible becomes tangible, and where the boundary between life and death often becomes blurred. Popular culture, from fiction to film and beyond, has been instrumental in continuing Transylvania's long-standing fame. The stories about Transylvania's abilities to channel the supernatural are so persuasive, however, that they often cast a shadow on the important networks of identity formation that provide Transylvania with its social, historical, and political foundations.

Every year, thousands of eager tourists travel to Transylvania, in search of any connection to the famous vampire that came alive in the pages of Stoker's novel, and later, continued to thrive in the broader network of transmedia adaptations. While some of the tourists simply enjoying visiting the locations mentioned in Dracula, a good number also come looking for proof of the vampire himself, and flock to the areas that hold supernatural appeal. One of these locations is Bran Castle, a fortress which sits in a strategic position in Transylvania, on the historical border with Wallachia. Fans of *Dracula* will recognize the presentation of Bran Castle, and the names of its surrounding areas, as truly befitting those penned by Stoker when giving a description of Castle Dracula, the ancestral home of the famous vampire. Stoker describes the castle as being "built on the corner of a great rock" and overall "quite impenetrable" (2004 [1897], 49). The castle's impenetrability is certainly emphasized, as Stoker indulges in descriptions of how "it sits on the very edge of a terrible precipice" and "a stone falling from the window would fall a thousand feet without touching anything!" (38).

There is evidence to suggest that Stoker may have encountered sketches and descriptions of Bran Castle—then known by its German name of Terzburg Castle—while conducting his research on Transylvania. It is widely purported that Stoker became fascinated with an image of Bran Castle as presented in Charles Boner's book *Transylvania: Its Products and Its People* (1865). The descriptions of the castle provided by Boner are distinctly romanticized, likely in an attempt to appeal to the sensibilities of a potential traveler. Boner presents Bran Castle as being a natural barricade, "built on a rock rising just where the mountains on either side slope down and meet as if to barricade the way" (278). Boner also seems to be channeling the castles of Gothic horror fiction that were widely popular at the time, mixing his travel memories with the power of the Romantic imagination (Crișan 2008, 12). While sensationalized, Boner's descriptions certainly hold a level of truth, as many details reported in his travel narrative can definitely be identified as part of the construction and outlook of Bran Castle. Boner even indulges in musings over the appealing sense of Otherness—although not so named—of the fortress, stressing that within its walls lie "narrow passages and galleries, strange nooks and zigzag stairs, and dark corners irresistibly attractive, and in the thick wall was a low prison where no ray could ever enter" (278–279). "Irresistibly attractive" is, arguably, a fitting description for many vampires in a myriad of texts, so one can only appreciate the unintentionally vampiric nature of Boner's descriptive lexicon.

Indeed, the physical and geographic similarities between Castle Dracula and Bran Castle are difficult to deny. Like Castle Dracula, Bran Castle is located high upon a rock on top of a valley, with a river flowing beneath it. The former also possesses the narrow passages and galleries that are typical of several Romanian castles, of which Bran is a typical example. The descriptions provided by Stoker via the character of Jonathan Harker in *Dracula*—the first to encounter the building and introduce it to the reader—provide much of the visual details for the Count's abode. Harker's details do not shy in relaying how the castle holds a mysterious atmosphere, together with many darkened areas. Like Boner in his travel book, Harker also has a penchant for the dramatic, and describes the dungeon of the castle in similar terms. Harker continuously describes the castle as a "prison" (2004 [1897], 38), commenting on the lack of light within its walls.

Beyond Boner's romanticized descriptions, more accounts of the look and feel of Bran Castle were also reported in other Victorian texts, which Stoker is known to have consulted. One of these was Nina Elizabeth Mazuchelli, *Magyarland* (1881); this particular travel book dedicates a good amount of attention to Bran Castle, and openly identifies it as an ideal tourist location for those with an interest in Eastern European folklore and Romantic literature. Mazuchelli portrays Bran Castle as mysterious and picturesque, which "with its many turrets and towers, is a mixture of the Byzantine and Gothic architecture" (151). Although it is quite generous in its tempting and authentic descriptions of Bran Castle, Mazuchelli's book is rather different from Boner's. What the two do share, however, is the identification of this particular castle as a mysterious and appealing place, carrying the feel of many centuries of history. Mazzucchelli, in particular, seems clear about her evaluation of Bran Castle as a "gothic place," and "the ideal spot of a fairytale world" (Crișan 2008, 13). Without being tempted to make unsubstantiated claims, it is possible to see how these travelogue descriptions might have had an impact on Stoker's writing, as the home of the infamous undead vampire slowly began to take form. Gothic tourism was clearly already successful in the Victorian era.

Regardless of their established provenance, the similarities between Castle Dracula and Bran Castle have been pointed out on numerous occasions, in a variety of texts, from tourism brochures to academic scholarship. Therefore, it is not surprising to see that Bran Castle has established a strong connection to the Dracula myth, and has even earned the contemporary appellative of "Dracula's Castle." Its colloquial name is clearly enough to attract tourists to the site. "Dracula Tours" are a common feature of the events surrounding the castle. One should only type these words in the search bar of any internet engine to be presented with a variety of options to go and visit the now famous location. Many tour operators offer a number of tours focusing—allegedly—on the paths and salient locations that were visited by Dracula. The most prominent group recommending all manners of vampire tours is fittingly named "Dracula Tours: Transylvania Live" (www.dracula-tour.com). On offer are visits to locations such as Borgo Pass, Sighisoara Citadel—openly named "the birthplace of Dracula" by the web site—and, of course, the legendary Bran Castle. No claims of actually encountering any vampires are included in the tour offers of either Bran Castle, or the other locations visited as part of the tours—unfortunately. What is clear, however, is that Bran Castle is presented as the "actual" castle described in Stoker's novel, together with its alleged connections to the mythical Count. It is truly incredible to witness the popularity of Bran Castle as the home of Dracula. After all, Dracula's Castle is, as imagined by Stoker, "undoubtedly a fictional building" (Crişan 2016, 47). The descriptions and outlook are substantial enough, however, to attract groups of willing tourists, who are—at the very least—keen to see the location that inspired Stoker in his novel.

Vampire tourism is a very successful part of the cultural industries of Romania. However, in its reliance on the figure of Dracula, it has "long presented" the nation with "a quandary" (Light 2016, 2). While Romania has embraced vampire tourism because of its lucrative outcomes, it is important to remember that its very existence is a point of contention for Romanians. One might be tempted to think that the reluctance to fully embrace vampire tourism as a part of the country's identity may be due to the fact that, with Dracula as its most prominent figure, it promoted a cultural association with villainy. There is, however, much more to be said on this. For sure, the Western obsession with Dracula appears strange to the average Romanian, as the famous Count was simply the creation of a foreign writer and owes very little to the history of Romania itself. The overarching association with the undead and the supernatural, and the image of the country that derives from it, is "starkly at odds with the way Romania sees itself and wishes to be seen by others" (Light 2016, 2).

The tourism narratives of Transylvania are further complicated by the fact that two versions of Dracula exist within the cultural folds: on the one hand, one will find many sites associated with Vlad Țepeș (1431–1476/77), an actual historical figure whose life is amply documented by the abundance of constructions—such as impressive castles—that he left behind. On the other hand, however, the industry thrives on the cultural reliance on Count Dracula, the vampire from Stoker's novel who, it would seem, has become one of the most well-known Romanians of the contemporary era.

The two figures are, across the board, greatly at odds with each other. In spite of the suggestions that Count Dracula was in fact based on the history and exploits of Vlad himself, very little evidence of this can actually be found. It might be worth remembering, *en passant*, how Coppola's controversial cinematic version of the Dracula narrative in 1992 did in fact merge the two figures into one, openly diverging from Stoker's novel, and infuriating many historians and literary observers alike. Indeed, the contrast between the historical Vlad and the fictional Dracula is closely felt in Transylvania, but its effects are limited by, it would seem, the hold of commercial imperatives. Catalin Gruia suggests that Romanians in general hold what she terms a "schizophrenic attitude towards Dracula" (Gruia 2014, 2). Unable to reconcile history with fiction, and historical prince with vampire, the common attitude is to allow them to coexist in a fluid and malleable fashion. The reason for this difficult relationship lies both in culture and in history. Firstly, Dracula is, broadly speaking, a literary invention originating in a land far away from Transylvania, or even Romania, itself. Secondly, and perhaps most importantly, it is well known that the Communist regime in Romania did not allow the circulation of "vampire fiction" until 1990. Therefore, the Count remained, as far as the broader population was concerned, largely unknown in his homeland until relatively recently (see Gruia 2014).

While tourism focused on the documented figure of Vlad Țepeș is clearly attuned to the country's historical narrative, Dracula and vampires in general are not. Vlad himself was, in fact, from Wallachia—another region of modern-day Romania—and not Transylvania. Here, the exploits of "Vlad Dracula" are often "commemorated in popular ballads and peasant folktales," keeping the historical memory alive, albeit in a narrative fashion (McNally and Florescu 1992, 34). These bear, unsurprisingly, virtually no connection to the Dracula of Stoker's novel. As far as the international tourism industry goes, however, the two figures are often indivisible. Vampire tourism tends to promote Dracula and Vlad Țepeș as one and the same, suggesting—in a strange, but overall logical development—that one simply evolved into the other. The conflation of the two figures within the tourism narrative proposes a complex issue, not only for Romania itself, but for those wishing to evaluate the impact of media and popular culture on the broader socio-historical and political fabric of the country. Vampire tourism, with its reliance on the fictional narrative of the ever-famous Count Dracula, represents a clear identification of the "identity versus economy" paradigm (Tunbridge 1994), where the potential to attract tourists manages to overcome the overarching cultural confusion that has surrounded the establishment and thriving of a fiction-based industry. The "inauthentic" vampires of the Transylvanian tourism industry provide a very "authentic" cultural association for those willing to travel to the much-coveted Gothic locations of the region.

Conclusion

As a cultural notion, vampire tourism is, it would seem, both a trans-historical and trans-media entity, mixing and mingling cultural motifs, Gothic tropes, folkloristic myths, and historical figures with the aim of providing a sellable product for the willing traveler. Historical narratives collide with the appeal and impact of the fictional world, where vampires live and operate in the midst of attractive suggestions and imagery. For the purpose of this essay, only salient, and perhaps arguably most-famous, examples have been considered—from New Orleans to Transylvania. The aim has been to construct conceptual links between history and popular culture, and the establishment of cultural entities that rely on transmedia representations of the undead. Indeed, many more examples exist, in many different locations around the world. For instance, "Twilight tours" are on offer in Forks, USA, as the location that inspired the vampire exploits in Stephenie Meyers' vampire saga of the same name. Evidence of vampire tourism can be also be found in Whitby (United Kingdom), exploiting the connection for the town provided in Stoker's novel, as the location of the vampire's arrival point into England. In the late twentieth century, and with the rise of Goth culture, Whitby "reinvented itself" to "tap into the mythology of Dracula" (Spracklen and Spracklen 2018, 139). For sure, the Whitby vampire industry is not quite comparable in size to the one thriving in Transylvania, but its existence still proves the impact of transmedia vampire narratives on a broader scale. Count Dracula is, of course, one of the most renowned figures from the vampire world, and it is not surprising to see that so many tours, especially in Transylvania, focus on his exploits. What is of note, however, is the constant conflation of real-life figures with fictional characters, merging worlds and blurring boundaries as the process of familiarizing the vampire takes place. Vampire tourism certainly encourages visitors to "behave in a certain way," and fully immerse themselves in the experience (Ek 2016, 142). Vampire tourism confronts participants with imperatives of enjoyment that largely rely on the imagination of fictional creatures, and the suspension of disbelief when it comes to the intermingling of historical and made-up narratives. Within this, the vampire itself emerges as a molded figure that is fully commodified and finds a new life in the folds of consumerist desires. The blood may indeed be the life, but, in the twenty-first century, the vampire finds its most sustaining form of nourishment in the interwoven narratives of media, culture, history, and consumerism.

Works Cited

Boia, Lucian. 2001. *Romania: Borderland of Europe*. London: Reaktion.
Boner, Charles. 1865. *Transylvania: Its Product and Its People*. London: Longmans.
Bram Stoker's Dracula. 1992. Film. Directed by Francis Ford Coppola. Los Angeles: Columbia Pictures.
Cohen, Robert Z. 2011. *Transylvania: Birthplace of Vampires*. New York: Rosen Publishing Group.
Costin, Claudia. 2018. *Folkloric Aspects of the Romanian Imaginary and Myth*. Newcastle Upon Tyne: Cambridge Scholars Publishing.
Crişan, Marius. 2008. "The Models for Castle Dracula in Stoker's Sources on Transylvania." *Journal of Dracula Studies*, vol. 10, pp. 10–19.
_____. 2016. "The Old and New Dracula Castle: The Poienari Fortress in Dracula Sequels and Travel Memoirs." *Dracula and the Gothic in Literature, Pop Culture and the Arts*, edited by Isabel Ermida, Leiden: Rodopi, pp. 45–68.
Dracula. 1931. Film. Directed by Tod Browning. Los Angeles: Universal Pictures.
Ek, Richard. 2016. "The Tourist-Vampire and the Citizen as Ontological Figures: Human and Nonhuman Encounters in the Potspolitical." *Tourism Encounters and Controversies: Ontological Politics of Tourism Development*, edited by Gunnar Thór Jóhannesson, Carina Ren, and René van der Duim, London: Routledge, pp. 139–158.
Gelder, Ken. 1994. *Reading the Vampire*. London: Routledge.
Gotham, Kevin Fox. 2005. "Tourism Gentrification: The Case of New New Orleans' *Vieux Carre*." *Urban Studies*, vol. 42, no. 2, pp. 1099–1121.
Gruia, Catalin. 2014. *Searching for Dracula in Romania: Romania's Schizophrenic Dilemma*. Scotts Valley: CreateSpace Publishing.
Harris, Charlaine. 2007. *All Together Dead*. London: Gollanz.
Kaplan, Robert D. 1993. *Balkan Ghosts: A Journey Through History*. London: Picador.
Light, Duncan. 2016. *The Dracula Dilemma: Tourism, Identity and the State in Romania*. Lodnon: Routledge.
Mazuchelli, Nina Elizabeth. 1881. *"Magyarland": Being the Narrative of Out Travels Through the Highlands and Lowlands of Hungary*. London: Sampson Low, Marston, Searle and Rivington.
McAvoy, Emma. 2016. *Gothic Tourism*. Basingstoke: Palgrave.
McKinney, Louise, 2006. *New Orleans: A Cultural History*. Oxford: Oxford University Press.
McNally, Raymond T., and Radu Florescu. 1992. *In Search of Dracula: The History of Dracula and Vampires*. Boston: Houghton Mifflin.
Ní Fhlainn, Sorcha. 2019. *Postmodern Vampires: Film, Fiction, and Popular Culture*. Basingstoke: Palgrave.
The Originals. 2013–17. Television. Created by Julie Plec. Los Angeles: CBS/Warner Bros Television.
Piatti-Farnell, Lorna. 2014. *The Vampire in Contemporary Popular Literature*. London: Routledge.
_____. 2017. "'The Blood Never Stops Flowing and the Party Never Ends': *The Originals* and the Afterlife of New Orleans as a Vampire City." *M/C: A Journal of Media and Culture*, vol. 20, no. 5, pp. 1–9.
Spracklen, Karl, and Beverley Spracklen. 2018. *The Evolution of Goth Culture: The Origins and Deeds of the New Goths*. Bingley: Emerald Publishing.
Stoker, Bram. 2004. *Dracula* [1897]. London: Penguin Classics.
Tunbridge, J.E. 1994. "Whose Heritage? Global Problem, European Nightmare." *Building a New Heritage: Toursim, Culture, and Identity in the New Europe*, edited by Gregory John Ashworth and Peter Parkham, London: Routledge, pp. 123–34.

Thinking in Connections
A.A. Carr's Eye Killers
and F.W. Murnau's Nosferatu

SVETLANA SEIBEL

In her interview with Diné (Navajo)[60]/Laguna Pueblo writer and filmmaker Aaron A. Carr, Mathilde Arrivé describes his novel *Eye Killers* as "Nosferatu in Navajo" (2010, 8). This designation follows others of similar kind, such as "Dracula-meets-Geronimo" (Kratzert and Richey 1998, 6) and "Coyote-meets-Count Dracula" (Elliott 1995, 35), all of which recognize *Eye Killers*' generic ties to Eurowestern vampire fiction alongside the storytelling traditions of the Indigenous nations of today's American Southwest. Indeed, Carr's novel clearly displays far-reaching intertextual connections to various defining texts of vampire fiction, including, of course, Bram Stoker's *Dracula*, but also much earlier literary tradition of vampire narratives from mid-eighteenth-century Germany. As a literary text, the novel's associations with other works of vampire fiction are both most readily evident and most widely discussed.

Arrivé's moniker for *Eye Killers*, however, hints at the fact that the novel's relational framework is far more complex than mere literary intertextuality. Referring to Nosferatu rather than Dracula as a point of comparison, the interviewer invokes the novel's transmedial dimension and its relational linkages to the medium of film specifically. Indeed, before

---

60. To my knowledge, both *Diné* and *Navajo* are currently in use to refer to the nation in question, although *Diné* appears to have become the preferred term. Robert McPherson explains: "While the People often refer to themselves as Diné in formal discussion, the term *Navajo* is still the one most often spoken and written" (9). Since the publication of McPherson's book eight years ago, the word *Diné* evidently has become more common in formal as well as informal contexts, and this is the word I use in this essay when speaking in my own words. A.A. Carr himself, in his novel as well as the interview, uses the word *Navajo*, as do critics and reviewers from the 1990s and early 2000s.

becoming known as an author of fiction, Carr has made a career in documentary filmmaking, collaborating with Lena Carr, a Diné documentary filmmaker and his mother, on some of her projects in the role of co-producer as well as directing his own documentaries and acting as producer and director of Prairie Dog Films. As is evident even from this brief summary, Carr is by no means a stranger to the process of filmmaking; what is more, his filmmaking and his writing are inextricably linked. On a diegetic level, *Eye Killers* keeps comparing its vampire characters to silent film, thus subtly affirming *Nosferatu*'s transmedial presence in the text—Elizabeth interprets Falke's telepathic communication with her as "a silent film in my head" (Carr 1995, 118); Michael compares Elizabeth to "a girl he had seen in a film many years ago, a silent film lost between the thunder and song of a matinee showing of Tom Mix and Gene Autry films" (Carr 1995, 163). But also formal features of Carr's text continuously engage in a dialogue with film. "*Eye Killers* came out of my love of film," Carr states, and it shows (Arrivé 2010, 8). Time and again, Carr's writing style privileges the image over the narrative, going to great pains to describe the minutia of a scene for the sake of establishing the mood and triggering the reader's senses more so than to advance the action. Such passages encourage the reader to pause and savor the moment rather than to press on to chase after the development of the plot.

As I have argued elsewhere, *Eye Killers* "is not only intricate in language, it is also rich in elaborate and striking imagery. The text adopts a writing style that is expressly visual, connecting so to the horror tradition in general, which, across media, relies heavily on the affective power of a strong image" (Seibel 2019, n.p.). This affective power is arguably nowhere more defining than in the silent horror films of German Expressionism. In fact, Carr cites Friedrich Wilhelm Murnau's *Nosferatu: Eine Symphonie des Grauens*, a loose adaptation of Bram Stoker's *Dracula* that first hit the big screen in 1922, in particular as not only "one of the most beautiful films [he] ever saw" (Arrivé 2010, 9), but also as a major influence on the inception and development of *Eye Killers*: "in a sense, that expressionist style was the visual style I had for everything in *Eye Killers*—the vampires, the sheepherder Michael. For me the novel was almost like a film shot in that style, that expressionist style, more dramatic, less melancholy, but somewhat like this. There was a lot of this taking control of our history involved" (Arrivé 2010, 10). This statement does more than simply establish an explicit connection between *Eye Killers* and *Nosferatu*, it also refers to the multilayered nature of this connection. The form and style are important, but so are the particular cultural moments and discursive backgrounds that molded the film and the novel—post–World War I Germany and the ongoing settler colonial realities in the

American Southwest, respectively. A reading of *Eye Killers* against *Nosferatu*, therefore, has a potential not only to yield additional insights into Carr's text, but also to provide a snapshot of the possibilities a nuanced cinematic-to-literary line of influence has to offer. To undertake such a reading is the purpose of this essay.

In his responses during the interview with Mathilde Arrivé, Carr often emphasizes the importance of connections of different kinds— for himself as an individual and an artist, the Indigenous cultures he is a member of, and his novel *Eye Killers*. "There is a really huge connection," he states on one occasion, "not only between us and fiction, but between us and the fiction of other people" (Arrivé 16). Partly to reflect that, this essay is structured in "connections," the one at the center being the connection between Carr's *Eye Killers* and Murnau's *Nosferatu*. By doing so, I am interested in the insights that emerge when these two texts—one literary, one cinematic—are brought into a dialogue with one another. The following is my attempt of doing just that.

As a loose adaptation of Bram Stoker's novel *Dracula*, one of the most significant alterations to the plot that Murnau's *Nosferatu* makes is changing the setting from England to Germany, from the real-life English Whitby and London to a fictional German Wisborg. The time of action has also been shifted in the movie, pushing it back to the first half of the nineteenth century, compared to Stoker's 1897 (Massaccesi 2016, 33). Critics have pondered the motivation behind these decisions many times, usually connecting them to questions of copyright and explaining these changes as a strategy aimed at avoiding the necessity of taking steps in order to secure legal rights to use Stoker's material.[61] However, as Cristina Massaccesi points out, while the copyright explanation is certainly plausible, it is also crucial to pay attention to the narrative repercussions of the change in time and place and "to consider … how these changes also triggered in the film a series of consequences that are worth underlining" (33).

These consequences are weighty indeed, perhaps more so than appears at first glance. In fact, I argue that what the changes in time and especially setting in *Nosferatu* achieve is transplanting Stoker's vampire narrative into the context of German literary history where, as

---

61. Giesen, for one, speculates that the change of setting and characters' names and origin could be due to the fact that the creative team behind *Nosferatu* "might have been misled by bad legal advice that they wouldn't have to pay the copyright owners for the film rights if they changed the story and names considerably" (40). Massaccesi also mentions the copyright issue in relation to the change of setting (33).

Heide Crawford argues, the literary vampire figure originates. In her book *The Origins of the Literary Vampire*, Crawford pinpoints mid-eighteenth-century Germany as the moment and place when the vampire moved from folklore to literature and became an expressly literary figure rather than a folktale. Her study, thus, "trac[es] the development of the literary vampire from its first appearance in literature with the German poem, 'Der Vampir,' by Heinrich August Ossenfelder in 1748, to its introduction into prose by German authors of the early nineteenth century" (Crawford 2016, xii). It was also the German poets of mid-eighteenth century who "added new traits to the literary vampire by connecting it with specific motifs, such as the *femme fatale* and the 'dead lover returns,' that modern readers automatically associate with the vampire" (Crawford 2016, xii). German literary tradition, Crawford explains, not only added these by now iconic traits to the vampire figure, but also infused it with complexity that allows for moral ambiguity (9) as well as for the vampire tales to function as a social and political commentary (11). She also highlights one particular feature of German Gothic stories, including vampire narratives, that sets the German tradition apart:

> Despite their varied contributions to the development of Gothic horror literature German authors' stories are unique in their reluctance to offer a final explanation for the Gothic horror they present. This is in contrast to the common model of British Gothic horror literature, in which the horror, mystery, and supernatural elements in the story are often explained in the end, a feature known as the "explained supernatural" and usually associated with Ann Radcliff's novels. In German Gothic horror tales, however, the mysterious events and supernatural occurrences are not always explained, at least not in a satisfactory manner for the reader, and nobody lives happily ever after; in fact, the protagonists usually die or they go insane. The achieved—and intended—effect of this common German narrative style that leads the reader along the same uncertain path as the protagonists without the luxury of clarity is one of limitless horror. The everlasting horror in the German stories may explain their international popular appeal, especially among British readers towards the end of the eighteenth century [Crawford 2016, xvii].

Into this narrative tradition *Nosferatu* is brought at the beginning of the twentieth century. If we consider *Nosferatu* the first cinematic incarnation of a vampire, it seems that this figure had come back to Germany to make another transmedial leap. Situating the film's action in a German cultural space naturally invokes this tradition and it is not hard to see parallels between German Gothic conventions as described by Crawford and the narrative choices the film makes when compared to Stoker's novel[62]: Count Orlok's mysterious origins and unspecified motives, the ineffectiveness of both civic and medical authorities in addressing or even correctly identifying the vampire threat, the necessity of a willing human sacrifice—a pure female, no less—in order to stop the vampire postulated as a given but never explained, the vampire's grotesque and alienating appearance are all features reminiscent of the features of German Gothic.

At the end of the movie, no explanation is given for any part of the Nosferatu phenomenon, and although the vampire is vanquished and the plague lifted, the cost is too much and there is no sense of victory. In fact, the closing shots of *Nosferatu* are a picture of despair and defeat: "We do not know what exactly *is* salvaged or restored, only that the plague has ended…. We are left with no restoration or the triumph of the living, but the ruins, the synecdoche for the vampire absence" (Waller 2010, 195). These parallels suggest a significance to the change in setting which goes beyond simple pragmatic copyright considerations and which infuses Murnau's free adaptation with a surplus meaning derived from German literary conventions and specificities and fitted to the historical moment Germany is living through at the time of *Nosferatu*'s release—a historical moment defined by the devastation of World War I and its aftermath, characterized by uncertainty and instability, as well as a sense of helplessness in the face of the Spanish flu pandemic of 1918.[63] The anti–Semitic subtext of the movie—in Giesen's words, its "hidden anti–Semitic ingredients" (2)—reveals the dark side of this connection.

Writing his vampire novel, A.A. Carr, of course, is very much aware of the vampire figure's cultural connections to Europe and its history, epitomized for him by the image of Murnau's Nosferatu character "in this expressionist style where it is distorted with these windows that are not straight" (Arrivé 2010, 9). This stark image of Nosferatu crisscrossed by

62. Stoker himself was obviously more than aware of the literary origins of the vampire's affinity to German cultural space and its literary tradition. Stoker's short story "Dracula's Guest," published in 1914, for instance, is set in Munich and the surrounding area, seemingly at a time that predates the events of *Dracula* in terms of narrated chronology. Apart from mere German setting, however, the similarities between *Nosferatu* and "Dracula's Guest" also include a reluctant carriage driver who refuses to venture into what is known as a vampire-infested territory, which in each case ends with the determined passenger proceeding on foot. Tellingly, both Waller in relation to *Nosferatu* and Sims in relation to "Dracula's Guest" point out the consequences this behavior has for characterization of the character known in *Dracula* as Jonathan Harker, and these consequences are very similar: for Waller, Murnau's Hutter, as he laughs at the driver's concerns, is revealed as "a shortsighted, foolish egotist" (181), while Sims calls similar attitude of the narrator of "Dracula's Guest" a "reckless disregard for danger" (447). Such correspondences beg the questions whether Murnau's creative team had possibly made use of *Dracula*'s "minor canon" such as "Dracula's Guest," and is therefore not only an adaptation, but also, as it were, a compilation.

63. For the historical context see, for example, Massaccesi 2016, 13–6.

irregular windows connects in Carr's imagination to the sense of "a mesa at Laguna" (Arrivé 2010, 9): "This is why I had a connection with that type of imagery, with what I saw of Europe, what I understood of this tragic past" (Arrivé 2010, 10). With *Eye Killers*, Carr transplants a master vampire of European origin into what is now New Mexico, where he had set up a small vampire coven and is hunting local women especially. At the beginning of the novel, the vampire seduces a Diné teenager Melissa Roanhorse into joining him as one of his companions, with the intent of making her his new vampire wife. Melissa's mother is eventually killed by the vampire and her English teacher Diana Logan joins forces with her Diné grandfather Michael Roanhorse in a quest to find Melissa, and, once they realize that the creature responsible for the girl's disappearance is a vampire, to destroy him.

How does all this connect to *Nosferatu*? In order to answer this question, it is necessary to look at the narrative makeup of Carr's master vampire and his background story in some detail. His name is Falke, a German word for "hawk," which immediately creates a link to a bird of prey as a metaphor for the predatory practices of a vampire, as well as places the origins of this particular vampire in a German-speaking territory. So does the invocation of the Nibelungs, figures of the most famous Germanic heroic epic, when his servant, nicknamed Kuenstler (the German word for "artist"), finds the place for Falke to settle in the unfamiliar desert: "Surely, we have crossed the Rhine and come to the Nibelungland!" he shouts (45). Falke speaks English with a foreign accent that no one can place; his speech patterns are often antiquated. He is handsome: tall, tightly muscled, elegantly dressed, with long flowing blond hair and blue eyes. Falke's story, his human origins, and his motivation are revealed piecemeal in the course of the novel, usually in the form of flashbacks that give glimpses and images of various episodes from his past, but do not in themselves provide full insight; it is a puzzle readers have to put together piece by piece. One of the more informative of these flashbacks occurs about one third into the novel. It gives the most concrete information about Falke's homeland and backstory the readers will ever get:

> Dimly, Falke recalled a serrated, wind-blown country, far south of his own kingdom in the Semming Pass near Vienna, where Christiane waited for his return. The sky was a veiled gold. If he looked behind him, Falke could glimpse a pale blue sea—the Adriatic. Small bells on the mounts' bridles *changed!* merrily. Leather creaked. His knights' songs were youthful and engaging—except for the song, resting secretly, that Christiane had given him…. Falke's long shield, borne by a dusty page, had displayed a single black anchor, which swallowed the rays of a weary sun. A memory of one afternoon, nine centuries past, when he had been alive and king [99–100].

"The Semming Pass around Vienna" surely refers to the Semmering pass which today separates Lower Austria and Styria. Incidentally, Styria is a place associated with much vampire activity in literature, figuring both in Sheridan Le Fanu's *Carmilla* (1872) and Bram Stoker's "Dracula's Guest" (1914); and this is the territory whereabouts Falke was a king sometime around the year 1095. His memory shows Falke leading a presumably military expedition south, to the Mediterranean, perhaps to one of the countries of central Europe whose stories have inspired vampire literature in the first place, while his thoughts are consumed by an image of a woman—Christiane. Taking into account Falke's statements on several occasions throughout the novel that he is nine hundred years old, something must have happened around that time, probably during this same expedition, that turned him into a vampire.

Human or vampire, however, Christiane remains the leitmotif of Falke's existence. He had spent centuries looking for her in other women. Later in the novel it is revealed that Falke's abduction of Melissa was motivated by his belief that she is the reincarnation of Christiane because of Melissa's uncanny resemblance to her. Elizabeth, Falke's first vampire wife, is the one who recognizes her from the images she had glimpsed in Falke's memories through the vampire telepathy: "Same thick fall of dark hair and penetrating gaze, same shadowed smile—Melissa was the mirror-image of Christiane. Falke's convent girl. A woman so dead and gone she wasn't even dust anymore. Nine centuries dead, Christiane had risen with Falke in the form of this girl. To claim him" (118). Apart from Melissa's identification with Christiane, the crucial information this passage provides is the fact that Christiane died nine hundred years ago, so around the same time that Falke became a vampire. Although we never learn what exactly had happened to Christiane, more details about her relationship to Falke are provided by Melissa who, in the process of becoming a vampire, also develops an ability to look into Falke's mind:

> I saw Christiane in his mind, like seeing a face underwater. When he was sleeping. Falke holds my hand when he sleeps with me. And I think that makes it easier to slip inside his dreams. The connection, you know? ... In one of his memories, I saw Falke against a window. A forest was passing behind him. There was sunlight outside, and we were moving. He was holding my hand, not squeezing it or anything, gentle and warm. I felt like I became someone else. It wasn't you. It was Christiane. I felt creepy; lost in memory. *Her* memory. I don't know how I knew this. Then this hand reached out to touch his face, Elizabeth, and ... and Falke was warm. So warm.... He was going away. And I wanted him with me so much. I felt his passion; I could see it in his eyes. But that day, I was the stronger one; I was betrothed to the Son of God. I made him go away. Falke let my hand go, but he promised he would come back for me. To win my hand, he said. I knew I wouldn't be strong then, Elizabeth. And I hoped for that so

much. But Falke never returned to me. Into whatever dark place my God had thrown him, Falke never emerged. My soul became grey stone. My knight never came back to me [262–63].

Thus we learn that, despite their mutual feelings, Christiane had rejected Falke's advances in order to commit herself to Jesus and join a convent, a decision which Falke neither condoned nor accepted. And while, apparently, he was never able to return to her, Falke keeps searching for Christiane for almost a millennium, extinguishing women's lives in the process.

With this theme Carr's novel not only situates its vampire character in a Germanic cultural space physically, it also connects thematically to the "dead lover returns" motif Crawford refers to (xii), albeit with a twist hinged on the reincarnation theme. In her study Crawford identifies Gottfried August Bürger's long poem "Lenore" (1774), in which a dead soldier returns to claim his still living bride and carries her away to join him in death, as the representative text for the "dead lover returns" motif. Incidentally, "Lenore" is also mentioned in *Dracula*, when one of the passengers of the carriage driving Harker to the Borgo Path quotes to him the now famous line "'Denn die Todten reiten schnell' ('For the dead travel fast')" (17), which is an imprecise quotation of Bürger's recurring refrain "Hurrah! die Todten reiten schnell!" ("Hurray! the dead ride fast!"). Although Falke does not appear to have returned to claim Christiane after his mortal death, he functions as a dead lover whose affection is a pathway to death to other women that he turns into vampires in hopes of finding in them his Christiane—first Elizabeth, and then Melissa (almost).

However, the text of the German tradition to which Falke's story in *Eye Killers* arguably connects the most is Heinrich August Ossenfelder's poem "The Vampire" ("Der Vampir"), which was published in 1748 and which Crawford credits as the first literary text in Western literature to feature the figure of the vampire. The vampire speaker of this short poem addresses a woman to whom in the German original he refers as "Christianchen," a German diminutive form for Christiane. As Crawford points out, the etymological connection of the name to Christianity hints at the strong religious faith of both Christiane and her mother (26), to whom the poem's speaker also refers as "an ever-faithful mother" to whose "long-held teachings" Christiane "clingeth/Unbending, fast and firm." The vampire speaker of the poem then reveals himself as a lover spurned who comes back as a vampire to take his revenge through a vampire "kiss," so that Christiane may compare what he offers to the teachings of her mother. Crawford writes: "The vampire's use of the German diminutive form of her name, Christianchen, is the reader's first clue that he has an emotional connection to her. It is likely that he is (or was) a suitor whose love for her was not reciprocated or acknowledged because of her strong religious faith" (26).

Apart from the obvious—that the object of the vampire's affections in both cases is named Christiane—there are several parallels between Ossenfelder's poem and Carr's novel. Both Falke and the poem's vampire speaker are rejected by their respective Christiane on the grounds of faith and religious calling. In Falke's case, there is no evidence that points towards Christiane's mother as the person on whose authority Christiane decides to dedicate her life to God. However, Falke does display a notable behavior pattern towards the mothers of his supposed reincarnations of Christiane—he kills them first chance he gets. He explains his actions to the distraught Melissa as a necessary evil: "The price of our existence. I saved you the task of doing it yourself.... One of us would have forced you to take your mother's life. This is how vampires are. We cannot allow ourselves even one distraction" (327). This rationalization does not sound very convincing on its own terms, and Falke's actions do appear to have the aim of isolating Melissa and binding her to himself rather than springing from any considerations of sparing her a painful decision. The connection within which his explanation does acquire a more ceremonial meaning is within the context of Diné tradition associated with evil and witchery—in one of the interviews with members of the Diné nation regarding these practices historian Robert S. McPherson was told: "The 'knowledge is a dangerous thing to handle, and you do not teach anyone that you do not know. In return for this knowledge, you must kill your mother or brother or sister' as part of the covenant" (McPherson 2012, 87).

The vampire speaker of the poem is outwardly aggressive and threatening towards his Christiane, while Falke, at first glance, is never anything but gentle with his. When examined closely, however, there are deducible hints of denial and aggression in his refusal to accept Christiane's decision. Neither is this occasion the last one on which his temper flares up dangerously. Although Falke had never purposefully hurt Christiane (that we know of), he does attack her viciously through Melissa when, towards the end of the novel, she demands that he let her go: "Falke jerked her to him, hit her savagely across the face. 'I will never let you go,' Falke rasped. 'Never again! If I have to nail you to the bedpost, I will do that!'" (331–32). It becomes clear in this instance that Falke is capable of open abuse even towards his beloved Christiane if threatened with a loss of control over her. As for other women, he goes on killing them, sometimes in Christiane's name, often using sexual seduction to do so, similar to the vampire speaker of Ossenfelder's poem.

As with *Nosferatu*, it is important to situate the violence occurring in

Eye Killers in terms of the historical context of an ongoing settler colonial reality within which the events of Carr's novel unfold. As many scholars and activists have often pointed out, violence against Indigenous women in settler colonial societies "is systemic in nature and colonial in origin" (Hargreaves 2017, 1). A violent and murderous intruder, Falke routinely singles out Indigenous women in particular as his prey—Melissa is not the only example of that. The vampire figure and the specific way in which it is embedded in the European vampire tradition in literature and film in this instance help underline systemic social problems that concern the time and place in which the novel is written.

Finally, one of the most striking thematic parallels between Murnau's *Nosferatu* and Carr's *Eye Killers* is the importance of the sun. *Nosferatu* is famously the first cultural vampire text that introduces sunlight as a natural phenomenon deadly to vampires. Unlike Stoker's *Dracula*, no staking or decapitating is mentioned as an effective means of vanquishing the vampire, the only remedy against him is exposure to the sun. While a novelty during the time of the movie's release, since then the lethality of the sun for vampires has become a staple of popular vampire lore. Carr's novel is no exception; in fact, in one instance the novel speaks of "a television sun" of which Elizabeth thinks Hanna, her fellow vampire, would be afraid, while Elizabeth herself is not: "The sun in movies is frozen. It's not a real sun at all. And the movie landscapes are frozen. Artificial" (207). And then she recounts her visits to the cinema to watch silent movies at the beginning of the twentieth century. It is hard not to think of Nosferatu's profile poised starkly against the sun before disappearing out of existence when reading these passages.

But in the fight against Falke, Carr roots the vanquishing power of the sun in Diné storytelling traditions: the power of the sun in *Eye Killers* is conceptualized and harnessed in terms of the story of the Hero Twins, the Monster Slayers of Diné tradition whose father is the Sun (Kristofic 2015, 17). In Jim Kristofic's telling, the Twins have journeyed to the house of the Sun to meet their father and, after a series of trials to ensure their true relation, they were accepted by the Sun as his children and given strong weapons with which to fight monsters threatening Diné people: "He gave to each brother a helmet and body armor of hard flint scales. He gave them these weapons: chain-lightning arrows, mighty sheet-lightning arrows, deadly sunbeam arrows, and killing rainbow arrows" (Kristofic 2015, 23). These are the kinds of weapons and symbols, associated with the Sun and the Twins and blessed in ceremony by the Elders, that Diana uses against Falke and that finally succeed in destroying him.

The elements of the Hero Twins story—the colors, the symbols, the weapons, the racing, the hunting of monsters—are woven tightly into the fabric of Carr's narrative, interweaving with many aspects of European vampire lore, for, to rid the Diné land of this foreign monster the combined knowledge of different cultural traditions is necessary. But among all these accumulated aspects the sun maintains a special importance just as it does in *Nosferatu*, as it remains the most feared bane of vampires' existence. The same is true of the fact that this formidable weapon in both texts has to be wielded by a hunter with pure intentions and special knowledge. Incidentally, in both the film and the novel this hunter is a woman (in fact, in *Eye Killers* it is a combined power and diverse cultural knowledge of several women), but the crucial difference is that while in the film Ellen does not survive her act of the vampire slaying in *Eye Killers,* Diana is not only victorious and alive herself, but also successful in liberating the young girl held in vampire's thrall. Instead of a willing sacrificial lamb who accepts death to save a mostly male world, Carr's women are warriors. By the end of the novel, as the vampire is defeated, Diana and Melissa, formerly a teacher and a student in a commonplace American high school setting, call each other "sister" and form a new family unit which is transcultural and rooted in knowledge, experience, and care. This vision of a female-led future stands in stark contrast to the doomed, femicidal ending of *Nosferatu*, an ending that leaves the town of Wisborg standing dumbstruck over the corpse of a woman who, time and time again, had proven to be the most insightful, conscientious, and effective of its citizens, but who is gone in the end with no one to replace her. When these two endings are put side-by-side in conversation with each other, they reveal striking gender representation disparities between the two texts under consideration, and they speak volumes.

The correspondences and breakages uncovered by this exercise in dialogic reading, thus, prove to be most revealing. These connections are both intertextual and transmedial in nature—and transmediality can, after all, be understood as a kind of intertextuality. What this reading clearly shows is that intertextuality and transmediality are far from one-directional; on the contrary, they flow in multiple directions at once, creating ever more complex trajectories. Above all, a reading such as this demonstrates the multiplicity of traditions and influences that combine in complex entanglements in the vampire stories of the twentieth century. When these traditions are brought into an open dialogue, new meanings and insights emerge that testify to specificities but also continuities, linkages, and, perhaps most importantly, connections. *Eye Killer's* transmedial connection to *Nosferatu* reinforces on the meta-level the importance of transcultural cooperation that the novel stresses, and at the same time calls attention to the way stories adapt, interact, and acquire new meanings while moving in time and space and between cultural contexts.

Works Cited

Arrivé, Mathilde. 2010. "Interview with Navajo-Laguna Novelist and Filmmaker Aaron Albert Carr." *Revue de Recherche en Civilisation Américaine*, vol. 2, pp. 1–17, http://rrca.revues.org/328.
Bürger, Gottfried August. 1778. "Lenore." In *Gedichte*, 81–96. Göttingen: Johan Christian Dieterich.
Carr, A.A. 1995. *Eye Killers*. Norman: University of Oklahoma Press.
Crawford, Heide. 2016. *The Origins of the Literary Vampire*. Lanham, MD: Rowman & Littlefield.
Elliott, Michael. 1995. Review of *Eye Killers*, by A.A. Carr. *Explorations in Sights and Sounds*, vol. 15, no. 1, Summer, pp. 34–35.
Giesen, Rolf. 2019. *The Nosferatu Story: The Seminal Horror Film, Its Predecessors and Its Enduring Legacy*. Jefferson: McFarland.
Hargreaves, Allison. 2017. *Violence Against Indigenous Women: Literature, Activism, Resistance*. Waterloo: Wilfrid Laurier Press.
Kratzer, Mona and Debora Richey. 1998. "Native American Literature: Expanding the Canon." *Collection Building*, vol. 17, no. 1, pp. 4–15.
Kristofic, Jim. 2015. *The Hero Twins: A Navajo-English Story of the Monster Slayers*. Albuquerque: University of New Mexico Press.
Massaccesi, Cristina. 2016. *Nosferatu: A Symphony of Horror*. Leighton Buzzard: Auteur.
McPherson, Robert S. 2012. *Dinéjí Na'nitin: Navajo Traditional Teaching and History*. Boulder: University Press of Colorado.
Ossenfelder, Heirich August. 2016. "The Vampire." *The Origins of the Literary Vampire*, by Heide Crawford, translated by Heide Crawford. Lanham, MD: Rowman & Littlefield.
Seibel, Svetlana. 2019. "Aaron A. Carr." *Literary Encyclopedia* 3.2.6: n.p. https://www.litencyc.com/php/speople.php?rec=true&UID=752
Sims, Michael. 2010. "Bram Stoker." *Dracula's Guest: A Connoisseur's Collection of Victorian Vampire Stories*, edited by Michael Sims, London: Bloomsbury, pp. 446–448.
Stoker, Bram. 1997. *Dracula*, Norton Critical Edition, edited by Nina Aurbach and David J. Skal. New York: Norton.
Stoker, Bram. 2010. "Dracula's Guest." *Dracula's Guest: A Connoisseur's Collection of Victorian Vampire Stories*, edited by Michael Sims, London: Bloomsbury, pp. 449–462.
Waller, Gregory A. 2010. *The Living and the Undead: Slaying Vampires, Exterminating Zombies*. Urbana: University of Illinois Press.

From Revenants to Vampires

The Transmedia Evolution of the Jiangshi

Katarzyna Ancuta

The *jiangshi* (Mandarin), or *goeng si* (Cantonese)[64] is a term used to describe reanimated stiff corpses that hop around attacking people to absorb their *yang* energy and suck out their life essence—*qi*. Most commonly known as the hopping vampires, in reference to the film *Mr. Vampire* (Lau 1985) that introduced them to international audiences, and occasionally branded as zombies due to their semi-decomposed condition, they are consequently depicted in early texts as a variety of ghost, or revenant. In Chinese belief, ghosts are created out of lingering aspects of the soul that remain earthbound or refuse to leave the body. The soul is the balance of *yin* and *yang*—the *yang* force is present in the *hun* soul that rises to heaven as a benevolent spirit (*shen*), while the *yin* force is attached to the *po* soul that accompanies the corpse to the grave and dissipates after the body has decomposed (Sumegi 2014, 236). Both types of soul can remain earthbound after death. Since the *hun* soul is associated with consciousness and intelligence, the *gu hun* ghosts are the souls that linger on due to personal reasons—driven by unfinished business, desire to communicate with the living, concern for the loved ones, resentment caused by an untimely death, attachment to life, or confusion as to where to go next (Lim 2005, 54). The *po* soul can become *ye gui* (the wandering ghost) when its grave is disturbed, uncared for, or when the body is not buried at all. It can also prove troublesome to humans (Lim, 54; Sumegi, 236). When the *po* soul fails to leave the body of the deceased it creates a *jiangshi* (Santangelo 2003, 52–3).

The most enduring representations of the *jiangshi* combine their literary portrayals known from works of the Qing Dynasty scholars with a reference to the folk practice known as "transporting a corpse over a thousand li" (*qian li xing shi*), where families would hire a Taoist priest to perform a

---

64. Alternative spelling *geong si, geung si*, also hyphenated.

ritual reanimating the corpse and forcing it to hop all the way home, seeing that in Chinese culture, a burial away from one's home was inauspicious. Corpse drivers leading solemn processions of hopping cadavers were said to be a particularly common sight in the mountainous region of Xiangxi in the Hunan province, where the practice was known as *Xiangxi ganshi* (driving corpses in Xiangxi). Contemporary explanations of this tradition disregard its supernatural dimension and speculate instead that the corpses were transported strung upright along bamboo poles, which created an illusion of their hopping (*Chuang* para. 2), or simply carried on the back of a living person hidden underneath a large black robe enshrouding the corpse (Lian Yiwu 2008, 32). Regardless of the method, to the witnesses the transported cadavers appeared to be the *jiangshi*—voracious creatures that feed on the life force of the living.

The *jiangshi* is a dangerous and deadly creature, unsophisticated and awkward but malevolent, nonetheless. Describing it as a vampire, however, is a gross overstatement, even if it bears some similarity to the *vampir, upir* of *vrykolakas*—monstrous revenants from European folklore said to have influenced the creation of literary and cinematic vampires. The vampire as a cultural icon, a creature of fiction popularized by its recurrent portrayals in literature, film and popular culture, is inseparable from the concept of blood-drinking with all its religious, philosophical, medical, sexual, racial, or ideological connotations that do not make much sense when applied to their hopping cousins. Obviously, on a certain level both blood and the *qi* energy can be said to represent the life force, but their symbolism is rather different. Yet there is no doubt that over the centuries, as a result of various media transmutations, the representations of the *jiangshi* have become progressively more vampiric. Contemporary renditions of the creature, especially in popular media with active fandom participation like *manga, anime*, cosplay, games, or webnovels have contributed to the creation of new hybrid creatures that blend Asian and European folklore with popular depictions of vampires in literature, film and popular culture re-constructed to maximize their global appeal.

This essay examines the transmedia evolution of the *jiangshi*—from their ghostly origins in Qing literature, through the cinematic portrayals that defined them as comic martial arts icons, to their recent appearances as hybrid creatures in popular fan-powered media, where their representations oscillate between cute and erotic and draw on the aesthetics related to the European vampire and Japanese *anime* characters. The essay begins with the discussion of portrayals of the *jiangshi* in Yuan Mei's eighteenth-century collection of strange tales, *Zibuyu*, then moves on to examine the cinematic construction of the "hopping vampire" in classic *jiangshi* films like *Encounters of the Spooky Kind* (Hung 1980) and *Mr. Vampire*

(1985) and, more recently, *Rigor Mortis* (Mak 2013) and *Vampire Cleanup Department* (Chiu and Yan 2017). Finally, the essay focuses on the creature's hybridization in fan-friendly contemporary texts like James Duvalier's light novel *Night Flowers* (2015), collaborative webnovels, and drama CD series *Midnight Jiang Shis* (2016).

Troublesome Corpses: The Ghostly Origins of the *Jiangshi*

Some of the earliest records of the *jiangshi* can be found in collections of strange stories written by the Qing Dynasty (1636–1912) literati. Chinese literature of the strange evolved from short accounts of anomalous phenomena known as *zhiguai* that solidified as a genre during the Six Dynasties period (220–589) and from their Tang Dynasty (618–907) poetic elaborations known as *chuanqi*. Stories about ghosts depicted encounters with the spirits of strangers and contemplated complex relationships between the dead and the living. Ghosts in the Chinese tradition are conceived of as revenants that are virtually indistinguishable from humans. This allowed for a multiplicity of plots in such stories that involved human-ghost interactions—telling tales of male scholar ghosts discussing poetry, training imperial exam candidates, playing games or enjoying a cup of wine with their human companions, and female virgin ghosts pursuing human lovers, engaging in sexual relationships, exchanging marriage vows, and giving birth to half-ghost-half-human children. Depicted as intelligent and emotional, such ghosts were capable of love and compassion, but also of jealousy, hatred, or greed. They protected their loved ones, divulged secrets, avenged their misfortunes, and showed cunning and calculation in their attempts to reincarnate, or to resurrect themselves. Although considered a type of ghost, the *jiangshi* were greatly limited in such stories by their attachment to the corpse, often in advanced stages of decomposition. Unlike regular spirits, they were considered primitive creatures, commonly denied a voice, driven by primal instincts to attack humans.

Conceived of as the *po* soul trapped in the deceased body, the *jiangshi* are reduced to their basic functions, driven by the desire for the *qi* and the *yang* of the living to counteract the unbalanced *yin* of the dead. In his collection of tales, *Zibuyu* (1788, translated as *What the Master Would Not Discuss*), a significant source or early *jiangshi* fiction, Yuan Mei (1716–1798) depicts the exact moment when a spirit is transformed into a stiff corpse. In a story called "Scholars of Nanchang," a young man is visited by a ghost of his friend who asks for help to complete his earthly responsibilities. The man asks his dead friend to stay for a while. The ghost obliges but eventually his demeanor changes: "he stood there without moving forward, staring wide-eyed. His features grew ugly and slowly began to decay" (Yuan Mei 2003, 168). When the frightened host attempts to escape, the corpse begins to chase him. Unable to climb a wall, the revenant is reduced to a brainless drooling monster, saliva dripping continually from his mouth. This sudden transformation is explained in the text as a result of the uncoupling of the dead man's *hun* and *po* souls. "When the heavenly soul left and his worry was resolved, the heavenly soul dissolved while the earthly soul remained. As long as the heavenly soul stayed, he kept his human personality; but when it left, he lost his human personality" (169). Without personality and consciousness, only the corpse remains.

The physicality and corporeality of the *jiangshi* are its defining features. Unlike ghosts that are often praised for their refinement and beauty in similar stories, the *jiangshi* are commonly depicted as disturbing and grotesque. The appearance of corpses ranges from relatively ordinary to disgusting and horrifying, and they are often distinguished by an unhealthy skin color—from green and white to black and purple, furry or covered in hair (Santangelo 2003, 53–54). Some corpses possess an ability to fly, other are under the influence of the moon or endowed with special powers (55). Yuan Mei's stories describe the *jiangshi* as "emaciated" (2003, 388), though often sporting "a bulging belly" (691), fat at night when they feed but "thin and withered" (1213) during the day when they sleep in their coffins. They have "disheveled" (358) and "unkempt" hair (485) and faces "as white as a whitewashed wall" (485), "blue and purple" (691), or "withered and black like dried meat" (689). In "Stiff Corpse Holding Weituo Buddha," "The corpse was covered from head to toe in white fur, as if wearing a coat made of snow weasel fur that had been turned inside out. His face too was covered in white hair, framing the darkest of eyes: however, his pupils were a dazzling green" (1068). Additional details include eyes "deeply set in their sockets" (689), or blood flowing out from their eyes (358). They may also have a particularly unpleasant breath whose odor is described as "unbearably foul" (1115).

Despite the cinematic tradition of dressing the *jiangshi* in the robes worn by the Qing Dynasty imperial officials, the corpses in Yuan Mei's stories wear all kinds of clothing—from an unassuming outfit comprised of "a hemp hat and straw sandals" (691) to the formal Tang Dynasty attire (657). In "Stiff Corpse Looking for Sacrifices," a corpse of a man who died childless and therefore will never become an ancestor spirit, is described as wearing his funerary offerings: "Across his shoulders were strings of paper money folded into the shape of silver ingots [buried with the dead for use in the netherworld], and they rustled slightly as he headed along the same path as before" (689). The characteristic activities of stiff corpses include copying people's movements (361), staggering (689), "jumping forwards" (485), running and chasing after people (168, 691), and biting (1069). The *jiangshi* are generally described as dangerous and malignant creatures. "A Flying Stiff Corpse" recounts the story of a cave-dwelling corpse that would fly down the mountain to attack the villagers and eat their babies (655–6). In "Strange Retribution for Digging Up a Grave," a grave-robbing monk meets a grisly end when "the stone coffin opened by itself. A blue arm over a *zhang* long stretched out and pulled the monk into the coffin, where he was torn to pieces and eaten. Not only were his flesh and blood sprayed about everywhere, but his bones clanked to the ground as well" (515). The *jiangshi* in the stories are eventually pacified or disposed of by sweeping them away with a broom (361), preventing their return to the coffin through a ritual involving ringing a bell (656), stealing the coffin lid (657) or placing red beans, pieces of iron and rice inside the coffin (690), and setting their corpse on fire (656, 1069, 1115) upon which, "they made a sound like a chirr" (1213).

Only two of the stories ascribe some form of higher emotions or intelligence to the creatures. In "Two Stiff Corpses Make Love," the narrator follows an elegantly dressed corpse to a mansion. He witnesses the dead man communicate with the lady of the house who invites him to climb up to her window. When the corpse returns to his grave in the morning, he cannot enter his coffin because its lid has been hidden. In panic, the *jiangshi* returns to the mansion but collapses at dawn on the roadside. The mansion is identified as an ancestral temple of another family and a corpse of a woman is found inside. The by-standers then realize that "oddly enough, the two corpses must have got out of their coffins to make love" (657) and decide to cremate them together. In "Stiff Corpse Looking for Sacrifices," the *jiangshi* is given a voice and allowed to plead with Ren San, the man attempting to destroy it. The corpse calls out to Ren: "I am the one who has been sleeping all along in the temple. I have no children, so I haven't received any sacrifices for a long time. To satisfy my hunger, I must go out in search of something to eat" (689–90). The *jiangshi* implores Ren to allow him to return to his coffin, asking: "Why are you being so cruel? I bear no animosity towards you" (690) but Ren disregards the request afraid that the creature may decide to kill him in revenge. The lifeless corpse is discovered outside the temple in the morning and destroyed.

Collections like Yuan Mei's *Zibuyu*, served as creative models of correct relations between the living and the dead in accordance with the Taoist and Confucian principles. The creation of the *jiangshi* in such stories is always connected either with the unnatural sudden death of a person—particularly through murder or suicide—or with improper burial rites (or the lack of thereof). The latter was often the result of the deceased dying far away from home and without any descendants to perform the mourning rites and ensure a continuous supply of offerings. The grave could have been disturbed by robbers, or as a result of an environmental disaster like an earthquake. A corpse belonging to a suicide or murder victim could have been left undiscovered and unburied. The return of the cadaver as the *jiangshi* prevents the deceased from reincarnation. In this sense, the stories could be read as a double warning: filial descendants should ensure their ancestors are sent into the afterlife in a proper manner to prevent their monstrous return, but also every person should ensure they produce descendants, otherwise there will be no-one left to care for their grave. In this sense, the appearance of the *jiangshi* in strange stories could be said to have a didactic dimension. Its entrance into the world of the cinema, however, marks its transition into a figure of entertainment.

Martial Arts, Magic and Mayhem: The *Jiangshi* as a Local and Global Horror Icon

The *jiangshi*'s gradual shift from revenant to vampire begins when it establishes itself as a distinct cinematic trope in Hong Kong movies in the 1980s. Most film scholars attribute the sudden surge in the *jiangshi*'s popularity to two movies, Sammo Hung's *Encounters of a Spooky Kind* [*Gui da gui*] and Ricky Lau's *Mr. Vampire* [*Goeng si sin sang*], both mixing supernatural plots with *kung-fu* stunts and laughter. While the first film features a variety of non-human creatures, part of its plot revolves around a bet that makes Sammo Hung's character, Bold Cheung, sleep next to a coffin, the inhabitant of which returns each night as a tenacious *jiangshi*. *Mr. Vampire* devotes more screen time to stiff corpses, beginning with the visit of a corpse driver and his hopping customers to a local Taoist temple and constructing the film's main storyline around the botched re-burial ritual that creates the titular *jiangshi* and the attempts to confine it.

The popularity of this second film, according to Stephen Teo, spurred a whole new genre of *jiangshi dianying*—Hong Kong cinema's answer to Western vampire movies, particularly the lush Gothic productions of Hammer Film (1997, 219). As noticed by Teo, *jiangshi* movies draw primarily on the rich Chinese ghost lore and literary sources, such as Pu Songling's *Liaozhai zhiyi* (1740, translated as *Strange Tales from a Chinese Studio*) and their connection with Western films is merely allusive (219). Yet, the decision to market Lau's film as *Mr. Vampire* promoted a reading of such films that favored direct comparisons with Western horror movies and resulted

The Vampire (Wah Yuen). *Mr. Vampire*, directed by Ricky Lau (Golden Harvest, 1985).

in the ongoing misunderstanding that sees the *jiangshi* as a type of Western vampire with Chinese characteristics.

Following this logic, in her *Historical Dictionary of Hong Kong Cinema* (2007), Lisa Odham Stokes includes *jiangshi* films under "Vampire Movies" category, listing *Midnight Vampire* (*Wuyi jiangshi*, Kung-Leung Yeung, 1936) as the first production of this kind. Jess Nevins argues that despite having a *jiangshi* in the title, the movie in question was more likely inspired by the 1935 Chinese screening of Tod Browning's *Dracula* (1931) rather than local folklore and places it alongside two similar productions: *The Three-Thousand-Year-Old Vampire* (*Sanqian nian didi jiangshi*, director unknown 1939) and *Vampires of the Haunted Mansion* (*Guiwu Jiangshi*, Wai-man Leung 1939). The plots of these films that see their characters return from the grave to avenge their deaths or plan the annihilation of humankind suggest that their monsters possess at least a degree of intellect, which makes them different from the usual portrayals of the *jiangshi*. Still, whether *jiangshis* or vampires, these early monsters proved unable to compete with ghosts, which dominate Hong Kong horror cinema, and made only sporadic appearances until the 1980s. By the mid–1980s, Stokes concludes, the *jiangshi* films became a staple, with 24 films made between 1986 and 1990 (2007, 448). The numbers are likely to be even higher. A user-generated list of *jiangshi* films on IMdB.com mentions 94 titles (including one Japanese and two Western productions), 52 of which were made between 1980 and 1990.[65]

65. Chinese Hopping Vampire (*jiangshi*) films https://www.imdb.com/list/ls006751934/.

Most scholarly discussions of the 1980s–1990s *jiangshi* films do not problematize the vampire label attached to the creature. The *jiangshi* is categorized as a Chinese vampire with a set of local peculiarities that draw on Chinese folklore and relevant religious worldviews, and the films themselves are often read through the prism of Western horror/horror-comedy genre. In his essay on vampires in transnational horror, Dale Hudson argues that vampires "migrate" into non-horror genres, like the Chinese *wuxia pian* telling stories of martial chivalry and sword-fighting heroes of ancient times (2014, 467). While the essay calls for the development of new critical frameworks through the study of non–Hollywood/European films, the idea that vampires can simply "migrate" into new genres suggests that while the genres may differ, the definition of vampire is rather fixed. The discussion of the *jiangshi* films that follows is therefore more focused on reading them as a generic hybrid, blending together genre conventions of Hammer vampire films, Chinese *jiangshi* literature, Chinese opera, and Japanese *samurai* films (476), rather than debating the characteristics of the monster itself.

Hudson's evaluation of the *jiangshi* is based entirely on their portrayal in the discussed films, observing that a corpse turns into a *jiangshi* due to "a lack of air" (478), or that because the creatures are blind they "locate victims by sensing breathing patterns of inhalation and exhalation" (478). He describes them trying to steal their victim's breath, biting humans, choking or piercing their throats with long fingernails. He does not fail to notice that the design of the creatures in the films appropriates "fangs and bloodlust from vampire films to add an 'exotic' European quality" (476) and help promote the *jiangshi* as a "hopping vampire." Teo similarly argues that "The vampire motif is a variation on the Western form which Hong Kong cinema assimilated with the release of *Mr. Vampire*" (219), and attaches a problematic dual label "cadaver or vampire" to the creature to distinguish it from an inanimate corpse. Teo attributes the creation of the *jiangshi* to an "extra breath" of life that gets trapped in a body: "When one does not die an auspicious death, an extra breath is retained in the body and the cadaver awaits an opportune moment to reactivate itself, searching for life forces to absorb" (223–4). The discussion of the films then follows a similar pattern, highlighting the hybridity of Hong Kong cinema as a whole "freely mixing elements from East and West" (219) and the hybridity of the Hong Kong horror genre "combining aspects of Western vampire movies, Chinese ghost stories and Hong Kong's own kung-fu and comedy genres" (219) but paying little or no attention to the figure of the *jiangshi* itself.

Taking a broader cultural perspective, Hudson notices that the emergence of *jiangshi* movies in the mid–1980s coincided with "[accelerated] awareness of uncertainties and certainties regarding Hong Kong's future"

(2009, 204) and argues that the later films in the cycle, especially those that placed the *jiangshi* in a dialogue with more Draculesque foreign vampires "pose questions about Hong Kong's crisis in a more urgent way [...] moving from the spectrality of ghosts to the corporeality of vampires as the handover became imminent" (204). It is, therefore, interesting to examine what has changed for the *jiangshi* in the years after the handover and the two films that must be mentioned here are Juno Mak's *Rigor Mortis* [*Goeng si*] and *Vampire Cleanup Department* [*Gau goeng cing dou fu*]. Made in the wake of the global demand for Asian Horror films spurred by the unprecedented international success of Japanese and Korean horror movies in the late 1990s/early 2000s, *Rigor Mortis* offers a well-balanced mix of local folklore and generic horror tropes that finally acknowledges the *jiangshi*'s potential as a figure of fear. Set in a run-down apartment complex, where humans and ghosts coexist in relative harmony, the film tells a story of a retired actor, Siu-ho Chin, who rents an apartment with an intention of committing suicide. He is rescued by a former Taoist exorcist, Yau, who now runs a small restaurant in the building. When one of the elderly residents dies and is resurrected by a practitioner of black magic as a *jiangshi*, Siu-ho joins Yau in his battle against evil.

Although taking a more serious approach to the subject, the film clearly ties itself to its predecessors. The cast includes several seasoned actors—Anthony Chang, Chung Fat, Siu-ho Chin, Richard Ng, and Billy Lau—who all starred in at least one of the numerous *Mr. Vampire* movies. The ongoing musical motif running through the film is a slower and sadder version of the Ghost Bride theme song composed by On-tat Lee for the original *Mr. Vampire*. The design of the creature, however, differs significantly from the earlier films which all tended to dress their *jiangshi* in the uniform of Qing Dynasty officials complete with a hat adorned with a peacock feather, perhaps to account for the *jiangshi*'s association with Qing literature, or to acknowledge the increased labor migration in the period that created the profession of corpse drivers in the first place. Here, the creature is dressed in a plain black robe and the most outstanding costume feature is a mask made of Chinese coins commonly used in *feng shui* charms. When the mask binding the *jiangshi* breaks and the creature awakens the ingenuity of the design is revealed, as the monster's bald head, claw-like bony fingers with extended fingernails, and long black robe place it also in direct connection with Nosferatu—the one version of European cinematic vampire that sees it as a revenant rather than a demonic lover.

The *jiangshi* also returns to its earlier characteristics, depicted as a mindless but malevolent and highly dangerous monster that literally tears its victims to pieces, and its attacks on humans resemble those of a feral beast. While it is unclear whether the creature actually drinks blood, or

The *jiangshi*-Nosferatu (Richard Ng). *Rigor Mortis*, directed by Juno Mak (Fortissimo Films, 2013).

consumes human flesh, it is certainly capable of ripping its victims apart and in this aspect, it does not resemble the bumbling hopping vampires of the 1980s that could be fooled by holding one's breath.

If *Rigor Mortis* establishes the *jiangshi* as the figure of fear and upgrades its position to a global horror icon, *Vampire Cleanup Department* steers towards the romantic comedy genre with its story of a female *jiangshi*, Summer, and her quest to become human again. The plot introduces an ancient secret society devoted to eradicating the *jiangshi* menace, whose members have been successfully disguising themselves for centuries as low-class street cleaners—a nod to early *jiangshi* literature that suggested the creatures could be swept away with a broom. One particular mission leads to a discovery of two *jiangshis*—a vicious corpse of an old male landowner and his young wife who was buried alive to accompany him into the afterlife. Unlike the master *jiangshi*, whose appearance is predictable, Summer revives into her former cute self with an addition of one fang (the other one missing during the fight). She follows her human rescuer like a lost puppy and learns to live again by meticulously copying his movements—a familiar behavior noted in early texts. Summer's humanity comes at a price as she eventually sacrifices herself to save her friend and defeat her former master but the appearance of a new recruit that looks exactly like her suggests that she might yet get a chance to reincarnate. With its blend of martial arts, slapstick comedy, and Taoist rituals the film fits the conventions of the *jiangshi* genre set by the 1980s productions. What is new, however, is that through the introduction of Summer, the *jiangshi* is repackaged as a cute and adorable character to suit the taste of the younger audience whose pop-cultural references are more likely aligned with the Japanese *anime* and Korean drama of today than with Hong Kong films made thirty years ago.

Summer (Min Chen Lin) learning to smile with Tim (Baby John Choi). *Vampire Cleanup Department,* directed by Sin-Hang Chiu and Pak-Wing Yan (Media Asia Distribution, 2017).

The *Jiangshi* Redux: New Media and New Audiences

Like any horror icon, the *jiangshi* has appeared in a wide variety of media forms. It featured in television shows like *My Date with a Vampire* (Chan, Poon and Tang 1998) from Hong Kong with a plot that pits vampire hunters against a *jiangshi* horde; *Hao Hao! Kyonshi Girl* (Hamatani and Nishiumi 2012) from Japan in which a member of an idol group becomes a Taoist exorcist to fight the undead she accidentally released; or more recently *What We Do in the Shadows* (Clement 2019–) from the USA, which includes the *jiangshi* in "The Orgy" episode 9, season 1. The creature made appearances in *manga, manhwa,* and *anime,* as well as all types of games from Nintendo's beat 'em up game *Phantom Fighters* (1988), or Line drop puzzle game *Spirit Catcher* (2012), to a Korean casual phone game *Mandrake Boys* (2017) in which you grow cute plant boys from seeds. There are even two Pokémon characters, Norowara and Kyonpan, based on the *jiangshi.* In popular fiction, perhaps the most notable *jiangshi* appearance can be found in Kim Newman's *Anno Dracula* (1992), where the *jiangshi* is cast as the most relentless and virtually invincible undead assassin. What all these characters have in common, is that they are mostly derived from the 1980s Hong Kong films. They have also become gradually more hybridized—merging Eastern and Western characteristics, while remaining attuned to specificities of various Asian cultures.[66]

66. More contemporary designs of the creature incorporate cuteness, often presenting the *jiangshi* as children or teenagers and adhering to the *bishōnen* (beautiful boy) stylistics.

The extent to which the *jiangshi* can embrace hybridity can be seen in texts, like James Duvalier's self-published vampire novel *Night Flowers* (2015) which blends the *jiangshi* motif with American vampire tropes and African witchcraft. The novel's main heroine, Liz Young, a white American teenager who grew up in Chinatown in Boston and therefore (obviously) can speak fluent Cantonese, moves with her mother to Exeter, Rhode Island, and finds work at a mysterious Chinese restaurant that seems to make a lot of money despite having almost no customers whatsoever. Liz soon discovers that the wealth of her employer has supernatural origins. The secret lies in enslaving a *jiangshi* and keeping it appeased with blood offerings, which apparently brings prosperity to its owners. Naturally intrigued, Liz learns about Lian Hua, the *jiangshi*, unaware that Lian Hua's vampiric spirit is planning to move into her body to escape her captors. Liz is eventually saved by a group of elderly Chinese vampire hunters and a ghost of Sarah Tillinghast—a young American woman who died in 1799 and, according to historical records, in death was accused to be a vampire.

The monster portrayed in the novel is a mix of the *jiangshi*, vampire and witch. Identified early as a "stiff corpse" (2015, 9), Lian Hua/Elvira[67] is said to be "a creature of darkness. A vampire. A *geong-si*" (112) created through a Palo Mayombe[68] black magic ritual that involves a consumption of the concoction known as *pó dos mortos* (dust of the dead) containing a mixture of night flowers, graveyard dust and pulverized human bone. This upgraded *jiangshi* is described as "intelligent, sharp and calculating" (92), possessing superhuman strength and the knowledge of magic. In its spectral form it feeds on life energy just like a regular *jiangshi*; in its physical form, however, it drinks blood: "She sat on the edge of my bed, lifting my wrist to her clay cold lips and licking the crimson trickle that her razor sharp fangs drew to the surface of my ailing flesh" (71). Like a European vampire she is weakened by Christian symbols and sleeps in a coffin filled with her native soil, hoards gold, obsessively counts scattered grain, leaves behind a dead body with "two puncture wounds on his neck" (81), and eventually dies with a wooden stake in her heart. While the simplification of both Asian and African culture to a few "exotic" horror tropes in the novel can easily be seen as an Orientalist gesture, it also demonstrates that since its introduction to the international audiences courtesy of Hong Kong cinema, the *jiangshi* has continued to evolve and through assimilating a number of features from its vampire cousin, it has reshaped itself as an Eastern/Western hybrid monster.

67. In the novel, Lian Hua is the second incarnation of the original vampire-witch Elvira from the island of São Tomé.
68. Palo Mayombe is a collection of beliefs and rituals originating from the African Congo based on the veneration of the dead.

Closer to home, the *jiangshi* theme is popular with the writers of webnovels—an online serial literary form that evolves through feedback and discussion on internet forums and can be written by individual authors or as a collaborative effort. Websites like Full Novels (www.fullnovels.com) or Novel Updates (www.novelupdates.com) feature translated versions of Asian *jiangshi* webnovels (mostly Chinese) and while the quality of translation is not always the best and most of the texts are forever ongoing productions, a quick look at the current offering can give us an idea as to the direction this type of *jiangshi* fiction tends to take. *I Woke Up Pregnant with an Undead Child* (ongoing, currently 63 chapters), for instance, is a tale about an undergraduate student in archeology who falls into a tomb during a field trip, faints, and wakes up miraculously impregnated. To make matters worse, the main character is actually a man, and the novel's *yaoi* (boy love) label can give us a hint as to what kind of supernatural romance is brewing. *My Husband is an Undead* (ongoing, currently 54 episodes) is an adventure story about a woman who gets reincarnated after a miserable life and joins forces with her new *jiangshi* husband to fight against all kinds of evil supernatural creatures. *Zombie Evolution* (ongoing, currently 48 chapters) is a supernatural comedy following an attempt of a low-class *jiangshi* to improve himself through following a "refining manual." The text is categorized as a *xianxia* novel—a fantasy genre devoted to stories about characters in pursuit of immortality.

The shortest and the only complete novel featured on the site is a 9-chapter story called *Grave Digger*, advertised with a tag "The lighthearted love story of a (vampire) zombie and an idiot." A boy called Sixteen is forced to dig up an old grave that happens to contain a beautiful female *jiangshi*, Zhuning. The girl attempts to drink Sixteen's blood but is not satisfied because it does not taste good. Zhuning asks the boy to help her exact her revenge on her fiancé, Xiaoran, she blames for her death. The couple travel together with the boy feeding her rabbits and helping her grind down her teeth. Zhuning finally finds the latest reincarnation of Xiaoran who is now a woman. When it becomes clear that the main fault of Xiaoran was simply moving on after her death and marrying another woman, Sixteen persuades Zhuning not to harm his current reincarnation. In the final chapter of the story, Sixteen saves Zhuning from a Taoist who attempts to separate them and the couple remain together.[69] While the *jiangshi* in each of these novels bears some resemblance to its folklore predecessors, it is clear that the monster has been thoroughly humanized—endowed with intelligence and human drives, desires and motivation. The appearance of the *jiangshi* in romance novels in both hetero- and homosexual relationships

---

69. All the novels can be read at https://fullnovels.com/tag/jiangshi/ or https://www.novelupdates.com/stag/jiangshi/.

affects the representation of the creature, which is now expected to conform to whatever standards of beauty are currently in trend. The inclusion of fantasy/martial arts motifs is a nod towards the *jiangshi*'s *kung-fu* past but curiously many of the creatures are described as blood-drinkers, which may have been influenced by the global popularity of Western vampire Young Adult fiction exemplified by the *Twilight* novels (Meyer 2005–8) and movie (Various 2008–12) franchise.

Vampire-Taoist romance is also the main theme of the Japanese drama CD series *Midnight Jiang Shis*, originally released by Rejed in a series of six CDs in 2016. Drama CDs are basically audio dramas that are sometimes referred to as "*anime* without pictures," as the only images they include are CD covers and additional art. The first six volumes are devoted to six *jiangshis*: Meimei, Rinrin, Leilei, Honoka, Riei and Iroha, who are released from their tombs and show up at a local school as transfer students. The cover art portrays all the boys as *bishōnen*, or beautiful androgynous slender boys with delicate features. Each character represents a certain type popularized by Japanese high-school drama—Meimei is a bad boy known for his strength, Rinrin is the popular kid with charisma, Leilei is a playboy that gets all the girls, Honoka is an idol famous for his looks, Riei is moody and hates everybody, and Iroha is fragile and emotional. Each of the stories is recorded as a monologue with only the voice of the character and occasional sound effects. Each of them also follows a very similar scenario in which the *jiangshi* wakes up, arrives at school, meets a girl who is a descendant of the Taoist that imprisoned him, and lures her to a secluded location where he attacks her. The attack takes a form of a mild rape fantasy where biting and sucking blood replaces an intercourse, the girl becomes "addicted" to being bitten and inevitably falls in love with her attacker.[70] With the genre of the story set as a soft sadistic erotica, the *jiangshi* transforms to a full-fledged vampire, since blood-drinking carries more sexual connotations than blindly hopping around sniffing out one's prey. It is at this point that the *jiangshi* catches up with the dark romantic Western vampire heroes of today.

Conclusion: Hopping into the Future

The *jiangshi* case illustrates that popular culture is a formative force that can reshape centuries-old traditional beliefs for its purpose and that globalization inevitably leads to the hybridization of cultural material and sometimes also to the infantilization of its tropes. What started as a

---

70. Character information and plot summary based on the translation provided by Akui Chansera https://akuichansera.tumblr.com.

misidentification seems to have become reality—the *jiangshi* has transformed into vampire, even though in doing so it has opted for the most recent version of the creature—a hyper-sexual blood-drinking morally ambiguous darkly-romantic lover luring young girls/boys with a promise of eternal love. The turn towards Asian Horror, a marketing brand that favors a mix of Western body horror with Asian folklore themes, has promoted a closer re-examination of older *jiangshi* lore but like its European cousin, the *jiangshi* has to adapt to remain relevant. Split between the two extreme portrayals that make it either terrifying or cute, the *jiangshi* of today appears to be hopping around in circles, staying put but also not exactly going anywhere.

WORKS CITED

Duvalier, James. 2015. *Night Flowers*. Middletown, DE: Self-published.
Encounters of a Spooky Kind [Gui Da Gui]. 1980. Film. Directed by Sammo Hung. Hong Kong: Golden Harvest.
Grave Digger. 2017. Webnovel. Retrieved from https://www.novelupdates.com/series/grave-digger/
Hudson, Dale. 2009. "Modernity as Crisis: *Goeng Si* and Vampires in Hong Kong Cinema." *Draculas, Vampires, and Other Undead Forms: Essays on Gender, Race and Culture*, editors John Edgar Browning and Caroline Joan Picart, Lanham, MD: Scarecrow, pp. 203–34.
____. 2014. "Vampires and Transnational Horror." *A Companion to the Horror Film*, edited by Harry M. Benshoff, Oxford: Wiley Blackwell, pp. 463–82.
Liao Yiwu. 2009. *The Corpse Walker*. Transl. Wen Huang. New York: Anchor Books.
Lim, Jonathan. 2005. *Between Gods and Ghosts*. Singapore: Marshall Cavendish Editions.
Mr. Vampire [Goeng Si Sin Sang]. 1985. Film. Directed by Ricky Lau. Hong Kong: Golden Harvest.
Nevins, Jess. 2014. "Women in Pre–1947 Chinese and Indian Horror Fiction and Film." *Apex Magazine*, 7 January. Retrieved from https://www.apex-magazine.com/women-in-pre-1947-chinese-and-indian-horror-fiction-and-film/
Rigor Mortis [Goeng Si]. 2013. Film. Directed by Juno Mak. Hong Kong: Kudos Films.
Santangelo, Paolo. 2003. "An Introduction to *Zibuyu*'s Concepts and Imagery: Some Reflections and Hypotheses." *Zibuyu, "What the Master Would Not Discuss," According to Yuan Mei (1716–1798): A Collection of Supernatural Stories*, edited by Paolo Santangelo with Yan Beiwen, Leiden: Brill, pp. 1–146.
Stokes, Lisa Odham. 2007. *Historical Dictionary of Hong Kong Cinema*. Lanham, MD: Scarecrow.
Sumegi, Angela. 2014. *Understanding Death: An Introduction to Ideas of Self and the Afterlife in World Religions*. Oxford: Wiley-Blackwell.
Teo, Stephen. 1997. *Hong Kong: The Extra Dimensions*. London: BFI Publishing.
A Thousand Li. 2016. Editorial. *Chuang* 1. http://chuangcn.org/journal/one/a-thousand-li/.
Vampire Cleanup Department [Gau Goeng Cing Dou Fu]. 2017. Film. Directed by Sin-Hang Chiu and Pak-Wing Yan. Hong Kong: Media Asia.
Yuan Mei. 2003. "*Zibuyu*." *Zibuyu, "What the Master Would Not Discuss," According to Yuan Mei (1716–1798): A Collection of Supernatural Stories*, edited by Paolo Santangelo with Yan Belwen, Leiden: Brill, pp. 161–224.

Part IV

Interventions, Fandom, Ownership

Transmedia Interventions and Palimpsestuous Relations

Carmilla *Meets Carmen Maria Machado*

NATALIE WILSON

The 2019 Lanternfish version of *Carmilla*, edited and introduced by Carmen Maria Machado, adds intriguing layers to Joseph Sheridan Le Fanu's already multi-layered 1872 original novella. The primary conceit of Machado's introduction is made clear from the outset: Le Fanu's text is based on fact. Claiming the novella has its basis in the real-life love story of Veronika Hausle and Marcia Maren, Machado uses a learned, academic tone in her introduction, never indicating that what she documents is anything but truth. At the outset, she informs readers of a discovery made in 1973 by Dr. Jane Leight: a stack of correspondence between a doctor and woman only identified as "V." "Accompanying these letters," Machado explains, "was the famous introduction to *Carmilla*, penned in Le Fanu's hand." This discovery, she posits, proves Le Fanu's tale was not fiction but appropriated fact—or, as she puts it, "the narrative artifice literary scholars had been admiring for well over a century was not artifice at all" (Machado 2019, ii).

As Machado tells it, Le Fanu's characters are based on historical figures, Dr. Hesselius on Doctor Fontenot, Laura on Veronika Hausle, and Carmilla on Marcia Maren. Noting that Leight's research was "extraordinary thorough," Machado, by way of reference to a faux text on the subject, *The Professor and the Vampire*, excuses herself from going into a lengthy overview of the history (ii). She does, however, provide us with specifics that result in key revelations. First, that *Carmilla* and *Dracula* are both based on true events. Second, that Veronika (Laura) was "married off" only to die in childbirth. Third, that Veronika's correspondence with Fontenot (Hesselius) makes no reference to any fear or repulsion regarding her feelings for Marcia (Carmilla), something that frames Le Fanu as grievously misrepresenting the queer history he bases his text upon.

"When Joseph Sheridan Le Fanu's magnum opus, *Carmilla*, was first published in installments in *The Dark Blue* in 1871, readers everywhere received it as fiction" (i), Machado reports in her opening salvo. She continues, "Each new edition, adaptation, and re-imagination of *Carmilla* has treated the correspondence between Doctor Hesselius and Laura as a fictional artifact, an epistolary fabrication nested in layers of metacommentary like a set of Russian nesting dolls" (i). Here, the insinuation is that all the "metacommentary" surrounding the text has only served to hide the true tale nesting within. Machado then builds a nesting doll textual edifice of her own, adding layers to restore the "truth" behind the tale. At the outer-edge of this matrix is Machado herself, at the core, her anagrammatic double, Marcia Maren (the "real" Carmilla) whose name just happens to be comprised of the same letters as Machado's first and middle names—Carmen Maria. Drawing upon what Jordan Hall (co-creator and writer of the *Carmilla* web series) deems her "Borgesian imagination,"[71] Machado's textual interventions add to the many existing versions and adaptations, doing so in a way that contribute to the transmedia components of *Carmilla*.

According to Henry Jenkins definition, a transmedia narrative is one which "unfolds across multiple media platforms, with each new text making a distinctive and valuable contribution to the whole" (Jenkins 2006, 149). Though the concept is usually linked to digital media and its contemporary manifestations, transmedia storytelling, as Matthew Freeman argues in his monograph *Historicizing Transmedia Storytelling*, is "perfectly viable without using new digital technologies" (2017, 4). Jenkins also contends transmedia narratives have a long history, noting that "initial claims that transmedia was emerging from a particular moment, at the place where old and new media collide, has given way to a recognition that transmedia has a much longer history" (2016, n.p.). Most pertinent to what follows, Jenkins posits that transmedia storytelling "encourages playful participation" and "creative reworking," both of which he links to a "process of dispersal" that "creates gaps which require our active speculation" (2018, n.p.). Machado's introduction to the Lanternfish edition of *Carmilla* encourages such participation, prompting readers to consider what components of *Carmilla* might be based in historical fact and to puzzle out the connections between *Carmilla* and Bram Stoker's *Dracula*.

The vampire, as this monograph posits, is a figure particularly conducive to transmediation. As Simon Bacon explores in "The Transmedia Vampire: From Bram Stoker's *Dracula* to HBO's *True Blood*," the vampire

71. Borgesian is used here in relation to the Latin American writer Jorge Luis Borge and his particular style of writing.

"is virtually indistinguishable or inseparable from the media technology through which it makes itself known" (2014, 56). Arguing a key component of the figure is its two-fold power: one, to "invite us into its world," and two, to prompt us to "willingly bring it into our own" (56). Bacon's reading interprets vampire texts as promoting a transcendence of the narrative frame, a jumping through the fourth wall, if you will, one that provides an immersive experience and promotes *becoming vampire* via textual consumption. This becoming vampire lends itself to experiencing vampirism beyond the world of the text, to bring the figure to (undead) life in more ways and across more media platforms so as to commune more thoroughly with the vampire and vampire mythos. Such a communion is fostered by Machado's transmediation of *Carmilla*, one that not only adds further layers to the novella in terms of narrative form and function, but which also urges readers to engage with the vampire as a historical (and historically misunderstood) figure.

Machado's contributions to *Carmilla* prompt readers to become textual vampires of a sort, ones eager to drink in and chew over the perplexing claims her introduction and footnotes present. Her editorial additions to Le Fanu's text are offered up in non-linear, puzzling fashion, energizing what Jenkins names as integral to engaging with transmedia texts: "curiosity, exploration, experimentation, and problem solving" (2013, n.p.). In constructing an elaborate back-story to the novella, Machado's work not only heightens its transmedia components, but also adds to the palimpsestic nature of the text, effectively erasing layers of "newer text" (the narrative's many adaptations as well as the layered narrative of the original) to restore the "true" story beneath.

In its literal form, a palimpsest is a manuscript, usually consisting of parchment or vellum, whose markings are scraped or chemically erased so as to be used again. The most compelling factor regarding palimpsests is that they retain traces of earlier, imperfectly removed writing. The palimpsest came to be used as a literary metaphor after Thomas De Quincey's writing on the subject in 1845. The lengthiest work to date since, *The Palimpsest: Literature, Criticism, Theory,* by Sarah Dillon, illustrates the usefulness of the concept for theoretical and literary analysis. Drawing on de Quincey's work, she argues palimpsestic texts offer "an involuted phenomenon where otherwise unrelated texts are involved and entangled, intricately interwoven, interrupting and inhabiting each other" (2007, 3–4). If we apply this notion to *Carmilla*, we might consider how, within the novella, Laura's narrative is interwoven with information provided by Generals Spielsdorf, the Woodman and Baron Vordenberg. Their narratives interrupt hers, entangling it in tales of the vampire history of Styria. Dillon, like De Quincey, also emphasizes the literary palimpsest as one in which underlying or older scripts reemerge, using the term "palimpsestuous" to describe what she names as key, the "simultaneous relation of intimacy and separation" (3). Within the novella, Laura and Carmilla share this type of relationship, doing so in a very writerly way. We might, for example, attribute the qualities of parchment to Laura. Camilla's bite writes upon her body, leaving "a small blue spot" below her neck (Le Fanu 2019 [1872], 83). Laura's flesh, in some senses, functions as the parchment upon which the "strange subject" of the vampiress Carmilla is made known—she is the blank slate, the virgin page, inscribed with the transgressive markings of a vampire coded as sexually and racially other. To "write over" this dangerous tale of love and lust, the men of the story set out destroy Carmilla, to erase her presence in Laura's life. However, Laura, in writing the narrative which comprises the novel, writes Carmilla as she sees her, as lover and friend, as beautiful and enigmatic. This sentiment is conveyed up until the very last line, a sentiment that proves she has not let the men of the tale fully erase Carmilla.

Machado enters with ink of her own, some 150 years later, to inhabit the text, doing so in a way that resuscitates the queer underpinnings of Le Fanu's tale. In effect, her intervention erases the many layers of artifice wrought by the males within the tale (Laura's father, the General, the Baron) as well as authors outside of it (such as Stoker). Returning the narrative to its queer roots, that of a love story between two women, Machado spins an intriguing tale of the purported real-life figures that appear in fictional form in *Carmilla*. In so doing, she positions Laura and Carmilla as done wrong by the heteronormative voices that effaced and misinterpreted their story. Referencing research projects, professional alliances, odic forces, museum exhibits, the invention of synthetic dye, Nabokov's *Lolita*, and a Japanese lesbian magazine also named *Carmilla*, Machado approaches Le Fanu's text with an encyclopedic attention to detail so as to prove the veracity of her queer reclamation. Though she admits some of her annotations do not have particular bearing on the introduction or the text, annotate she does, both within her introduction and in the body of the text itself. This accumulation of detail mocks academese on the one hand and calls for a reconsideration of what "counts" as proof/legitimacy on the other.

A key aspect of Machado's transmedia intervention, albeit a well-hidden one, is her allusion to The Museum of Jurassic Technology in Los Angeles, a "faux museum" that passes itself off as a real one. By referencing Veronika (Laura) as the great-granddaughter of Madelini Delani, a vocalist said to have inspired neurophysicist Geoffrey Sonnabend's work, Machado invokes one of the primary collections housed at the museum. One must connect the dots to unearth her obfuscated nod to this museum, one that is "a very real place that showcases some not very real things—although neither the artifacts nor the scripts indicate otherwise" (Downing 2009, 48). Though hinted at in the very name of the museum (the Jurassic period was of course not a technological one), the displays, including those linked to Delani and Sonnabend's, are presented as historical fact. In referencing Sonnabend's *Theories of Forgetting and the Problem of Matter,* Machado nods to *Carmilla* as a text comprised of Laura's memories yet, rather than questioning the veracity of her tale in response, she grounds it in fact—in the work of an academic researcher (Leight), a doctor (Fontenot), and a neurophysicist (Sonnabend). Just as the Museum of Jurassic Technology toys with knowledge production, expecting its attendees to take for granted its claims due to their placement within a museum, so too does Machado expect readers to accept her faux introduction as fact precisely because it is a published artifact.

In claiming Veronika is the great-granddaughter of Madelina Delani, Machado also gestures towards the use of anagrammatical naming in Le Fanu's text. *Carmilla*'s true name according to the introduction is Marcia Maren, itself an anagram of Machado's first and middle names—Carmen Maria. Maren, claimed to be of Cuban descent, also shares a similar lineage to Machado. These puzzles within Machado's introduction align to Jenkins description of transmedia narratives as "like pieces of a puzzle" which require "our active speculation" (2013, n.p.). In this regard, the original novella might also be considered as containing transmedia components given Laura encourages readers to participate in questioning her narrative via calls such as "Judge whether I say truth" or "Listen, and wonder!" (Le Fanu 2019 [1872], 4). Shelby LeAnn Wilson in "The Bitten Word: Feminine Jouissance, Language, and the Female Vampire" asserts such calls reflect Laura's attempts to make language her own. Laura uses her narratorial pen, Wilson argues, "like *Carmilla*'s fang," puncturing language rather than flesh. More specifically, she interprets Laura's narrative as involved in a "wrestle with phallocentric language," one enacted so as to free her experiences from the linguistic prison house of the male symbolic, a claim that speaks intriguingly to the various framing devices deployed in the novella (2015, 3).

Of note is that while modern imprints include a prologue, when *Carmilla* was initially published in the literary periodical *The Dark Blue* it did not contain any introductory framing. It was not until it appeared in Le Fanu's 1872 collection *In a Glass Darkly* that a prologue was added, one initially attributed to the unnamed medical secretary of Dr. Hesselius, Le Fanu's occult detective figure. The addition of a prologue added a new layer to the narrative, one which positions Laura as penning the story at Hesselius' request. Though the prologue indicates Laura acts as his "informant," her narrative is addressed to a "town lady like you," not Hesselius (2019

[1872], 38). This inconsistency is not addressed in the prologue or elsewhere, leaving readers to wonder *why* Laura directs her story to the town lady and *who* this town lady is. Machado's introduction gestures towards what has been excised from the text, suggesting that the narrative Le Fanu presents is both truncated and inadequate. Citing this as the grounding her decision not to "restore the original complexity and length of Veronika's letters to this edition," Machado continues:

> There are a few reasons: First, there is reason to believe that even the collection of correspondence discovered by Dr. Leight was not complete, and I remain eternally hopeful that Veronika's uncensored voice will one day have its due. The second is more complex, and infinitely more petty: I wished this edition to bear LeFanu's shame. I wish the reader to come to the book with a complete understanding of its inadequacy [2019, vii].

If the excised portions of Veronika's/Laura's letters were indeed restored, Machado suggests, the tragic story would be revealed as one of love cut short by "senseless slaughter," a revelation that renders the account of the "ecclesiastics and doctors and fathers and uncles and barons and vampire hunters" within the text "highly suspect," as voices which *write over* and reinterpret Veronika's/Laura's voice (vi).

In addition to asserting the male voices within the text are not to be trusted, Machado's introductory framing mines the linkages between writing a memory, troubling the divide between fact and fiction. Like Laura, Machado exhorts readers to participate in the construction of meaning, as when she encourages us in a footnote to "Imagine it, reader: a river of blood" (25). This exhortation comes just before Laura reads the letter General Spielsdorf sent to her father detailing his niece Bertha's mysterious death. The river of blood imagery inserted by Machado evokes the female body and its menses as well as the vampire's associations with blood. Metaphorically flowing between Laura, Bertha, and Carmilla, the stream muddles the general's thinking, resulting in a letter Laura's father presumes was "written in distraction." That Laura further speculates about "the violent and incoherent sentences" from the general's letter further positions her as an interpreter of male language (Le Fanu 2019 [1872], 12–3).

In the scenes detailing the carriage accident that follow, women's language and their capacity to interpret is also favorably represented. As Laura, her father, and her two governesses take in the full moon, Laura notes being "pleased with the tinkle of the ladies' conversation" (15). She references a story told by Mademoiselle DeLafontaine about a cousin of hers who dreamed of an old woman who clawed his face as he slept. Soon after, the carriage crash brings three more women into the story—"a lady with a commanding air" (presumably *Carmilla*'s mother), her daughter

(Carmilla), and "a hideous black woman with a colored turban" described as "grinning sinisterly towards the ladies, with gleaming white eyeballs and teeth set as if in a fury" (25). This woman, generally interpreted to be the "Matska" Carmilla refers to later in the narrative, is represented in ways more akin to a vampire than is Carmilla. Yet, unlike the Count, she appears only briefly in the text. Perhaps more than in this one scene, however. As Machado suggests in a footnote, she may be the old woman referenced in De Lafontaine's story. Citing Valerie Guyant's article "What or Who is 'Matska' in *Carmilla*?," Machado entertains the idea this women could very well be the vampire bringing death to Styria, an idea that supports a claim footnoted in her introduction, that Marcia/Carmilla "may have been innocent of the more devious charges laid against her" (2019, viii).

Asserting "[i]t seems as though Marcia/Carmilla falls somewhere in the historical record alongside Countess Elizabeth Bathory ... either an unrepentant predator or an ambitious proto-feminist" (vii), Machado refuses to display Carmilla as villain or victim. In gesturing towards the wildly divergent accounts concerning Elizabeth Bathory, Machado questions the veracity of history, hinting that its "facts" are subject to the whims of who is doing the telling. The suggestion that narratives should not be taken at face value gibes well with the content of *Carmilla* itself, wherein it is unclear whether Carmilla is the fiend others claim or if she is viewed as such due to her "too close" relationship with Laura (and perhaps, offstage, with Bertha as well). Take, for example, the claims of General Spielsdorf. Given he is overcome with grief, are we to trust his account of Bertha's death? Laura's father is puzzled by his claims and views him with suspicion. When the general announces, "I mean to decapitate the monster," Laura's father becomes "more bewildered than ever" (Le Fanu 2019 [1872], 115). In the exchange, the general is described as trembling with rage and stomps his foot, as if a toddler having a tantrum. Soon after the Woodman arrives on the scene followed by Baron Vordenberg. Vordenberg is described by Laura as "one of the strangest looking men" she has ever seen with "long and grizzled" hair, a "shambling gait," and hunched over comportment. What are readers to make of the "grotesque" Baron Vordenburg, one who appears far more monster-like than does Carmilla? Are the "imaginary lines" he traces on a scroll of paper he rests atop a tomb or the words he reads from a dirty little book, whose yellow pages were crowded with script "meant to be trusted?" (127–8). All of these suspicious men—the general, the Woodman, and Vordenburg—along with Laura's enigmatic father—converse out of Laura's hearing. We, along with her, are thus kept out of the conversation that seals Carmilla's fate. Though Laura later admits "it is difficult to deny" the voluminous testimony regarding the existence of vampires, she reports as much in a markedly detached voice (132).

In the final chapter that follows, she summarizes more of Vordenberg's "curious lore," before concluding her narrative with the revelation: "And to this hour the image of Carmilla returns to my memory with ambiguous alternations—sometimes the playful, languid, beautiful girl; sometimes the writhing fiend I saw in the church. Sometimes, I start from a reverie, certain I heard the light step of Carmilla at the drawing-room door" (135). In these closing lines, Laura's passionate tone returns as she admits she remains unsure about Carmilla's "true" identity. Significantly, this identity is referenced as an image, as something Laura *sees* rather than something Carmilla *is*. The ambiguous image of Carmilla harkens back to the refurbished painting Laura discusses earlier in the text, one that similarly depicts the mystery of Carmilla in terms of a palimpsest. Recall that palimpsests involved the erasure or "painting over" of older markings to make way for new inscriptions. New text was sometimes inscribed at a right angle to the older text, meaning the parchment would be turned again and again, creating a box-like layering of text. The square shape of the portrait Laura discusses in the narrative can be likened to this box-like layering, as can the process of layering oil paint to achieve a particular image/color. The restoration process of such portraiture involves "erasing" discoloration with the use of solvents or, in some cases, removing overlaid images to reveal the original work below. The portraits, previously "blackened by age" are "brought to light," much as the dark and foreboding women that frame Carmilla when she arrives (her presumed mother and Matska) are "erased," leaving only the "quite beautiful and startling" Carmilla the unframed image presents (49–50).

The restoration processes the painting of Camilla undergoes is similar in some regards to Machado's "unfinished" framing of the novella, one in which "history" is "refurbished." Like the paintings, which have their blackened images erased away, *Carmilla*, in Machado's hands, undergoes a distinct transformation, one which "brings to light" the queerness at the heart of the tale on the one hand, and writes her own queerness into the tale on the other (most literally, as noted above, by turning Carmilla's name into an anagram of her own). Recall this unframed portrait is initially misread by Laura's father as depicting "Marcia Karnstein." Once restored, however, the gold-lettering clearly reads "Carmilla, Countess Karnstein." The erasure/transformation of the original image can be associated with linear time, with the changes in color and hue that occur as paintings age. In terms of the portrait as palimpsest, the passage of time "writes over" the original image yet its traces remain—the original image can, in other words, be "brought back to life." That Laura refers to this image as an effigy of Carmilla that "seemed to live" is telling given the connotations of "effigy"—a word often associated with an image or model of a hated person (50). However, Laura describes the image as a beautiful one, even asking if she can hang it in her room. Here again, we encounter a doubled, or layered, version of Carmilla.

To turn to layers beyond the text itself, another "palimpsestuous" aspect of *Carmilla* is its relationship to the text that most overtly effaced it, *Dracula*. "Palimpsestuousness" between texts, defined by Dillon as "a simultaneous relation of intimacy and separation" (2007, 4–6), certainly speaks to that between *Carmilla*, an intimate and slim novella, to *Dracula*, the imposing textual edifice that overshadows it. Stoker clearly had intimate knowledge of Le Fanu's text, though he never admits as much. This plundering and subsequent forgetting of *Carmilla* aptly links to Shelley Reese's argument that "there is certain violence inherent to the palimpsest, as texts are invaded and reformed through interference and interpenetration by others" (2015, n.p.). Reese's choice of words, "invaded" and "interpenetration," are of particular interest here. While Stoker *invaded Carmilla*, extracting numerous bits of its vampire mythos to repurpose in *Carmilla*, Machado's interventions are more aptly linked to *interpenetration*. She merges and comingles the texts in two distinct ways, firstly, by claiming Dr. Hesselius and Van Helsing were contemporaries and, secondly, by compiling an archive similar (though much briefer) to the one Mina Harker compiles in *Dracula*. Regarding the first, Machado references Van Helsing as "another 'character' whose real-life counterpart had his life's work undermined by the guise of fiction" (2019, ii). That his work was "undermined" implies that Stoker did a disservice to the "real" Van Helsing, as did Le Fanu to Fontenot according to Machado. In a footnote, she further comments "There is no doubt that the events that inspired *Dracula* would have interested Doctor Fontenot tremendously, but he died of pulmonary tuberculosis in 1885, over a decade before its publication and well before its central events took place" (ii). This footnote hints at the linkages between tuberculosis and vampire mythos, a disease that clearly informs *Dracula* yet, like LeFanu's influence, is never noted within the novel itself.[72]

Regarding the second area of "palimpsestuousness" between *Carmilla* and *Dracula*, the compiling of an archive to "prove" the veracity of one's tale, Machado incorporates various types of "proof"—academic research, unearthed correspondences, factual minutia, relevant texts, and so on. This archive, though much briefer, is akin the one compiled and

72. There is speculation that the widespread reports of outbreaks of vampirism in New England, America, in the early to mid–19th century and which have subsequently been attributed to tuberculosis, might have influenced Bram Stoker's depiction of the vampires in *Dracula* (see Crystal Ponti, 2019, "When New Englanders Blamed Vampires for Tuberculosis Deaths," *History.com*, 28 October, https://www.history.com/news/vampires-tuberculosis-consumption-new-england. Accessed 21 August 2020).

edited by Mina Harker. Comprised of numerous recording methods—journals, letters, legal documents, invoices, news stories, shipping logs, ledgers, deeds, transaction records, and so on—*Dracula* reads as a vast archive. The recording and organizing of the documents that comprise the novel rely on technology (typewriters, gramophones, photographs), resulting in a text that unfolds via the incorporation of multiple media types—or, in other words—a transmedia text. Mina then transcribes these texts in triplicate form. This narrative multiplication, made possible via carbon paper, attempts to make permanent the "proof" she and the crew of light have amassed regarding Count Dracula. Machado overlays her own proof over this archive in her introduction by implying the "central events" featured in *Dracula* were, like *Carmilla*, based in historical reality.

Allow me to add another layer to this textual matrix—the brief essay "A Note Upon the 'Mystic Writing-Pad,'" penned by Sigmund Freud in 1925. In the essay, Freud suggests the above-named apparatus functions in ways similar to human memory. The writing pad consisted of a thick waxen or resin board covered with a thin transparent sheet. One could use a stylus to write on the pad and then lift the plastic sheet to "erase" the resulting text. Yet, traces of the text remained in the waxen board underneath. Freud used this writing device as a metaphor for how we create, store, and (partially) erase memory. If we apply Freud's ideas about the Mystic Writing-Pad to the text at hand, we might think of the interrelationship between *Carmilla* and *Dracula*. *Carmilla*, written first, would comprise the original etchings and *Dracula* those overlaying them. To put it another way, Stoker writes (and writes!) over *Carmilla*, yet traces of Le Fanu's tale remain. Then along come several films, televisual productions, and digital content that "write over" these tales, and, most recently, Machado's own etchings. It is thus apropos that, near the close of her introduction, Machado references fiction itself in a way conducive to the Mystic Writing-Pad. She writes, "The act of interacting with text—that is to say, of reading—is that of inserting one's self into what is static and unchanging so that it might pump with fresh blood" (ix). Here, texts are akin to permanent traces in the waxen board—they cannot be erased but can be altered and edited as readers interact with them and/or authors adapt and build upon them.

Concluding Thoughts

In the last lines of her introduction, Machado calls upon readers to unearth the layers of *Carmilla*, to mine its "palimpsestuousness." She writes:

> Having read this introduction, I hope you enter into *Carmilla* thusly, using your fingertips and mouth and mind to locate the lacunae where Le Fanu excised pieces of Veronika's account, the hallways haunted by the specters of truth and phantoms of passion. See if you cannot perceive what exists below: the erotic relationship of two high-strung and lonely young women. The shared metropolis of their dreaming. An aborted picnic in the ruins [ix].

Importantly, she encourages readers to take what they have learned in from her introduction about the "truth" behind the tale, the erasure and excision of queer female voice, the suspect motivations of "learned men" such as Fontenot and Le Fanu, and apply them to the original novella. One small but important component of this textual revisioning is Machado's account of the wild roses passed between Veronika/Laura and Marcia/Carmilla. As she tells it, Veronika, in one of the unpublished letters, "revealed that the wild rose was a symbol of affection between herself and Marcia," that the lovers "left clipped branches for each other on their respective pillows" (iv). When Veronika dies in childbirth after being "married off," Machado reports, she dies with "her fingers curled around the branch of a wild rose." Machado refers to this as an "unextraordinary death" not in keeping with her "extraordinary life" (iv). This linkage of marriage/motherhood to death puts the termination of their relationship in the context of heteronormativity and compulsory motherhood. It also offers another chiding of Stoker's appropriative authorship (in *Dracula*, Van Helsing explains placing a wild rose upon a vampire's coffin will bind them there, eventually using this tactic against the count).

Overall, Machado's engagement calls for both a "palimpsestuous" and transmedia approach to *Carmilla's* legacy. In addition to reclaiming a more overtly queer version of the tale, Machado puts the narrative in conversation with feminism by highlighting Veronika's "advocacy for women's agency," suggesting we might think of Marcia as "the victim of a political conspiracy" (iii, vii). Here, the suggestion is the two lovers may have been targeted not only for their micro queer desire, but because of the macro political threat they posed to patriarchal systems. In one sense, her introduction adds more "permanent traces" to the Mystical Writing-Pad of *Carmilla*. In another, it effaces later works to reveal the original parchment, taking apart, as it were, the nesting doll nature of *Carmilla's* legacy to get to the "original doll" housed within. In overturning *Dracula's* status as ur-text, troubling the tenuous split between fact and fiction, and encouraging the reader to take on the role of detective, Machado provides not only a post-structural approach to the novella and its legacy, but also a queer and feminist one. She both erases the plundering of *Carmilla* rendered via Stoker's tale and creates *Carmilla* anew, transforming the phallic bite of patriarchy into a wild rose of queer desire and female agency.

Works Cited

Bacon, Simon. 2014. "The Transmedia Vampire: From Bram Stoker's *Dracula* to HBO's *True Blood*." *Words, Worlds, Narratives: Transmedia and Immersion*, edited by Yawnya Ravy and Eric Forcier, Oxford: IDP, pp. 55–75.
Byrne, Katherine. 2011. *Tuberculosis and the Victorian Literary Imagination*. Cambridge University Press.
De Quincey, Thomas. 1845. "Suspiria De Profundis, Being a Sequel to Confessions of an English Opium Eater: The Palimpsest." *Blackwood's Magazine*, pp. 739–43.
Dillon, Sarah. 2007. *The Palimpsest: Literature, Criticism, Theory*. London: Continuum.
Downing, Spencer. 2007. "So Boring It Must Be True: Faux History and the Generation of Wonder at the Museum of Jurassic Technology." *Specs: Journal of Arts and Culture*, vol. 2, pp. 46–63, https://scholarship.rollins.edu/specs/vol2/iss1/23.
Freeman, Matthew. 2017. *Historicizing Transmedia Storytelling*. New York: Routledge.
Freud, Sigmund. 1976. "A Note Upon the 'Mystic Writing Pad.'" *General Psychological Theory*. New York: Collier Books, pp. 207–212.
Guyant, Valerie. 2014. "What or Who Is 'Matska' in *Carmilla*?" *The Explicator*, vol. 72, no. 3, pp. 185–8.
Jenkins, Henry. 2006. *Convergence Culture: Where Old and New Media Collide*. New York: New York UP.
_____. 2016. "Transmedia What?" *Immerse*, November 15, https://immerse.news/transmedia-what-15edf6b61daa
_____. 2013. "T Is for Transmedia." *Confessions of an Aca-Fan*, March 18, http://henryjenkins.org/blog/2013/03/t-is-for-transmedia.html
Le Fanu, Joseph Sheridan. 2019. *Carmilla* [1872]. Philadelphia: Lanternfish Press.
Machado, Carmen Maria. 2019. "You Are Mine: Obsession, Odylic Influences, and LeFanu's *Carmilla*." Introduction to *Carmilla*. Philadelphia: Lanternfish Press, pp. i–ix.
Radick, Caryn. 2013. "'Complete and in Order': Bram Stoker's *Dracula* and the Archival Profession." *The American Archivist*, vol. 76, no. 2, Fall/Winter, pp. 502–20.
Reese, Shelley. 2015. "It's Alive: Penny Dreadful as Palimpestic Creature" Southwest Popular Culture Conference.
Wilson, Shelby LeAnn. 2015. "The Bitten Word: Feminine Jouissance, Language, and the Female Vampire." Master's Thesis, University of Santa Cruz. https://escholarship.org/content/qt7vgl10pg/qt7vgl10pg.pdf.

The Originals and Family History Two-Fold

Caught Between Two Worlds

Verena Bernardi

Introduction

Transmedia storytelling is not a new concept but has taken on a new level in the twenty-first century. Adapting books to movies and television series has become a common practice for many genres—vampire fiction is no exception (e.g., *Twilight* novels [Meyer 2005–8] and films [2008–12]). However, transmediality has also moved on to character vlogs (e.g., *True Blood* [Ball 2008–14]), comics, computer games (e.g., *Vampire: The Masquerade—Bloodlines* [Roika Games 2004]), and social media. These different media outlets provide viewers and readers with deeper insights into the characters' inner workings. Transmedia narratives enable the audience to have a stronger connection with, and better understanding of, character behavior. To be more precise, fans can more easily justify, or even comprehend, actions committed out of compassion or cruelty. In turn, in-depth character treatment and discussion eventually leads to a more devoted and loyal fan base. It is important to note that this extended engagement particularly benefits the figure of the sympathetic vampire. While acceptance and use of varying media outlets can be read an indicator of how involved fans really are, the interrelation between different storylines, as told through different media platforms, allows for the formation of more complex and likable characters.

In this paper, I will investigate how the television show, *The Originals* (Plec 2013–18), tells the life story of the original vampires through different media formats. I aim to primarily focus on how these differing formats foster a strong bond between the audience and the characters. Ultimately, this bond allows the audience to empathize with the ruthless siblings Klaus (Joseph Morgan), Elijah (Daniel Gillies), and Rebekah Mikaelson (Claire Holt). This intense connection and sympathy between audience and characters paved the way for *The Original's* narrative/world to spill over into additional media outlets. This overflow created a far-reaching transmedial story world contained within three novels, all published just two years after the television series aired in 2013. Focusing on the dynamics between the televised and literary versions of *The Originals*—with brief references to its originating series *The Vampire Diaries* (Plec and Williamson 2009–17)—I seek to shed light on how transmediality influences the audience in its endeavor to discern between the Mikaelson siblings' barbarity/inhumanity and their benignity/humanity.

Transmedia Appearances of *The Originals*

In her work, *The Postmillennial Vampire*, Susan Chaplin argues that "postmillennial vampire films such as *Blade, Underworld, Daybreakers,* and *30 Days of Night* have taken vampire narratives into darker, more apocalyptic territory" (2017, 2). In contrast to vampire films, much of the traditional fabric-like representation[73] in these movies changed, especially concerning the adaptation of vampire stories into television series. Vampires are no longer creatures who roamed dark alleys hunting innocent victims. Instead, the power dynamics between humans and vampires became more attuned to one another by "humanizing" vampires' behavior and desires. While the pre–2000s bore witness to a renewed interest in vampire fiction,[74] their popularity soared in the post–2000s through an explosion of novels, movies, and television series.[75] In these new narratives, vampires became somewhat functioning members of society and mostly kept their vampiric nature a secret from humanity (e.g., *Moonlight* [Koslow 2007–8]; *The Vampire Diaries*; *The Originals*), or openly tried to blend in with society (e.g., *True Blood*[76]).

73. E.g., vampires as evil creatures who roam in the shadows of dark alleys preying upon their unsuspecting victims.
74. E.g., well-known examples of novels: Anne Rice, *Vampire Chronicles* (1976–); Laurell K. Hamilton, *Anita Blake: Vampire Hunter* series (1993–); Tanya Huff, *Blood Books* series (1991–1997); etc. Probably the most popular television series was *Buffy The Vampire Slayer* (1997–2003), which followed Joss Whedon's movie *Buffy: The Vampire Slayer* 1992.
75. Here, Stephanie Meyer's *Twilight* series (2005–8) or Charmaine Harris's novels adapted into *True Blood* mark an infamous starting point of the post–2000 "vampire hysteria."
76. In *True Blood*, vampires formed the so-called "American Vampire League (AVL), which is an organization mainly focused on the public relations of the vampire community in the United States, and the promotion of vampire rights" (*American Vampire League*, original emphasis).

The original family, Klaus, Elijah, and Rebekah were able to live among humans due to their daylight rings.[77] The siblings had their debut appearance in the second season of *The Vampire Diaries (TVD)* and were introduced as the main characters' antagonists. Portrayed as ruthless killers, the siblings caused a lot of upheaval for the town of Mystic Falls due to their infighting, as well as Klaus's desire to break the Doppelganger curse.[78] The siblings are mostly shown to antagonize the "good" vampires and humans in *TVD*, it is only on rare occasions that viewers can catch a glimpse of their emotional and kind sides.

The fact that the characters were well received by fans of *TVD*, resulted in the creation of the spin-off series, *The Originals*. The series traces the Mikaelsons' life in New Orleans, and portrays the more sympathetic sides of Klaus, Elijah, and Rebekah by regularly employing flashbacks, as well as the occasional character crossing between the shows. One prime example can be found in *TVD* ("Moonlight on the Bayou," season 7, episode 14) when Caroline Forbes (Candice King) heads to New Orleans to seek out Klaus's assistance and protection. Although Klaus is reported to have been absent for more than three years, and the two are not reunited, a time jump to an instance a few years ago manages to demonstrate Klaus's soft spot for Caroline. When Stefan (Paul Wesley), Caroline's boyfriend at the time, requested to hide from the vampire huntress Rayna Cruz (Leslie-Anne Panaligan) in New Orleans, Klaus refused his help and forced Stefan to leave the city as his arrival also endangered Klaus's family. It was not until Klaus answers Caroline's call on Stefan's phone, that he succumbed to her charms, and eventually saved Stefan's life. In this episode, the audience discovers that Caroline refers to Klaus as "mommy's friend" when speaking with her children.

Aside from such small exceptions, *The Vampire Diaries* tends to paint an unfavorable picture of the Mikaelsons. However, *The Originals* focuses on their almost pathological desire for a happy family and home, which brings their emotional and passionate side to the forefront of their story. The use of flashbacks, spanning over a thousand years, not only shed light on the origins of the characters' present behavior, they also elicit viewers to

---

77. Daylight rings are rings (or other pieces of jewelry) with a lapis lazuli gemstone. When carried by a vampire, this ring enables them to be out in daylight without suffering burns or bursting into flames.

78. The Hybrid Curse: When Esther Mikaelson (Alice Evans) turned her children, and husband, into vampires, she additionally bound Klaus's werewolf side (suppressing his ability to turn into a werewolf) in an attempt to offset the imbalance her magic had caused. In order for Klaus to break this curse, he needs to perform a ritual channeling the power of the full moon. During the ritual, a vampire and werewolf need to be sacrificed (signifying both sides of the hybrid's nature) before Klaus drinks the blood of a doppelganger (e.g., Elena Gilbert [Nina Dobrev], main character in *TVD*, love interest of the Salvatore brothers and treasured member of the Mystic Falls community).

feel boundless empathy for the family. Following the Mikaelsons' successful reception, Julie Plec, producer of the show, published the three successive novels: *The Originals: The Rise, The Originals: The Loss,* and *The Originals: Resurrection* in 2015. These novels provide readers with an in-depth narrative of the siblings' past from 1713 to 1788.[79] This period significantly impacted the siblings' ability to create, and maintain, emotional, interfamilial, and interpersonal bonds, which will be the focus of the second half of this essay.

In *The Originals*, the Mikaelsons are constantly caught between two worlds: one that is often cruel and dangerous, replete with merciless conflict, and painful memories. The other offers the only reliable constant, their oath "Always and Forever."[80] When the viewers and/or readers immerse themselves into the characters' struggles, they are unsure if they should sympathize with the siblings or recognize them as the egocentric tyrants. Across different media platforms, the story ensures that the audience remains at a crossway to decide what to make of the siblings, as the other characters tend to see the siblings in a negative light. While fans struggle to make up their minds, they might only find a solution by travelling across the two media—television series and novels. In his work *Convergence Culture*, Henry Jenkins explains this phenomenon stating, "Transmedia storytelling is the art of world making" (2006, 21). He continues to say that: "To fully experience any fictional world, consumers must assume the role of hunters and gatherers, chasing down bits of the story across media channels, comparing notes with each other via online discussion groups, and collaborating to ensure that everyone who invests time and effort will come away with a richer entertainment experience" (21). This is very much the case for *The Originals*. Viewers that only know the characters from *TVD*, lack a deeper understanding of, and emotional investment in, the Mikaelsons than those who have followed the story across media platforms.

In similar fashion to Jenkins, Simon Bacon comments on the influence of transmediality in his essay "The Transmedia Vampire: From Bram Stoker's *Dracula* to HBO's *True Blood*," stating:

> it is important to remember the technology and the media platforms brought into play here as well, as they too become carriers of power. Subsequently, it is the technology, … which facilitates the production and delivery of ideological messages that become the true owners of power. The vampire's alignment and

---

79. The events of the first novel, *The Originals: The Rise*, take place in the year 1722, nine years after the sibling's arrival in New Orleans. The second novel, *The Originals: The Loss*, begins in the year 1766, 44 years after the events of the first novel. The events in the last novel, *The Originals: Resurrection*, take place 22 years after *The Loss*, in the year 1788.

80. E.g., season 1, episode 1, "Always and Forever," Elijah: "This is us. The original family. Now we remain together always and forever."

symbiotic development alongside it then becomes one of inevitability rather than coincidence [2014, 65].

Bacon's statement essentially articulates the effects of the two media platforms on the audience, which makes the Mikaelsons powerful outside of their fictive story world. Suddenly, they are no longer the most powerful creatures in the universe of *The Originals*. Yet, the Mikaelsons do exert power over their fans by simultaneously exuding confidence and vulnerability. In turn, this fascinates and enthralls the audience into watching their televised story on a weekly basis, or letting the vampires enter their home by reading the novels.

The Rise of *The Originals*

Bacon also identifies the transmedia vampire, that "*Dracula* ... was the first 'talking' horror film" where "for the first time on screen, the vampire was allowed to speak for itself" (64). Since Anne Rice's novel *Interview with a Vampire* (1976) and its screen adaption in 1994, vampires were also given the opportunity to voice their emotions directly and explain their state of mind.[81]

In the late-twentieth and early twenty-first century, depicting vampires' agency through romance and vulnerability became common practice. Vampires are no longer portrayed as antagonists to humanity or through a divide of monstrous evil versus human good. Vampires are characterized through their ability to experience human emotions and interpersonal challenges. These qualities are often emotionally charged or dimmed in comparison to human existence. The series *The Originals* follows this trend by depicting its main characters' relentless search for love and acceptance, belonging and loyalty.

In *The Vampire Diaries*, viewers catch rare glimpses of the Originals' emotions and their capability for kindness towards their own kind and occasionally a few others (e.g., humans, witches, werewolves). In the series, viewers are presented with the odd flashback and rare occasions when one of the siblings utters a few words of emotional wisdom or displays mercy towards the other fellow beings (e.g., Bonnie, the witch, or Hayley, the werewolf). Each episode of *The Originals* opens with a voiceover monologue by one of the main characters and is somewhat reminiscent of the recordings of Louis's interviews in *Interview with the Vampire*.[82] In "All Dark Inside: Dehumanization and Zombification in Postmodern Cinema,"

---

81. Louis de Pointe du Lac tells his life story and expresses his dislike for his vampiric existence to a reporter who records their interview sessions.
82. It is mainly the members of the original family whose voiceovers open the episodes, but sometimes also their extended family members, such as Hayley Marshall or Marcel Gerard, can be heard.

Sorcha Ní Fhlainn explains that "Vampire subjectivity is the ultimate postmodern achievement ... [where] the vampire in using the term 'I' is immediately empowered and provides a distinct point of view" (2011, 260*n*29). The pilot episode, "Always and Forever," also made use of this strategy, which sets the tone for the series. Opening with a voiceover by Elijah, viewers become immediately aware of the more personal and emotional mood that the series assumes for the Mikaelsons, when Elijah states: "Over the course of my long life, I have come to believe that we are bound forever to those with whom we share blood. And, while we may not choose our family, that bond can be our greatest strength or our deepest regret. This unfortunate truth has haunted me for as long as I can recall" ("Always and Forever" season 1, episode 1). Elijah's introduction points out some of the major themes of the series. Viewers will find out about the strengths and weaknesses of each of the Mikaelson siblings and will be privy to their personal stories through flashbacks to and memories of bygone times.

While season 1 begins with Klaus's return to New Orleans, and the ensuing problems his and his siblings' arrival cause in the supernatural community, the siblings are shown to work together in their attempt to protect Klaus's child. Being one of a kind, the only offspring to ever exist, hybrid between an original vampire (the creation of a powerful witch) and a werewolf, and hence possibly capable of ruling and/or destined to rule all races (vampires, witches, werewolves), the siblings work out their initial differences upon their return to the Big Easy. In their pursuit of this common goal, viewers will, slowly but surely, become aware of Klaus's, Rebekah's and Elijah's quests for personal fulfillment. As is visible throughout the telling of current events, as well as said flashbacks and memories, each one of the siblings has experienced an unerring longing for a certain ambition or purpose in their lives. Bacon explains that the use of transmedial storytelling results in "the audience becom[ing] hyper-attentive, no longer passive but fully engaged with the narrative and the environment within which it takes place" (2014, 63). Following Bacon's assertion, I will explain how the television series, *The Originals,* addresses Klaus's and Rebekah's search for self-realization (as ruler of all races and the ability to have a family of her own), how the ensuing novels reveal their origins and how the employment of different points of view provided for the viewers/readers helps to achieve their continuous engagement with the characters and their experiences.

Rebekah's Search for Love

Upon the originals' introduction in *The Vampire Diaries*, Rebekah, the youngest of the siblings, is depicted as an impulsive young woman with a conniving streak. Although she is already more than a thousand years old, she still longs for human (teenage) experiences, such as going to prom (e.g., "A View to a Kill" season 4, episode 12). Rebekah is portrayed as the everlasting teenager. She tends to be ruled by her temper and emotions, instead of the maturity one would expect of someone with her considerable age and life experience. Throughout her appearances on *TVD*, viewers cannot escape Rebekah's romantic escapades and constant flirting when she engages with reoccurring characters: Damon Salvatore (Ian Somerhalder) (season 3), his brother Stefan, as well as Matt Donovan (Zach Roerig) (Season 4). Unlike in *TVD*, Rebekah's love life in *The Originals* takes a more mellow turn when she unexpectedly faces her former lover, Marcel Gerard (Charles Michael Davis) who was believed to be dead. Although viewers only see her engage in futile romantic relationships with a few men throughout the series and its flashbacks,[83] Klaus regularly hints at her promiscuity and poor choice in men. Justifying, for example, his murdering of most of her suitors, he states, "I was trying to protect you from imbeciles and leeches, not to mention your own poor judgment" ("Le Grand Guignol" season 1, episode 15). As the series will show, Rebekah and Marcel have a somewhat complicated on-and-off relationship, which uncovers Rebekah's relentless search for true love and romance. She is the only sibling to express her explicit desire to live a human life, which as she is aware, would only last one lifetime. Nonetheless, she believes human life would provide her with a chance at having a family of her own and allow her to experience true love.

In her reference to *Dracula* as the prototype of vampires, Judith Halberstam states, "He is the deviant or the criminal, the other against whom the normal and the lawful, the marriageable and the heterosexual can be known and quantified" (1993, 334–5). Unlike *Dracula* and a long tradition of ensuing depictions of vampires,[84] Rebekah is the ultimate romantic, the antithesis to traditional vampires. As stated earlier, *TVD* and *TO* play at Rebekah's experiences with heartbreak and disappointment, showing that Klaus is often responsible for her suffering. However, it has always been ultimately her vampirism that caused her pain. When Rebekah has not had to hide her true nature or lineage from her suitors (e.g., Emil Gerard [John Redlinger]), she has had to worry about their possible motivations instead of their interest in her personality. While *The Originals* provides its viewers with several examples of Rebekah's longing for true love, the novels explore the reasons for her relentless search for happiness.

83. E.g., Alexander, a vampire hunter, in the 1100s; Emil Gerard, during the early 1800s; Stefan Salvatore in the 1920s; Marcel Gerard, in the late 19th/early 20th century.

84. E.g., Joseph Sheridan Le Fanu's Gothic novella *Carmilla* (1872), Richard Matheson's novel *I Am Legend* (1954), Stephen King's horror novel *'Salem's Lot* (1975).

The first book, *The Originals: The Rise* (Plec 2015a) from the trilogy takes readers back to the year 1722, nine years after Klaus, Elijah, and Rebekah had arrived on the shores of the Mississippi River. During this time period, the siblings were well-established in New Orleans as powerful antagonists, even enemies, to the city's witch and werewolf communities.[85] However, the witch and werewolf communities announced their intention to unify their fractions through marrying a female witch and a werewolf. The Mikaelsons realized their combined power would soon pale in comparison to this potential union and would force a dangerous and challenging future on the family in New Orleans.

Rebekah plotted to turn humans against the werewolves, to weaken their ranks, in an attempt to protect her family. While executing her plan, Rebekah falls in love with the human Captain Eric Moquet. During their courtship, Rebekah attempts to objectively assesses her feelings for the Captain, thinking to herself, "She really *did* love her dashing soldier-boy, at least as much as she could call any of those doomed infatuations of hers 'love'" (128, stress in original). Later, Rebekah exposes Eric to be one of her father's spies and executioners. When Rebekah reveals her true nature to Eric, he unexpectedly proclaims his love for her. The two of them face her brothers to inform them of their intention to leave New Orleans in the midst of the war between werewolves and witches. Through conversations between Rebekah and her brothers, as well as Rebekah and Eric, her longing for love becomes apparent to the readers. Explaining that she found "something more. Something *real*" (247, stress in original) and that she feels free (270) when she is in Eric's company. Rebekah even goes so far as to say that she does not see her immortality as a curse now that they have found each other (271). However, when the war between the factions was in full motion, the witches called forth a hurricane that destroyed much of New Orleans. As the storm hit, Rebekah and Eric attempted to sail out of Louisiana waters. In a twist of fate, they shipwrecked and only Rebekah survived. As the harsh reality set in, Rebekah stated, "For a few short days, she had believed that an Original vampire could be entitled to a life of her own choosing, but [that] it all had been a girlish fantasy" (Plec 2015a, 295). Rebekah not only suffered the loss of a lover, but was forced to cope with bitter disillusionment, which would be a more difficult experience to bear.

The readers of the second novel, *The Originals: The Loss* (Plec 2015b) discover that after forty-four years after the shipwreck, Rebekah holds on to the memory of her lost lover in the form of a necklace Eric had given to her. Although she continues to keep this physical reminder of their love,

---

85. "They had built their legend through a surplus of brutality and made sure they were always prepared to reinforce the lesson" (*The Rise*, 2015, 169).

Rebekah appears to have recovered from the loss rather quickly. Commenting on Klaus's strong, borderline insane infatuation with the young witch Vivianne Lescheres, Rebekah states that she "had followed her own heart to disaster a time or fifty" (76), recognizing her "tiresome obsession with love" (Plec 2015c, 242), as Klaus calls it.

All three novels continuously remind their readers of Rebekah's inability to find love and happiness. As the novels take place before the Originals' appearances on *TVD,* and the events covered in *The Originals,* loyal fans of the series gain a deeper understanding of Rebekah's wish to be human. Ultimately, the combination of facts presented across the three different media paints a fuller picture of Rebekah's character, as well as her desire to be human. In *Fantastic Transmedia* Collin Harvey claims, "We ordinarily think of adaptation as retelling *existing* stories, whereas transmedia storytelling tends to be characterized as telling new stories in different media but set within a consistent diegetic world" (2015, 3). While viewers of *TVD, TO,* and readers of the ensuing trilogy all follow the story of the Mikaelsons, they find themselves to be observers of different periods of their lives. Similar to the characters' different life stages, the different media also provide fans with different modes of information. While viewers of the series take most of their information from conversations between Rebekah and other characters, the novels provide additional insights into their inner thoughts, and assessments of actions and situations. In turn, viewers either find themselves to be observers, maintaining a certain distance to the story, or are plunged into the characters' inner musings and emotions, making it harder to remain an objective observer.

Klaus's Hunger for Power

Klaus does not appear to pursue the goal of finding ever-lasting love like his sister. Although Klaus experiences a few romantic encounters,[86] he appears to only feel true love for his daughter, Hope, and his family. As viewers become aware in *The Originals,* Klaus's focus lies on the acquisition of power and voices his pathological need to make New Orleans his home again in the first episode of series one, explaining to Elijah: "This town was my home once and in my absence Marcel has got everything I ever wanted. Power. Loyalty. Family. I made him in my image and he has bettered me. I want what he has. I want it back. I want to be king ("Always and Forever" season 1, episode 1). As viewers of *The Vampire Diaries* know,

---

86. Namely his on-again-off-again relationship with Caroline Forbes, a fateful one-night-stand with Hayley Marshall (Phoebe Tonkin) in *The Vampire Diaries,* as well as his infatuation with Camille O'Connell (Leah Pipes) in *The Originals.*

and followers of *The Originals* find out through flashbacks that Klaus is a hybrid. He is half vampire and half werewolf. Due to this hybridity, and his inability to turn into a werewolf, (caused by his mother Esther's binding spell), Klaus feels disconnected from both groups, vampires and werewolves, and does not consider himself to be an equal member of his family as he is only a half-brother to his siblings. Moreover, Klaus's tries to subject everyone in his environment to his rule, including his siblings to compensate for his feelings of not belonging. Viewers of *TO* see Klaus's obsession with power when he attempts to wrestle his former protégé, Marcel Gerard, and his army for the rule over New Orleans in an attempt to create a kingdom of his own choosing ("The River in Reverse," S01/08). Previously, the Mikaelson siblings migrated from Viking era in Norway to the New World. They only became "real" members of the nation of the New World when they are reborn as vampires, or Klaus as a hybrid. When the Mikaelson's first arrived in New Orleans in the early 1700s, Klaus built a reputation of wielding "overwhelming force" (Plec 2015a, 169), which is why neither one of his siblings "had tried too hard to slow Klaus's killing spree when they had first landed [t]here" (169), as Rebekah muses in the first novel.

Through flashbacks of Klaus's past in *TVD* and *TO*, viewers learn to understand the origins of Klaus's trust issues.[87] However, until the end of the series it remains unclear why the hybrid longs for loyalty and solidarity in his life, but does not actively pursue a meaningful relationship. Instead of trying to find happiness, or openly proclaiming his feelings for Caroline or Camille, Klaus always puts his desire for power and authority first. It is only readers of the three novels eventually become privy as to why Klaus's pathological hunger for power and control dominate his life. Surprisingly, this hunger is linked to love.

The television series rarely openly displays or states Klaus's emotions or feelings for a romantic partner, whereas the first novel, *The Rise*, quickly immerses readers into Klaus's psychological inner workings. In 1722, while attending a ball (12), in honor of the betrothed coupling between the young witch Vivianne Lescheres and the werewolf Armand Navarro (son of the werewolf chief), Klaus feels drawn to the bride-to-be. He engages in conversation, dances with her and realizes that Vivianne herself is also a hybrid. The daughter of a witch and a werewolf, Klaus finds Vivianne "extraordinary, indeed" and thinks her "far too good to waste on a werewolf" (13). Over the course of first few chapters of the novel, Klaus's interest

---

87. Klaus's complicated relationship with his "father," Michael, and the discovery of his mother's betrayal by magically preventing him from being able to turn into a werewolf are just some of the reasons why it is hard for Klaus to trust anyone and to form deeper relationships.

in the witch-hybrid grows. He begins to feel a strong bond between the two of them through their mutual hybridity. It is a kindredness/kinship that he had not known with another being before explaining to Vivianne, "you make me want to be different" (68). His infatuation even comes between him and his siblings as they do not understand or support his feelings for Vivianne. In an argument with Rebekah over both of their love interests, and the danger they both pose to the Mikaelson family, Klaus states matter-of-factly, "I will not hesitate to put her [Vivianne's] well-being above yours, and you already know I will do the same when it comes to my own" (Plec 2015a, 130).

Although both, Klaus and Vivianne, declare their love for one another, Vivianne clandestinely decides to marry Armand in the name of peace between the werewolf and witch communities. However, shortly after having been turned into a werewolf, Vivianne regrets her decision and finds her way back to Klaus. Klaus was devastated by Vivianne's abandonment, yet, his love for her quickly help him to overcome his feelings of betrayal. Recognizing the torment they both suffer through their hybridity, he explains to her, "Being half one thing and half another makes you neither, not both" (280) and declares, "this unending life of mine is meaningless without you" (281).

As a consequence of Vivianne leaving Armand for Klaus, she, Klaus, and his siblings then face the wrath of the werewolves. Vivianne attempts to stop the fighting alone and dies. Just as Rebekah had lost her lover, Eric, the previous night, also Klaus faces a loss that lets him feel like "he had nothing left to protect" (Plec 2015a, 306). Readers are plunged into Klaus's emotions when they read his thoughts and inner declarations of despair. Thinking he "found himself alone, the world around him as barren as his own heart" (306) and pondering that "With her gone, I do not think my happiness will ever depend so entirely on one woman again" (308), readers are once more reminded of the intensity of Klaus's love for Vivianne, a depth of emotions, to which viewers of *TO* are not privy.

Ultimately, as book two will reveal, Klaus feels incapable of living without Vivianne. He even goes so far as to bring her back from the dead with the help of the witches. Unfortunately for him, this results in disastrous consequences for his family and all of New Orleans. He is quickly forced to end her life, suffering her death for a second time. In the face of her second demise, Klaus and Vivianne proclaim their ever-lasting love for one another, and Vivianne explains that she wants to die at Klaus's hands and no one else's. Shortly before ripping out her heart, Klaus professes "Goodbye, Vivianne, […] I'll never love another the way I love you" (Plec 2015c, 273). Again, readers gain further insight into his deepest thoughts when they read:

He had told her the absolute truth at the end. It would never be possible for Klaus to love this way again. The suffering he felt now left no room for it, and that was a lesson Klaus would never forget. Losing Vivianne forced him to face eternity alone, because an eternity full of this kind of loss would be unbearable. The love of Klaus Mikaelson's life was gone, and there was nothing ahead of him now except for more life [273].

Judging from the Mikaelsons' representation in *TVD* and *TO*, one would have expected this kind of blind devotion and all-consuming love from Rebekah, not from Klaus. However, as the first two books of the trilogy have shown, Klaus was once capable of experiencing, and even openly declaring, his love. Book three, *The Originals: The Resurrection*, does not focus as much on Klaus's love and mourning as the two previous novels. Instead, the third novel deals with the importance of *family* for the siblings, and how their solidarity is what ultimately keeps them alive. Yet, towards the end of the novel readers peek into Klaus's mind as he comments on the difference between his sister and himself: "That was the difference between her and Klaus: Rebekah always had hope for the next great love she believed was waiting around the corner for her. Klaus had lost that hope decades ago. There was no more life-changing, earth-moving love out there for him, and that left only power" (242). Nina Auerbach once stated that "Vampires go where power is" (1995, 6). In her assessment, Auerbach connects power to locations, i.e., nineteenth century England. In this observation, she creates a connection between power and nationhood. This connection is also visible in Klaus's strive for power in *The Originals*. Klaus feels disconnected from all supernatural groups, as well as his own family. Yet, the moment he found love and kinship in Vivianne Lescheres, his short reprieve is quickly ripped from his hands. Readers of *The Loss* and *The Resurrection* know that the loss of his love was something Klaus would never fully recover from, which is why he directed his attention to something he felt he could achieve: power.

Conclusion

At the beginning of this essay, I set out to focus on the dynamics between the televised and literary versions of *The Originals*. In this endeavor, I sought to shed light on how transmediality influences the audience in its attempt to discern between the Mikaelson siblings' barbarity/ inhumanity and their benignity/humanity. Through an in-depth analysis of the reasons and origins of Klaus's and Rebekah's search for self-fulfillment, it is clear that only fans who engage in the transmediality of Mikaelsons' story are able to gain a full understanding of the characters. Viewers and readers are enabled to see different sides of the characters as well as situations when they are supplied with differing viewpoints. True to Ní Fhlainn's claim that "Vampire subjectivity is the ultimate postmodern achievement" (2011, 260, note 29), the transmedial story world of *The Originals*, does not only employ direct speech in terms of conversations and interactions viewers and readers are privy to. Instead, through the use of opening monologues (TV series), and the plunging of readers into the characters' private thoughts, fans gain "a tantali[z]ing insight by the very creature that was previously marginalized" (Ní Fhlainn, 2019, 4). As Sorcha Ní Fhlainn aptly puts it, the strategy of the vampire's "subjective insight essentially destroys the boundaries between us and the monsters we encounter" (2019, 3). Ultimately, Julie Plec has told the Mikaelsons' story in reverse. From their emergence in *The Vampire Diaries*, fans were given a glimpse at a plethora of stories these thousand-year-old vampires would be able to tell. With the creation of the spin-off series, *The Originals*, viewers of *TVD* were given the opportunity to become fans of the Mikaelsons. Most likely this interest, or even fascination with the siblings, was due to their continuous humanization. In a world full of terrorism and hate, viewers can be captured by the opportunity to find the good in the evil.

Works Cited

"American Vampire League." 2019. *True Blood Wiki*, https://trueblood.fandom.com/wiki/American_Vampire_League.
Bacon, Simon. 2014. "The Transmedia Vampire: From Bram Stoker's *Dracula* to HBO's *True Blood*." In *Words, Worlds and Narratives: Transmedia and Immersion*, edited by Tawnya Ravy and Eric Forcier, Oxford: IDP, pp. 55–75.
Chaplin Susan. 2017. *The Postmillenial Vampire: Power, Sacrifice and Simulation in* True Blood *and Other Contemporary Narratives*. London: Palgrave Macmillan.
Halberstam, Judith. 1993. "Technologies of Monstrosity: Bram Stoker's 'Dracula.'" *Victorian Studies*, vol. 36, no. 3, pp. 333–52.
Harvey, Collin. 2015. *Fantastic Transmedia: Narrative, Play and Memory Across Science Fiction and Fantasy Storyworlds*. London: Palgrave Macmillan Limited.
Jenkins, Henry. 2006. *Convergence Culture*. New York: New York University Press.
Ní Fhlainn, Sorcha. 2011. "All Dark Inside: Dehumanization and Zombification in Postmodern Cinema." *Better Off Dead: The Evolution of the Zombie as Posthuman*, edited by Deboarh Christie and Sarah Juliet Lauro, New York: Fordham University Press, pp. 139–58.
_____. 2019. *Postmodern Vampires: Film, Fiction and Popular Culture*. London: Palgrave Macmillan.
The Originals. 2013–18. Television. Created by Julie Plec. Burbank: Warner Brothers Television.
Plec, Julie. 2015a. *The Rise*. Buffalo: Harlequin Sales Corp.
_____. 2015b. *The Loss*. Buffalo: Harlequin Sales Corp.
_____. 2015c. *The Resurrection*. Buffalo: Harlequin Sales Corp.
The Vampire Diaries. 2009–17. Television. Created by Kevin Williamson and Julie Plec. Burbank: Warner Brothers Television.

Transmedia Vampire Stories and Their Consumers in Anne Rice's *The Vampire Chronicles*

Laura Davidel

> No vampire must ever reveal the history of the vampires to a mortal and let the mortal live. No vampire must commit to writing the history of the vampires or any true knowledge of vampires lest such a history be found by mortals and believed. And a vampire's name must never be known to mortals, save from his tombstone, and never must any vampire reveal to mortals the location of his or any other vampire's lair.
>
> —Rice 2008, 302

Maintaining secrecy is one of the vampiric commandments that Armand mentions when telling his story to Lestat and Gabrielle in the last decades of the eighteenth century. According to the "old ways" of the satanic covens, the undead are required to cultivate invisibility and detachment from what they call the mortal world. However, it is precisely solitude and the burden of invisibility that prompt Louis and Lestat to come forth and share their stories with humans. These vampire narrators turn to humans in hope for understanding, acknowledgment, and, especially in Lestat's case, for adoration. Since media is inherently a tool for communication through which vampires assert the reality of their existence, it is important to look at the ways in which the undead disseminate their stories in order to step away from the shadows and reach the center of the human world. A focus on the transmedia circulation of vampires' stories within the narrative may seem contradictory especially considering that Rice has been remarkably protective of her undead characters and has manifested strong reactions to their transmedia proliferation in both cinema and fan fiction.

Nevertheless, Rice's vampires share an intrinsic connection to the cinematic medium as the author borrowed "the concept of vampires as tragic creatures with great sensitivity" (Rice 2012, interview) from the 1936 film *Dracula's Daughter*, in which a beautiful countess struggles with the curse of being a vampire. Rice explores this concept of the sympathetic monster throughout the thirteen volumes of the *Vampire Chronicles*—from *Interview with the Vampire*, published in 1976, to *Blood Communion*, released in 2018. The author was, arguably, defending this heightened sensitivity in her vampires when she initially expressed her disapproval of Neil Jordan's choice of Tom Cruise as Lestat in the film *Interview with the Vampire* (1994): "I was particularly stunned by the casting of Cruise, who is no more my Vampire Lestat than Edward G. Robinson is Rhett Butler" (Dutka 1993, n.p.). However, Rice changed her mind after having seen the film and stated that "[f]rom the moment he appeared Tom was Lestat for me" (Rice 1994, n.p.). As for the film *Queen of the Damned* (2002), Rice stated that she could not control or prevent it because Warner Bros. owned the film rights at the time (Rice 2009, interview). Another aspect that demonstrates Rice's control over the dissemination of material on her vampires from the *Vampire Chronicles* through other media is her war on fan fiction and the legal means she took to prevent such creations. In 2000, Rice's website published the following message: "I do not allow fan fiction. The characters are copyrighted. It upsets me terribly to even think about fan fiction with my characters. I advise my readers to write your own original stories with your own characters" (Anne Rice's website, n.p.). Rice's strong objections against the cinematic re-creation of Lestat and fan fiction iterations suggest that the author tries to prevent her vampiric universe from becoming diluted under the effect of someone else's vision.

This essay argues that, despite Rice's disapproval of the uncontrolled transmedia proliferation of her undead in the real world, the author uses the transmedia dissemination of the vampires' stories as a literary device that underpins the plot of *Interview with the Vampire* (1976), *The Vampire Lestat* (1985), and *Queen of the Damned* (1988). The medium through which the undead choose to present themselves and their monstrous nature to humans is indicative of the entertainment media at different points in time. If Armand and the Theater of the Vampires rely on the theatrical performances of the nineteenth century, Louis chooses the intimacy of the interview in the second half of the twentieth century, while Lestat "comes out" as a vampire in the guise of an eccentric Rockstar in the 1980s. The use of these different media within the narrative illustrates the "[t]ransmedia storytelling," which, according to Henry Jenkins, "represents a process where integral elements of a fiction get dispersed systematically across multiple delivery channels for the purpose of creating a unified and coordinated entertainment experience. Ideally, each medium makes its own unique contribution to the unfolding of the story" (Jenkins 2011, n.p.).

Through an examination of Louis's interview and Lestat's autobiography, music, and videos, I will demonstrate that Ricean vampires choose specific media for sharing their stories. Within the narrative, forms of media, such as the recorded interview, fiction, music, and videoclips, are particularly significant in underlining that fictive humans are oblivious consumers and discard vampires' stories as mere entertainment. I argue that the immortals' transmedia proliferation sustains a metafictional consumption of the text by its own characters, which in turn conveys the idea that the vampire storytellers become real to the extent that their material is consumed. What is interesting about the deployment of transmedia in Rice's narrative is the focus on fictive consumers, both human and undead. Therefore, this essay will also consider how other vampires respond to the stories circulated by Louis and Lestat, and most importantly, how the Talamasca, a secret order investigating the paranormal, collects the "transmedia remains" of the vampires in order to study and document their existence in the human fictive world.

Louis and Lestat have been interpreted as sympathetic monsters (Gordon and Hollinger 1997, 2; Botting 2007, 18) not only due to the fact that they are given a voice and command of the story they tell, but also on account of their subjective perspective on coping with self-loathing for their compulsive feeding. As Nina Auerbach argues, Rice's vampires are "compulsive storytellers" (1997, 154–5) whose existence is made sense of only to the extent of being recounted to another. As a result, each volume of the series depends on reworking the frame of a vampire storyteller and another human or a vampire listening and recording—either to memory, paper, or tape—the storytellers' experience of immortality. This framework is most evident when Louis tells his story to the interviewer, when Armand shares the history of his coven with Lestat and Gabrielle, and when Maharet recounts the unfortunate events that befell her and her sister. In addition to this "[v]ampiric community," based on "oral productions" and "oral consumption" (Wasson 2012, 208), the stories which permeate the fictive world of the living become eternal, although their storytellers are mockingly referred to as "the Coven of the Articulate" (Rice 1998, 280).

Since Rice's immortals are among the first vampires to be given a voice in order to narrate their stories, it is important to look at the medium and the technology employed to disseminate these accounts. The transmedia links within the first three novels of the series uncover metafictional elements that are essential to the development of the plot. Transmedia re-productions of the undead further emphasize the self-referential character of the narrative because Rice's vampire characters consume and react to the stories released into the human world by other vampires. For example,

Lestat reads Louis's account of *Interview with the Vampire*, and expresses his disapproval of how he is portrayed in Louis's story. This prompts him to release his own account in his autobiography, which is in fact the second volume of the *Vampire Chronicles*. In turn, Lestat's music and videoclips are consumed world-wide, including by the dormant Akasha, who awakens and aims to start a reign of terror through mass murder, as depicted in the third volume of the series. In this sense, the transmedia dissemination of vampire stories and their consumption by the narrative's own characters contributes to the heightened self-reflexivity characteristic to metafiction.

Metafictional Consumption

Rice's vampire novels are representative of the contemporary Gothic not only through the rewriting of the vampire as a sympathetic monster, the horrific attacks on humans or through the existential angst of the undead who are aware of their compulsive thirst; but also, through the self-consumption and the self-referentiality of the text. This constant return of the narrative to its own contents, either as artifacts or as references to previously presented events, illustrates Catherine Spooner's assertion that "Contemporary Gothic possesses a new self-consciousness about its own nature; it has reached new levels of mass production, distribution and audience awareness, enabled by global consumer culture; and it has crossed disciplinary boundaries to be absorbed into all forms of media" (2006, 10). Rice achieves the metafictional self-consciousness of the text that Spooner refers to through the use of transmedia circulation of the vampires' stories, which are distributed and consumed by mortals and immortals alike.

Metafiction, according to Patricia Waugh, represents "fictional writing which self-consciously and systematically draws attention to its status as an artefact in order to pose questions about the relationship between fiction and reality" (2001, 2). Rice utilizes metafiction to convey the idea that vampires populate the fictive world of humans, and that their stories, which humans believe to be mere art and fiction, are in fact strikingly real. This merging of the real and the fictional world is highlighted in *The Vampire Lestat* as the protagonist "wondered how many of our kind had 'noticed' the book [*Interview*]. Never mind for the moment the mortals who thought it was fiction. What about other vampires? Because if there is one law that all vampires hold sacred it is that you do not tell mortals about us" (Rice 2008, 16). Here, Lestat refers to Louis's book as an artifact, but also to the reality of vampiric rules, which he later details in his own autobiography. This mirroring effect and the focus on the (immortal) readers demonstrate what Linda Hutcheon calls "the text's own paradox [...] that it is both narcissistically self-reflexive and yet focused outward, oriented toward the reader" (2010, 7). Lestat's interest in how Louis's story was received by the vampire world reinforces the focus on a select group of *connoisseur* consumers and how these may contribute to the unfolding events. On the other hand, Lestat's disinterest in human readers portrays them as naïve consumers who do not follow the train of vampire stories in order to grasp the reality of their existence.

Since Rice's vampires are characterized by invisibility, if not a level of spectrality, they gain reality by producing material which can be distributed and consumed. Their existence is amplified through tape recordings, fiction, and especially through the repeated videos and music that give off the impression of omnipresence. As Justin Edwards argues, "technology alters the possibility of action, changing its range and timing and enlarging its consequences; technology can usurp the power often associated with human will" (2015, 3). What this means for Rice's vampires is that their immortal voices and stories are carried through electromagnetic waves, given substance and reality through their availability to being consumed by oblivious humans and shocked vampires. Conversely, for the humans of the Talamasca, the transmedia material represents not only the trace of the "passing of the vampire[s]" (Bacon 2014, 55), but evidence of their actual existence, provided that readers and consumers succeed in reading beyond the technological image of the vampire.

Louis's Interview

The medium through which the vampire's story is transmitted is at the heart of the novel as part of the title: *Interview with the Vampire*. The tape recordings of Louis's confessions to the then-unnamed reporter create an alluring sense of proximity to the supernatural as the vampire sits down and reveals his secrets. Louis's choice of a recorded interview to be later broadcast on the radio is intriguing and somewhat outdated considering that "the heyday of American radio (popularly called the 'Golden Age')" lasted between the 1920s and the 1950s (Hand, 2014, 464). Richard J. Hand stresses upon liveness and intimacy as two distinctive characteristics of the radio, but also on the imagination of the listener to immerse oneself in the invisible realm of sounds (2014, 464). While there is a certain ephemeral, if not ghostly, quality to the idea of capturing the vampire's voice on tape, Louis's recorded interview provides a sense of intimacy with the reporter and with the implied listener. Despite the delay between the time of the vampire's confession and the potential airing of the story, the tape has a double function: it enhances the spectrality of the vampire as his voice would resonate through the airwaves, and also provides proof of his existence. In other words, the recorded material, the technology behind it, and the radio allow the vampire to preserve a certain degree of invisibility and yet an auditive reality.

Unlike Bram Stoker's Dracula, whose story is documented and controlled by Mina and the "Crew of Light" (Craft 1984, 109), Louis is a highly sentimental blood drinker who willingly provides an extended account of his life both as a human and as an angst-ridden vampire. The interview, or rather the confession, is punctuated by the young reporter's questions and reactions, which invite the reader to identify with his curiosity and anxiety at questioning an immortal. However, it is not the interviewer who draws the elements of the story from the vampire, but rather it is the vampire who controls the sequence of the events he recounts. In other words, the interview is actually lead by Louis: "'No,' said the vampire abruptly. 'We can't begin that way. Is your equipment ready?'" (Rice 2008, 7). Interestingly, Louis's confession is interrupted by endings of tape, changing the tape, and the reporter's cigarette turning to ash. The ending of the tape occurs in symmetry with crucial ending points in Louis's story, such as the end of his mortal life, his giving up on Babette when she perceives his supernatural otherness as demonic, or when Claudia is transformed into a vampire. These elements convey the sense of ending, of human life fading away, and tapes reaching their end, which starkly contrasts the vampire's eternal existence and his ever-continuing story, marked by his question: "We are ready to go on?" (Rice 2008, 88).

The role of the human reporter is twofold: he provides a first audience to the vampire's story, but he is also in charge of the technological aspects of the interview by handling the tapes and the recording machine. The interviewer, referred to as "the boy," represents anonymity and youthful inexperience in comparison with the vampire's sensuous existence. Since the interviewer was collecting lifetime stories, which suggests his search for the extraordinary, it is not surprising that he refuses Louis's ending that emphasizes meaninglessness. The young reporter echoes the participatory culture's desire to consume the story just as much it wishes to contribute to it: "It didn't have to end, not in this, not in despair! [...] I beg you … give it all one more chance. One more chance in me!" (Rice 2008, 306). What this means is that the human reporter is fascinated by the highlights of the vampire's life and is so immersed in the story that he craves the vampiric "power to see and feel and live forever" (2008, 305), that is, be part of the extraordinary.

Rice's undead are not the first to give a first-person perspective of immortality. Fred Saberhagen's *Dracula Tapes* (1975) depicts the count as leaving a recording of his own story to Harker's descendants. However, it is important to note the role of the human in handling the technology meant to disseminate the vampire's story. The interviewer repeatedly manipulates technological devices for vampires: the tape recorder for Louis and, in *The Queen of the Damned*, the phone for Armand. As I have argued elsewhere, the boy reporter functions as "an intermediary body that operates a reality-testing for the vampire" (2018, 63). Just as Jonathan Harker manages the legal matters of Dracula's entrance to the British society, so does the interviewer ensure the vampire's technological incursion into the human world by publishing Louis's interview as a novel and by giving Armand an entrance point to the twentieth century.

Louis's story is both consumed and has the power to consume. There is a vicious circle in which the vampire's story is consumed by the interviewer, and by extension the reader, but also by the tape recorder, which captures the voice of the vampire on tape. Furthermore, the story itself has the power of consuming the tape and mesmerizing the reporter, who by the end of the interview wishes to become immortal. Louis, on the other hand, is acutely aware of the implied consumer when he asks the boy interviewer "I am not giving you what you want, am I? You wanted an interview. Something to broadcast on the radio" (Rice 2008, 63). This suggests that, in order to be considered authentic, Louis must end his story by performing as a vampire. Although he objects to the boy's desire to be immortal, Louis feeds on the interviewer in a move that provides the dramatic horror closure to the interview and confirms the vampire's compulsive thirst. In doing so, Louis repeats his question "Do you see?" (2008, 306) with its double meaning of seeing and understanding the pitfalls of living forever.

Lestat's Autobiography, Music and Videoclips

Even from the first pages of *The Vampire Lestat*, the immortal protagonist addresses the reader directly by describing himself and his vampiric nature. Lestat also stresses on the popularity he has as "a Rock Superstar" (Rice 2008, 3) and boasts about his accomplishments across media: his "first album has sold 4 million copies," his San Francisco concert has already been scheduled and "MTV, the rock music cable channel, has been playing [his] video clips night and day for two weeks. […] Video cassettes of the whole series of clips are selling worldwide"; also, his autobiography has recently been published (2008, 3–4). Lestat seems to have acquired a place in the fictive human world as a popular culture icon, as his face materializes through the multiple media platforms available. His voice is technologically amplified and his videoclips give him a spectral effect in that they are repeatedly broadcast even before he actually performs his "live" concert.

Lestat reads Louis's account, which triggers his desire to disseminate his own story and be known by the mortal world. The choice of fiction and music to make his story known is not arbitrary. Lestat is literally awakened by technology from his slumber: he listens to human voices over the radio or TV, but what prompts him to come back to life is the sound of the rock music played by a nearby band called Satan's Night Out. Furthermore, Lestat declares himself "enchanted by the world of rock music—the way the singers could scream of good and evil, proclaim themselves angels or devils, and mortals would stand up and cheer. [...] And yet it was technologically dazzling, the intricacy of their performance" (Rice 2008, 5–6). Essentially, Lestat chooses the rock genre for its artistic blending of theatrical effects in creating a stage persona to be adored by fans. He also perceives "something vampiric about rock music [in] the way the electricity could stretch a single note forever" (2008, 6). This "barbaric" form of art proves to be the perfect medium for his disclosure as a vampire whose music is played on repeat, even though the audience is oblivious to his supernatural stance.

Lestat's transmedia proliferation is employed as a literary device not only to convey the idea that the human world is driven by the lure of consumption, but also to mock the rationalism, and yet the superficiality, of contemporary culture. Rice reiterates that the fictive humans do not believe in the existence of vampires, and by extension, in the menace they represent, precisely because such creatures belong to the realm of fiction and art. However, one can argue that the human audience in Rice's novel does not pursue the transmedia work of consciously consuming Lestat's fiction, music and videoclips. As a result, they do not make the necessary connections between different elements of his multimedia material in order to grasp that vampires actually exist. As Edwards argues, "[t]echnological creations have left a void in personal experience; horror no longer has an impact on subjective experience but exposes the emptiness of its audience" (2015, 11). This emptiness is most apparent in the human fans who consume Lestat's stage image, hypnotized by the illusion of the rockstar vampire. Unlike the nineteenth-century Theater of the Vampires, who fooled its unsuspecting audience, Lestat's aim is to be visible and known as a modern monster. He is capable of both horrifying and charming the audience as he reveals ancient secrets through art, hoping to lead humans to the uncanny realization that "art ceased to be art and became real!" (Rice 2008, 17). Lestat's artistic persona can be read as a simulation of vampirism through which myth blends with the power of technology resulting in a disorientating artifice.

With the exception of one song dedicated to the transformation of his mother, Gabrielle, Lestat's songs that echo throughout *The Queen of the Damned* constitute a call to the dormant ancestors Akasha and Enkil and to other vampires throughout the world. In this sense, the technologically broadcasted admonitions within Lestat's music function as an occult summoning:

> Mother and Father.
> Keep your silence,
> Keep your secrets,
> But those of you with tongues,
> sing my song.[...]
>
> Make a chorus
> Let heaven hear us
> Come together,
> Brother and sisters,
> Come to me [Rice 2008, 83].

The merge between Lestat's rock music and the endless replay of the lyrics enhances the supernatural call as a subliminal message to the undead. This gothic summoning resonates with Friedrich Kittler's assertion that "there is no difference between occult and technological media" (1990, 229), an idea that is also alluded to through Gabrielle's opinion that Lestat's music "could wake the dead" (Rice 2008, 552). Rice further highlights the conceit of summoning the vampire ancestors by means of electrically amplified songs as these reach Akasha through the television installed by Marius in their shrine. Interestingly, Lestat's music wakes not one but two ancient vampires: Akasha, who begins her monstrous killing of vampires and humans, as well as Mekare, who rises and projects dreams of the injustice she and her twin, Maharet, suffered in the past. In this sense, Lestat's depiction of vampire myths through modern technology is answered to by Mekare, who also "transmits" images, albeit inadvertently, through dreams that torment the majority of the immortals.

Responses Among the Undead and Fictive Humans

If Lestat's concert constitutes the climax of *The Queen of the Damned* as it gathers humans and the undead, including Akasha, the multiple voices of the novel provide a multi-focal perspective of the events. The importance of the transmedia for the development of the plot is signaled as Lestat, the main narrator, promises his readers access to "the minds and hearts of other beings who were responding to [his] music and [his] book" (Rice 2008, 8). For example, Pandora is shocked by Lestat's disclosure of the ancestors' names (2008, 64), while Khyman admires Lestat and adopts his cliché vampiric attire: "the black cloak, the stiff white shirt, the fine black jacket with tails" (2008, 130). However, Lestat's omnipresence afforded by transmedia also attracts the hate of the "Vampire Connection"—young undead who gather in vampire bars and disapprove of Lestat's popularity. Interestingly, these immortals respond to Lestat's mass-produced material through the "Declaration in the Form of Graffiti—written in black felt-tip pen on a red wall in the back room of a bar called Dracula's Daughter in San Francisco" (2008, 13). This manifesto, presented among the first pages of the novel, echoes the subcultures' dissemination of zines, meant to reach a specific group of people within the same community. Rice employs the declaration as a metafictional commentary on the two books preceding *The Queen of the Damned* and as a means of portraying vampires who do not believe the very history they claim to protect. In addition to spelling out the plan of killing Lestat, the manifesto expresses fear regarding Lestat's over-dissemination of vampiric secrets across multiple media, making them readily available to humans: "what are his motives for the book, the album, the films, the concert?" (2008, 14). Although the vampires in the bar are suspicious with regards to the authenticity of their own history, their paranoid response to Lestat's breaking of rules highlights their superficiality in protecting their "secret prosperity" (2008, 14). What this suggests is that the blur between fiction and reality spreads even to the vampire world of the "Vampire Connection." This idea is further emphasized as these young vampires are unable to recognize Marius as he walks among them, even as they invoke him to punish Lestat. Conversely, Marius's perspective is invaluable in reading Lestat's transmedia disclosure and how it is perceived by the twentieth century's "faithless times": "Yes, he'd told the secrets he'd been warned to keep, but in so doing, he had betrayed nothing and no one" (2008, 18).

In addition to the oblivious humans, the elder vampires, or the faithless novices, Rice introduces another group that is interested in Louis's and Lestat's transmedia material. The Talamasca is a secret order that studies the paranormal and consists of the only humans who follow and document the vampires' existence. Talamasca holds files on different undead and collects objects that have belonged to them. In doing so, the members of the order are not dissimilar to the consumers of the transmedia storytelling, whom Jenkins defines as "consumers [who] must assume the role of hunters and gatherers, chasing down bits of the story across media channels, comparing notes with each other" (2006, 21). This collaborative aspect of the Talamasca is emphasized as the society co-opts members with shared interests in the paranormal, but who are willing to act as collectors of so-called vampire paraphernalia and extend the knowledge of the entire order. In fact, the order's files and collection of artifacts functions as an additional medium meant to make "a distinctive and valuable contribution to the whole [story]" (Jenkins 2006, 95–6). This becomes apparent when David, the Superior General of the Talamasca, shows Jesse, a young and promising scholar, "The Temptation of Amadeo," Marius's painting of Armand in Renaissance style (Rice 2008, 180). To this he adds "a tintype, a late-nineteenth-century photograph," and then "an old magazine, a nineteenth-century journal, the kind with narrow columns of tiny print and ink illustrations. There was the same boy again alighting from a barouche—a hasty sketch, though the boy was smiling" (2008, 182). David also draws Jesse's attention to a 1789 article about the Theater of the Vampires and Armand. As such, Talamasca's collection of artifacts and media from different centuries describes and attests the existence of Armand and the theater. Last, but not least, David refers Jesse to the order's own files which comprise "[c]ountless memoirs [that] describe the theater. We have the deeds to the property as well. [...] The name of the owner of the theater was Lestat de Lioncourt, who purchased it in 1789. And the property in modern Paris is in the hands of a man by the same name even now" (2008, 182). Talamasca's impressive collection of material on Armand corroborates the information provided by Louis in *Interview with the Vampire*, which leads David to the assumption that "[i]n all probability, there are no fictional characters in this little novel whatsoever" (2008, 179).

While the Talamasca is interested in vampires solely for research purposes, their surveillance and collection of different media and artifacts corresponds to Jenkins' concept of convergence whereby "consumers are encouraged to seek out new information and make connections among dispersed media content" (2006, 3). The order's interest in knowledge convergence regarding the undead is further emphasized through Jesse's assignment to go back to New Orleans and document the existence of Lestat, Louis, and Claudia—the characters in *Interview with the Vampire*. Jesse conducts her own investigation and confirms David's theory by tracking the property deeds belonging to both Louis and Lestat, together with Lestat's "signature appearing in records dated 1895 and 1910, [which] was identical to the eighteenth-century signatures" (Rice 2008, 185). Jesse also visits the flat in Rue Royale, mentioned in the novel, where she finds a mural and Claudia's diary. This artifact confirms, yet again, the authenticity of Louis's story in the interview. Interestingly, with every new piece of information that Jesse discovers regarding the existence of vampires in *Interview*, she also becomes aware that her eccentric aunt Maharet (introduced in *The Queen of the Damned*) is also an immortal. As such, the Talamasca, and Jesse's investigation provide valuable self-referential content that establishes links between the novels in another narcissistic return of the narrative to itself, to borrow from Hutcheon (2010, 7). The secret order and its extensive collection exemplify a transmedia engagement in gathering information, making the necessary connections, and contributing to the expansion of knowledge on vampires in order to uncover the real within the fictional.

The Transmedia Re-vamping of Lestat and His Immortal Companions

In the present age of streaming and binge-watching, the vampire has migrated to the home television screen, as the popularity of *True Blood* (Ball 2008–14), *The Vampire Diaries* (Williamson and Plec 2009–17) and *The Originals* (Plec 2013–18) can confirm. Not surprisingly, Rice's views about the transmedia re-vamping of Lestat have changed: "a series [and not a movie] is THE way to let the entire story of the vampires unfold. […] It is, more than ever, abundantly clear that television is where the vampires belong" (Facebook post on Anne Rice's page, 2016). In another 2018 Facebook post, Rice invites her fans to give a face to Lestat by suggesting which actor should portray him, as well as the other characters in the forthcoming TV series. Although she has not yet made any announcements regarding the final choice for Lestat's role, this marketing stunt is surely effective in refreshing the audience's memory of her vampire anti-hero (as of today, there are more than 527 replies with recommendations). This instance of author-consumer interaction provides valuable insights into which actors might crystalize the desires and the ideals of perfection of the twenty-first century (mainly female) audience. Furthermore, by asking what the modern monster would look like, Rice is channeling the imagination of fans though social media in order to contour Lestat's face. As such, this transmedia experiment echoes the creation of Frankenstein's monster from body parts; but in this case, the face of the monster is shaped based on virtual representations of male perfection. Such a direct involvement of the fans coincides with "the transmedia creative model," in which, according to Marta Boni, "consumers are granted a main role: they are allowed to explore these complex worlds and are encouraged to add content" (2017, 16). While Rice invites her fans to take part in the process of recreating Lestat and the other immortals on the TV screen, it remains to be seen to what extent she and her production crew will take the fans' suggestions into account.

Conclusion

This essay aimed to provide an analysis regarding the central role of the media chosen for the dissemination of the vampires' stories in Rice's first three novels of *The Vampire Chronicles*. If Lestat and Louis have been repeatedly referred to as sympathetic vampires, this is partly due to the different media they use to make themselves known and infiltrate the private lives of both mortals and undead. Rice's vampires rely on humans and on technology to fight the invisibility and the secrecy imposed by their old rules. In doing so, they employ tape recordings, radio, fiction, theater, television, and music with the aim of reconnecting to the world of the living. Louis and Lestat produce material readily available for consumption, which signals a vicious circle whereby vampires become real to the extent that their stories are amplified through technology and consumed by the audience within the narrative. In turn, mindless consumption wakes up monsters better left undisturbed, or causes a loss of identity and history, as signaled through the trope of the vampires oblivious of their own myths. What this transmedia approach to Rice's novels reveals is that the vampire may have become an omnipresent multi-media figure. However, the audience is required to make its own exploration and connect the dots provided in different media, by different vampires, in order to grasp how the stories weave into the larger world of the undead. Despite her earlier objections to the uncontrolled transmedia proliferation of her vampire characters, Rice invites input from her fans in order to understand how they imagine Lestat's portrayal in the forthcoming TV series. The vampire's transmedia visibility afforded by technology, or enhanced by fans, provides a commentary on the alluring but potentially deceiving powers of mass-media, especially in the present screen era as truth and deceit are continuously intertwined.

Works Cited

Anne Rice's website "Welcome to Anne Rice.Com!" http://www.annerice.com/Reader Interaction-MessagesToFans.html.
Auerbach, Nina. 1995. *Our Vampires, Ourselves.* Chicago: University of Chicago Press.
Bacon, Simon. 2014. "The Transmedia Vampire: From Bram Stoker's *Dracula* to HBO's *True Blood.*" *Words, Worlds and Narratives: Transmedia and Immersion,* edited by Tawnya Ravy and Eric Forcier. Oxford: IDP.
Boni, Marta. 2017. "Introduction." *World Building,* edited by Marta Boni, Amsterdam University Press, pp. 9–28.
Botting, Fred. 2007. "Hypocrite Vampire." *Gothic Studies,* vol. 9, no. 1, pp. 16–34.
Craft, Christopher. 1984. "'Kiss Me with Those Red Lips': Gender and Inversion in *Bram Stoker's Dracula.*" *Representations,* no. 8, pp. 107–33.
Davidel, Laura. 2018. "'Orphans of Ticking Time': Armand's Experience of Immortality as Duration and Desynchronization in Anne Rice's the *Vampire Chronicles.*" *Aeternum: The Journal of Contemporary Gothic Studies,* vol. 5, no. 2, pp. 54–67.
Dutka, Elaine. 1993 "A Look Inside Hollywood and the Movies: Interview with the Vampire's Picky Creator." *Los Angeles Times,* https://www.latimes.com/archives/la-xpm-1993-08-22-ca-26172-story.html.
Edwards, Justin D. 2015. "Introduction: Technogothics." *Technologies of the Gothic in Literature and Culture: Technogothics,* edited by Justin D. Edwards, New York: Routledge, pp. 1–16.
Kittler, Friedrich. 1990. *Discourse Networks 1800/1900,* trans. M. Metteer with C. Cullens, Stanford: Stanford University Press.
Gordon, Joan, and Veronica Hollinger. 1997. "Introduction: The Shape of Vampires." *Blood Read: The Vampire as Metaphor in Contemporary Culture,* edited by Joan Gordon and Veronica Hollinger, Philadelphia: University of Pennsylvania Press, pp. 1–10.

Hand, Richard J. 2014. "The Darkest Nightmares Imaginable: Gothic Audio Drama from Radio to the Internet." In *A Companion to American Gothic*, edited by Charles L. Crow, Chichester: Wiley Blackwell, pp. 463–74.
Hutcheon, Linda. 2010. *Narcissistic Narrative: The Metafictional Paradox*. Waterloo: Wilfrid Laurier University Press.
Jenkins, Henry. 2006. *Convergence Culture*. New York: New York University Press.
_____. 2011. "Transmedia 202: Further Reflections." *Confessions of an Aca-Fan*, http://henryjenkins.org/blog/2011/08/defining_transmedia_further_re.html.
Rice, Anne. 1994. "*From Anne Rice: On the Film, Interview with the Vampire*." Sharon Murphy. https://www.maths.tcd.ie/~forest/vamipre/morecomments.html.
_____. 1998. *The Vampire Armand*. New York: Alfred A. Knopf.
_____. 2008. *Interview with the Vampire* [1976]. London: Sphere.
_____. 2008. *The Vampire Lestat* [1985]. London: Sphere.
_____. 2008. *The Queen of the Damned* [1988]. London: Sphere.
_____. 2009. "*Opinion of the Movie the Queen of the Damned*," Interview by Mona Schnell. https://www.youtube.com/watch?v=PcX7aD2Pn1k&list=PL133614310A1ADFAE&index=9 1&t=1s.
_____. 2012. "*Anne Rice on Vampires, Werewolves and More!*" Interview by Morgan Doremus, https://www.youtube.com/watch?v=-9MlHLz-hs4&t=75s.
Spooner, Catherine. 2006. *Contemporary Gothic*. London: Reaktion Books.
Wasson, Sara. 2012. "'Coven of the Articulate': Orality and Community in Anne Rice's Vampire Fiction." *The Journal of Popular Culture*, vol. 45, no. 1, pp. 197–213.
Waugh, Patricia. 2001. *Metafiction: The Theory and Practice of Self-Conscious Fiction*. London: Routledge.

First-Person Gothic
Anne Rice, Vampirism, Authorship and Identity
Evan Hayles Gledhill

Anne Rice is a prolific instigator of text—not only as creator of her own fictions, memoirs, screenplays, microblogs, and social media posts—but as the subject of innumerable articles, reviews, fanzines, transformative works, internet forums, and online discussions. Her *Vampire Chronicles* began with the publication of her novel *Interview with the Vampire* (1976) and now span multiple platforms and media, including the film adaptation of the same novel in 1994, and a short-lived stage musical *Lestat* (2006). Though the vampire character Lestat might be described as a transmedia vampire, there is no sustained attempt to construct an interlinked story-world for the Vampire Chronicles across differing media as, for example, the Star Wars franchise has done. As defined by Henry Jenkins, a transmedia narrative "unfolds across multiple media platforms, with each new text making a distinctive and valuable contribution to the whole" (2008, 95–96). However, Rice is adept at constructing her own story as an author across multiple platforms; she interviews on television and in the press, writes opinion pieces on social media, makes announcements through her fan club, and contributes to documentaries on topics as diverse as human sexuality and horror fiction, becoming a transmedia phenomenon herself.

As Rice's vampires crossed media boundaries, in official adaptations and fan-created transformative works, their status as intellectual property, based on notions of originality and authorial invention, becomes a contested topic. Fans seeking to extend and develop this fictional world—through fanfiction, or unofficial events such as walking tours of New Orleans—ran afoul of Rice's stringent defense of her copyright. In a previous study of discussions about copyright by authors and their readers, Jennie Roth and Monica Flegel observe "that both claim ownership, but not within the discourse that underpins much of copyright law itself" (2014, 902).

Roth and Flegel analyze the ownership claims of fans and authors, consumers and prosumers, not only in terms of the philosophical underpinnings of the development of copyright law, but also through the language and imagery used by participants in these discussions. This previous exploration of Rice's engagement with discourses of copyright and textual ownership places her statement that she "does not allow fanfiction" into context with similar comments from sci-fi and fantasy authors, such as Diana Gabaldon, John Scalzi, and Robin Hobb. Roth and Flegel's study explored the metaphors deployed by authors regarding their work to understand why copyright law has been ineffective in preventing and deterring fan authors. The current chapter explores Rice's professional alignment with the figure of the vampire to try and understand her investment in authorial ownership.

In this essay, I seek to explore Rice's relationship with her creations within the specific contexts of Gothic fiction, to explore the monstrous potentials of authorship. Rice's fear of the producing-consumer, the "prosumer," suggests a view of that creator as a vampire-like monster that absorbs its substance from others, endangering the source, and that the resurrected, stitched-together tropes of fanfiction are too monstrous for even the author of horrors. Though Gothic has been a contested term since its inception in the eighteenth century, we can "specify some general parameters" for its genre fictions, following Jerrold E. Hogle (2002, 2): key elements would be the antiquated and/or potentially haunted setting (castles, ancient mansions, ruins, and decaying spaces), and the element of the past that "haunts" the main character, whether that be literally or metaphorically, and drives the narrative forward. The vampire story is thus quintessentially Gothic, as the undead protagonist or antagonist can be both haunted and haunting, themselves a relic of the past that persists in the present. The Gothic author, likewise, creates from the ruins of other eras, bringing older models of both form and content into their contemporary era. The roots of Rice's genre, her beloved vampire creation Lestat, and the philosophies of the copyright that she invokes, all trace back to the eighteenth century. Given the "haunting" nature of these relics of the past, I suggest that Rice's resurrected anti-hero—the vampire—perhaps provides a useful metaphor for exploring the complexities of authorial identity and textual ownership in a transmedia age.

"Just suppose that the art ceased to be art and became real!": Fashioning the Self Through Fiction and Fandom

The history of Gothic fiction in which Rice works is very much about the enjoyment of reading as a somatic experience, a bodily pleasure. In the earliest period of the genre's development the physical act of reading, and its effect upon the imagination and the body of the reader, were often discussed. The editors of a popular Romantic-era women's magazine defended their rejection of submissions of Gothic tales and love poems, declaring such to be "dangerous writings for youth to indulge in," as both readers and creators, as they "soften and enfeeble the mind" (*The Ladies' Monthly Museum*, iv). That the pleasures of reading and writing go beyond the page is a staple of the Gothic mode, and the desire to write oneself into one's favorite genre—or to "self-insert" in fannish terms—is a trope of the earliest Gothic; Jane Austen parodies the original Gothic fangirl in *Northanger Abbey* (1817). The trend continues in recent vampire fictions: in *Buffy the Vampire Slayer* (1997–2004) a teenage runaway, who calls herself Chantarelle in a mistaken attempt at sophistication, soon learns to fight—rather than entice—dangerously demonic vampires. Initially convinced that her life will be improved by proximity to vampires, hoping to be "turned" and become a vampire herself, in the end the delusional fangirl comes out ahead: rechristened Anne, the young woman is empowered by fighting real monsters to become fearless advocate for homeless youths like herself. Thus, for two hundred years, both the vampire and the Gothic novel have been positioned as pernicious influences that women would do well to avoid, but also as an exciting adventure of self-development, through which one makes friends and connections.

Anne Rice and her fans seem to share the same desire: to bring aspects of the fictional world into their own lives and explore new modes of self-fashioning. As Milly Williamson explores, through interviews with former and current members of the Anne Rice Vampire Lestat Fan Club in the late 1990s, every October the fan club throws an annual ball, and Rice herself occasionally attends. In 1995 the New Orleans–based event, titled the "Gathering of the Coven," was hosted by Rice herself in her home, the former St Elizabeth's Orphanage in the Garden District. This building also featured as a location in her latest novel, *Memnoch the Devil* (1995), the venue itself blending the author's identity into her fictions. Proximity to Rice was used to signify authenticity and status, as fan club officials had an office in the former Orphanage and there were extensive VIP privileges at the party. However, Williamson's interviews show a distinct divide in reviews of the event: between the official fan club statements praising Rice's hospitality and the experience of the "ordinary" fans. One participant says:

> There was nothing that I recognised from her books or wanted to be a part of … it was a lot of people getting drunk and it was very cold […] 3,000 people who were invited guests and they were treated so much better than the people who actually paid and stood in the line […] this is my world, she should have paid more attention to the fans [Williamson, 2005, 121].

The idea of an inner cabal who receive preferential treatment and disregard others might seem a clear reflection of various vampire covens that form around Rice's central characters, but this is clearly not the part of the book that this fan wanted to recreate, suggesting that reader responses are not as univocal as the majority of Rice's texts.

In the opportunities it offers for connection and self-fashioning, Gothic fandom is dynamic and diverse in its possibilities. Vampire fandom is not simply dominated by the desire for, or to become, a vampire, or to adopt the rebellious and luxurious styles in which fictional creatures of the night usually indulge. As Brigid Cherry notes, in her book on cult media fans and handcrafting, there are extensive forums in online knitting platforms dedicated to vampires and vampire fictions with names like "Blood and Yarn" (2016, 49). These crafting fans share patterns for obviously vampire-related items, but also for creating homewares "as seen on screen": "Props on screen are recognised by the fans as useful domestic items which can be appropriated for use within their own home, but which nonetheless bring the narrative and the characters of the storyworld into the personal and domestic space" (Cherry, 78). In the online forums, the homespun, rural–Southern aesthetic of the Stackhouse family home in *True Blood* (2008–14) is a popular source of inspiration, though its rag-rugs and faded quilts are styled in direct contrast to the dark and forbidding interiors of the vampire's "lairs" in the show. Vampire fans are as likely to connect with a supporting character, potential victim, and even a vampire hunter, as they are with the primary [anti]heroes.

Rice, however, has very much come to identify with the apex predator: "If I were a vampire, I would certainly want to be Lestat" (Ramsland 1997a, kindle 938). Although many of Rice's texts, and those inspired by her, are also about Catholicism, witches, romance, the art or craft of writing, the business of publishing and other topics, the dominant textual output from Rice, her critics and collaborators, is about, and written from the perspective of, the vampire. Her identity as an author, and literary celebrity, is enmeshed with the image and person of the vampire. Rice goes so far in identifying with her key protagonist, Lestat de Lioncourt, as to say, "I'm in love with him. He's my alter ego" (Stern, 2016). This may explain the difference in reception for the specially commissioned "Victim" branded beer at 1995's "Gathering," which some fans viewed as crude. Rice's increasing identification with the glamorous, powerful and exploitative "Brat Prince" of the vampires illustrates some of the conflict that has arisen within her own fan club over the years.

The fan's statement about the ball, that "this is my world," is in direct conflict with the official fan club, and Rice herself, who claim ownership over these spaces, both fictional and real. The fan pleasures taken from, and around, the texts are often at odds with the values espoused by fan club personnel and Rice. Williamson interviews Diane, the assistant manager of Rice's local book shop when resident in New Orleans, who promoted events and signings linked to the fan club. Diane collects pre-publication material and first edition books—"anything we get at the bookstore, that just booksellers get, you know, we always put it aside," then she asks Rice to sign these artefacts, making them "more valuable" (Williamson, 125). "Value" here is monetary; the bookseller specifically tells the interviewer the resale values of first editions. Diane scorns the fans who rifle through the bookshops castaways after signings for ephemera she deems "trash." Those fans more concerned with collecting ephemera, or the creative materials produced by other fans, and/or creating elaborate hand-made costumes for the balls, disrupt the formal ownership model Rice and her official fan club promotes. One fan interviewed by Williamson explicitly names and disrupts this (capitalist) model, saying the official fan club "don't take it at all seriously, they figure, 'we've got the product, we don't have to.' They've got Anne, and they're the only ones who do, they've got the coven ball, they've got New Orleans" (126–127). Anne is available for consumption like her writings: as the source, she is both product and a producer. This is a model of engagement predicated on traditional values of originality and ownership, and the philosophy, and copyright, upon which this mode of thinking rests is roughly of the same vintage as Lestat himself—which, I suggest, is no coincidence.

The Gothic After-Lives of Romantic Originality

Modern U.S. and UK copyright law, which enables Rice to assert authorial control over her creations, developed from eighteenth century origins. Though Roth and Flegel look to John Locke's philosophies of labor, and their impact on the very first copyright Act in England of 1710, Romantic-era ideologies about creative originality were hugely influential in the development of the late-eighteenth and early-nineteenth century copyright laws that form the basis of much of our modern provision. Peter Jaszi (1991) argues that it is not coincidental that key structures of modern copyright law developed in the late-eighteenth century, as they are linked to concepts of originality, identity and authorship prevalent in Romantic ideologies. As Robert Macfarlane explores in *Original Copy: Plagiarism and Originality in Nineteenth Century Literature*, "the neoclassical aesthetics of the earlier eighteenth century, which had recommended imitation as a compositional technique by which valuably new literature could be born," were replaced in the Romantic period by an idealization of authorial invention (2007, 22).

The influential 1759 essay *Conjectures on Original Composition* by Edward Young claimed originality was "of a *vegetable* nature; it rises spontaneously from the vital root of genius; it *grows*, it is not *made*" (Macfarlane, 18). Asserting authorial identity, claiming ownership of thought and mode of expression, becomes part of legal doctrines that seek to define what Jaszi calls the "talismanic quality of originality" (466).

However, the Gothic novel has always posed a challenge to the idealization of the unique, natural and original in its development as a genre that relies upon tropes, codes and conventions. The dominant model of late-eighteenth century literature, the Sentimental novel, certainly meant many novels shared common features: the epistolary model was popular, as was first-person fictional autobiography. However, Gero Guttzeit suggests that the authors of eighteenth-century Gothic fictions, and their "monstrous progeny" (in Mary Shelley's phrase), embody a specific challenge to the Romantic model of authorship as "individuality, originality and organic totality" (2018, 279). The monstrous undead body and the infectious vampire of the Gothic genre depict "authorship-as-influencing, authorship-as-copying and authorship-as-fragmenting" (289). Further, as Young equates original and "organic" authorship with the natural, we can see echoes of the vampire's unnaturalness also in the genre fiction that is a monstrous replication of corrupted forms, perpetuating an older model (of imitation) derived from before the modern era. Rice is more correct than she knows, when she says that "the vampire is the poet and the writer of the monster world" (Rose, 2010, n.p.). The origins of the Gothic monster, as disparate parts recombined into new life, or as a dying form given new life through new blood, can provide us with a useful lens for exploring the relationship between author and text.

The idealization of the vampire Lestat—a "man of reason, a child of the eighteenth century" (Rice, 1992, 3)—born, in human terms, in 1760, suggests that Rice is heavily invested in the ideals of the Romantic era. Jennifer Smith suggests that Rice's artistic "debt to the Romantics" (1996, 18) is great, based on a thematic reading of her novels focused on specific textual influence. I suggest, more broadly, that the very model and expression of Lestat's character demonstrates an investment in a Romantic conception not only of authorship, but of selfhood. The expression of self, and the importance of the first-person narrative for Rice, suggests an investment in certain Romantic ideologies.

Lestat's direct address to the reader as first-person narrator, and detailed self-portrait of a sensitive masculinity, echoes influential novels of the Sentimental school in the eighteenth century. Lestat explores his needs and desires, describes his emotional responses at length and, famously, weeps tears of blood regularly: "I like to weep. I must. Why else would I do it so much?" (Rice, 1992, 426). His response to the entire twentieth century is to take it as a personal affront, to be indignant that the world has moved on without him as he hibernated in a tomb: "This brilliantly lighted world where the value of human life was greater than it had ever been before. [...] It was enough to make an old world monster go back into the earth, this stunning irrelevance to the mighty scheme of things, enough to make him lie down and weep" (Rice, 1986, 10). Yet, even his oldest friends cannot take his emotions seriously, as Louis says in response to Lestat's self-pity and self-justification: "I'll take your brand of pain anytime, as they say" (Rice, 1992, 402). How like Yorick, the protagonist of Laurence Sterne's *A Sentimental Journey* (1768), or Harley in Henry Mackenzie's *Man of Feeling* (1771)—heroes whose self-awareness and emotional development underpin their autobiographical tales. However, these protagonists have themselves have been labeled "vampiric" by George E. Haggerty:

> [Harley] feeds on others, consumes them as it were, as a way of giving substance to his own responses. He is passive and self-involved for all his "interest" in others, and his "action" is a kind of unwitting aggression that emotionally "commodifies" whomever he encounters. Out of this "self" of pseudosuffering subjectivity emerges the "man of feeling" [1999, 86].

In this description it is easy to see the echo of Lestat, who constantly centers his own emotional response to the sufferings of others—of which he is very often the cause—and whose tale is always driven by his own desires.

That Rice identifies overtly with Lestat, and that he asserts his authorial and artistic identity in terms of individuality, complicates any separation of Romantic original authorship and Gothic disruptive monster. At the opening of his third first-person narrative, *The Tale of The Body Thief* (1994), the vampire rockstar narrator declares: "this is my book from start to finish" (3). Yet, it is Rice's name displayed prominently on the cover and copyright page: despite the in-text assertions, there is no attempt to subvert the fictional origin through pseudonym. Lestat revels in his individuality and originality, repeatedly declaring his difference from other vampires—from the ghouls of the Théâtre des Vampires, to his closest ally Louis—yet the pages of his "autobiographies" rebound with references to other authors. The preface of this volume alone name-drops Charles Dickens, Vladimir Nabokov, and Leo Tolstoy, and directly quotes William Blake (without attribution) (1992, 4–7). The use of bookish allusions to other authors and publications works to weave Lestat and his author into a history of textual production. The lack of attribution, the interlacing of fact and fiction in the historical record, also work to erase the boundaries of text and identity. Whose books, whose words, are these? The individuals and texts—vampire and author, original and derivation—become indistinct in

Rice's work, despite the investment in individual identity and self-fashioning autobiography.

Just like her favorite protagonist, Rice seeks to position herself at once within a literary history and as a true original. Rice recognizes that *The Vampire Chronicles* could not exist as they are without the influence of previous textual works, and not only other vampire fictions: she draws on her Catholic heritage, with references to the Bible and the lives of the saints, and cites the influence of authors and philosophers as diverse as Richard Matheson and Thomas Aquinas (Rice, 2010, n.p.). Lestat also acknowledges diverse influences, the very words he uses reflects a continuation of previous authorship:

> the language I use in my autobiography—I first learned it from a flatboatmen [...] about two hundred years ago. I learned more after that from the English language writers—everybody from Shakespeare through Mark Twain to H. Rider Haggard, whom I read as the decades passed. The final infusion I received from the detective stories of the early twentieth century in the *Black Mask* magazine. [...] When I write I drift into a vocabulary that would have been natural to me in the eighteenth century, into phrases shaped by the authors I've read [Rice 1986, 3–4].

Thus, it seems fitting that Lestat describes himself as a "full-fledged, post–Renaissance, post-nineteenth century, post-modern, post-popular writer" (Rice 2003, 3). Postmodernist authorship has been theorized as an ahistorical pillaging of previous representations, and as wholly subjective representation that refuses the possibility of universal symbols and thus deconstructs meaning (Bertens, 2019). Lestat might claim to "deconstruct nothin'" (2003, 3), refusing any link between postmodernist collage and the challenge to older models of identity, however the resurrected cadaver continues to move forward in time; through his first-person autobiographies, the Romantic author never dies, but is resurrected time and again, a consumed commodity and consuming narrator.

"You think I don't want new readers? My name is thirst, baby": The Author as Monster

From Marx's capitalist monsters, to infection panic at the time of the first AIDS crisis, vampires have long been recognized as metaphors of circulation. The vampire is a site of exchange between people, and between people and texts, and is a metaphor for both physical and cultural transformation. The novel, similarly, is a site of textual exchange, but I suggest that so, too, is the author. The very act of creating and writing the vampire can be an act of textual vampirism, in and of itself, as Patricia Skarda (1989) claims of John Polidori's relationship to Byron. The author is a vampire, turned by the act of reading, inspired to (re)create, and thus turn more reader/authors. Thus, the "spirit of the book" becomes separated from its textual origins, and like vampirism, seeks out new hosts. This is the origin myth Rice wrote for her vampires in *The Queen of the Damned* (1988), where the spirit Amel bonds to the human Akasha to create the first vampire. Rice acknowledges, through her monstrous narrator Lestat, the vampiric nature of authorship—the desire to be consumed, and the desire to consume in turn: "I want you to read every page I write. I want my prose to envelop you. I'd drink your blood if I could and hook you into every memory inside me" (2003, 8). This sentence highlights the links between the author, her narrator, vampirism and the importance of self-fashioning within a community of readers.

Thus, I suggest, Rice herself can be considered a vampire: converted by the act of reading, inspired to (re)create, and thus to turn others. Rice influences her readers in turn, to identify as vampires, as well as authors, in their own right; to use vampiric characters to enable their own identity-fashioning, on and off the page. In an article focused on the influence of Rice, K.M. Sparza speaks of his development as an author through his engagement with other people's writing, and through fanfiction, using the vampire as a repeated metaphor for this process: "I was Akasha, Queen of the Damned, the one from whom all the blood flowed. I had power over my words and myself and my genre" (2019). Sparza's words disrupt the easy alignment of identity between a singular author and their creation, and the concentration of power in the alignment of author/creator/vampire—he identifies with the vampire of another writer's creation, as the most powerful of all vampires, yet his words flow like the blood of the victim. The exchange, by which victim become vampire, and author becomes reader, is made explicit in this metaphor. The blood of the original vampire, in this case Akasha, must be drunk by the "victim" in turn to make a new monster—but who is Akasha here: Rice herself as the originator of this image, or Sparza who adopts this form in creating their own "monstrous progeny"?

There is, thus, a tension between Rice's acknowledgment of the necessity of exchange between author and reader, as in vampire and victim, and her refusal to acknowledge the monstrous offspring of fanfiction. Though Lestat desires that his prose "envelops" his audience, Rice wishes them to remain in thrall and not to be "turned." Sparza desired to inhabit, and to write about, Rice's characters and was prevented by Rice's insistence on defending her copyright: "I never got to write those stories, but that's okay because I wrote mine. After devouring hers—after desiccating like a vampire who hadn't fed for a decade. When I wanted more, I didn't wait for the Dark Gift. I wrote my own" (2019). Sparza uses vampirism as a metaphor for both identity and literary creation here. Though his words suggest he did not need to be inducted into authorship/vampirism, through the Dark Gift in Rice's terminology, yet Sparza has been transformed. Rice's copyright defense may have stopped one form of imitation and shared imagination, but the text is always a site of exchange, and the dominant tropes of possibility and renewal in genre fiction ensure that new texts and new monsters are originated and disseminated. Rice acknowledges that, after *Interview*, the focus of her later works became increasingly about "procreation [...] and it was about possibility and renewal" (Riley, 1996, 23). A shared investment, in both growth and identity, is expressed by both the fanfiction writers and Rice herself.

Though Rice proclaims postmodernist tendencies in interview (Rose, 2010), like her fictional alter-ego, she cannot fully embrace this model as a replacement for the singular Romantic genius in practice. Though willing to view a visual transformation of her own narratives, as the publications of graphic novel formats and official adaptations for stage and screen suggest, Rice's resistance to speculative textual works is absolute. Rice has repeatedly stated her pleasure in, and admiration for, fan art and other forms of creativity that draw upon her novels, yet pursues copyright infringement in textual form vigorously. She posted the following statement to her official website in 2000: "I do not allow fan fiction. The characters are copyrighted. It upsets me terribly to even think about fan fiction with my characters. I advise my readers to write your own original stories with your own characters. It is absolutely essential that you respect my wishes" (Rice, 2000).

Emailed letters from Rice's lawyers appeared on listservs and fan archives in the late 1990s and early 2000s to enforce this dictum, as far as was possible. The blog Corporate Bandwagon (2001) posted the full text of the take-down instruction, issued by Kleinberg Lopez Lange Brisbin & Cuddy LLP, that resulted in the removal of the Anne Rice Chronicles [sic] section of Fanfiction.net. The blog owner notices the inconsistency between formats, asking "does Anne have a right to ban all fan 'literary material' (poems, short stories) while lauding other fanworks (drawings, etc.)?" (Jekkal, 2001, n.p.). That Rice enjoys inspiring visual art, but seeks to curtail the writing of stories about her characters, is perhaps explained by her preference for the first-person narration that positions Lestat as the self-fashioning Man of Feeling, and herself as the unique Romantic originator. Rice's mode of stating her approval for Tom Cruise's performance of Lestat on film reveals this: "He became Lestat; he did his own Lestat without stealing my character from me" (1997b, kindle 2778). Cruise was speaking lines from Rice's own script and drawn from her novel, his difference to her vision of her character is primarily visual. What constitutes the "theft" of a character for Rice would seem, I argue, the "theft" of her voice, her self-expression, which is also Lestat's by proxy.

Rice's identification with her narrator is clearly expressed in the style, form, and content of the novels, as well as in interviews about her authorial practice. Rice constantly engages in first-person exposition, and extensive volumes of interviews with her have been published, such as Michael Riley's *Conversations with Anne Rice* (1996) and Nola Cancel's *Anne Rice, The Interviews* (2014), and in collections such as Katherine Ramsland's *The Anne Rice Reader* (1997). By comparing diverging narratives told at different times of the transformation of *Interview* into a Hollywood film, we can see the echoes of Lestat in Anne particularly clearly. In Ramsland's telling, Rice's distance from the production is presented as, in part, the result of decisions she had made: "Anne had severed relations with Geffen" (1997b, kindle 2613). Yet, in interviews with Riley, Rice claims it was "very plain to me that David felt intense animosity toward me personally. We clearly weren't speaking to each other" (227). She goes on to say, "I would have been happy to meet any actor connected with it, but I was never approached. I never received a phone call […] my phone was listed. I could have been reached at any time" (Riley, 231). By contrast, Ramsland quotes Tom Cruise saying he "had hoped to discuss the character with [Rice] but realised that any such meeting would be impossible: 'I would have asked her a lot of questions'" (1997b, kindle 2607). Rice's reframing enables her to contextualize her negative pronouncements about the film, which she recanted after seeing the finished product: "one has to realise […] that was the backdrop. It was silence, and it was animosity" (Riley, 231). Thus, Anne appears very much like Lestat, writing back to Louis, "for the lies he told about me. […] To write my story for him, not an answer to his malice. […] And it didn't matter that they didn't believe it" (Rice 1986, 15). Rice, like her anti-hero, seeks to be heard, to express herself, above all things.

However, Rice initially identified strongly with Louis, the brooding anti-hero of *Interview*, and this shifted in later installments of the *Chronicles*: "there was nothing to do but grow beyond that because it's a book about disappointment, disillusionment, and bitterness. […] *Interview with the Vampire* was a tragic, lyric book about nothing being possible" (Riley, 23). Rice thus starts writing as the victim of fortune, or circumstance, but from the second novel onwards, *The Vampire Lestat* (1985), the narrative voice shifts to the active shaper of destiny: Lestat, the antagonist from the first novel who makes Louis one of the undead. Rice speaks of the change in narrator as though it were inevitable: "Lestat grew as a character almost beyond my control. He spontaneously appeared in the corner of my eye while I was writing *Interview*, and then he took on great strength"

(Ramsland, 1997a, kindle 933). He who voices the narrative is able to exert control, and yet Louis refuses to take control, feeling too much the responsibility and guilt, and is thus a less attractive narrator for Rice. Rice is an author who seeks to assert control—a monstrous power over not only the narrative, but over its reception, and her own framing beyond the page also.

In a recent interview, Rice has reflected on the development of the first-person narrative, which now dominates the Vampire Chronicles: "When I came to write *The Vampire Lestat*, I had published several books. I had been to Egypt. I had been to places I dreamed of going and lived in houses I dreamed of living. I had more strength and energy, and that's how I saw Lestat. I saw Lestat as the male person I'd like to be" (Fessier, 2018). It would not be out of place to mark the class markers of financial and cultural capital, of property and travel, that Rice cites as linking experiences between herself and her idealized "man of reason." Rice depicts vampires, as many authors have before, as aristocratic parasites, not only in their preternatural after-lives but as humans also: the most successful converts, who thrive in monstrous form, are those willing to feed off the bodies and labors of others. Lestat de Lioncourt's human life started in genteel poverty in rural France, and he happily exploits the possibilities for long-term investment and property ownership born of an unnaturally extended life. By contrast, Louis du Pont du Lac is the owner of a slave-worked plantation in French Louisiana who becomes increasingly uncomfortable with his exploitation of others and returns to a melancholy solitude feeding not upon humans, but upon rats and livestock. Whereas Louis refuses also to turn humans, Lestat revels in his means to impose his will and vision, transforming others to vampirism: "Want to fight me? It's useless. There's no force on earth that can stop me from doing this" (Rice, 1992, 413). It is Lestat, then, who confers narrative worth, who makes subjects and authors of mere humans.

The Vampire Anne Rice: Controlling the Chronicle

The difficulty distinguishing between the voices of author and narrator, I suggest, demonstrates the links between Rice's explorations of both vampirism and authorship. The author's increasing investment in her authorial and narratorial voices as part of *her* identity, rather than Lestat's, is reflected in her increasing insistence on control over her text. In one respect, Rice has achieved complete ownership, as she is able to release her books exactly as she envisages them: "I have no intention of allowing any editor ever to distort, cut or otherwise mutilate sentences that I have edited and re-edited, and organized and polished myself. […] I fought a great battle to achieve a status where I did not have to put up with editors making demands on me (Lyall 2004, n.p.). Rice describes the editor's actions in monstrous terms, however, she has previously said that editing has helped her shape her work for the better. She states that when Knopf acquiring the novel *Interview* "they had some criticisms with it, and wanted to know if I would attack some of those problems. Of course, it was a foregone conclusion that I would" (Riley, 8). Rice acknowledges the flaws of the original manuscript, and her reflections suggest a younger author with less self-confidence and greater respect for the role of the editor: "if they had looked me in the eye and said we, the editors at Knopf, think it should be published exactly the way it is—I would have believed them" (Riley, 10). Rice once again rewrites her perceptions, her past, as befits her present. Issues of control are once again linked to issues of identity, expressed through control of the first-person narrative.

Yet, Rice cannot control what happens to her text in the hands of readers. Negative reviews for the novel *Blood Canticle* (2003) on online platforms prompted her to post a 1,200-word rant to her official website, claiming critics were "interrogating this text from the wrong perspective." Her public response was so extreme as to be quoted in the *New York Times*, when she claimed "stupid, arrogant assumptions about me and what I am doing are slander" (Lyall, n.p.). This inability to accept critique has become more pronounced over time: when retracting her objections to the film adaptation of *Interview* Rice lightly suggested "if you don't like the picture, let me know. Laugh in my face, write me letters. Call…. I can take it" (Ramsland, 1997b, kindle 2781). However, in April 2014, she railed against negative reviews on platforms such as GoodReads for the latest installment of the Chronicles, *Prince Lestat*, as the product of "notorious gangster thug careerist reviewers who seek to victimize [authors] for sport on GoodReads and on Amazon. […] These bully thugs make a mockery of honest book reviewing" (Trout, 2014, n.p.). Rice thus responds to critiques of her novels as though they were personal attacks on herself, which make sense in the context of her identification with her principal narrator and protagonist, Lestat. In *Blood Canticle* he and she merge as authors, fictitious and real, in their indignation at critique: "what the Hell happened when I gave you *Memnoch the Devil*? […] You complained!" (4).

In performing her endless interviews on video and in print, by taking out multi-page adverts in industry publications to discuss the adaptations of her work, and in her attempts to silence amateur authors and critics, Anne Rice ensures that her voice is the loudest. In her fictions, this is also true—Lestat is first and foremost a mouthpiece, as most clearly seen in the construction of *Memnoch the Devil*, a large portion of which is devoted to conversations between Lestat and other supernatural entities regarding theology and morality. Thus, in her most famous creation, we can trace the echoes of Rice's own beliefs and philosophies, not only about the nature of humanity as she would like us to, but about the pleasures and purposes of the text.

Rice's role as an author is as essential to her identity as his vampirism is to Lestat, though he needed two hundred years to realize it: "The Vampire Lestat—*c'est moi*" (Rice, 1992, 283). This paraphrase is, of course, is a play on the apocryphal utterance of Gustav Flaubert, referencing his novel *Madam Bovary* (1856) about a romance reading fan who reads reality through the lens of the text. Though seeming to have the sympathy of her author, Emma Bovary fails in her attempts to "self-insert" into the romance genre she desires to inhabit, resulting in her own death by suicide, her husband's social ruin, and their daughter's loss of all the potential for social success that the mother desired. This brief *bon mot* by Rice-as-Lestat then is a somewhat complex statement of identity. The figures of the reader, the author, and the narrator merge textually—Rice writes as Lestat, who cites another author who identified with his own character, who was also a reader, but who failed in integrating her reality with her desires. This is, thus, a complex metaphor of textual exchange reaching back into literary history; a Gothic act of textual vampirism if you will, in which the novelist exists in the ruins of a failed remaking of identity, haunted by the vampiric return of the undead Romantic genius.

Rice is, it seems, caught between two modes: she elevates the eighteenth-century Romantic ideal of authorial ownership, just as she idealizes its embodiment in her first-person narrator. Who embodies "organic totality" and "individuality" better than the eighteenth-century man, the self-sufficient gentleman of means and education? However, the vampire version of this author disrupts "natural" modes of reproduction, both textual and biological. As Rebecca Tushnet notes of the Gothic language used about prosumers' remix culture, in terms like reinvigoration and resurrection there is "the implication that the source was dead before being revived. The intervention of the artist brought it back to life, but that is not unqualifiedly a good thing" (2011, 2139). Rice's own preference for the phrase preternatural, over supernatural, for her vampires perhaps suggests a discomfort with being outside of nature, as does Lestat's continual grappling with his relationship to the "natural," his place within the "Savage Garden" of the earth. The concept of the natural is a social construct, linked to the same discursive frameworks of power and identity as ideas of gender, originality, and copyright. We can surmise, then, that there is nothing "natural" about the creation of the Gothic text, or its fanfiction spin-off, and this constitutes a further challenge to Romanic authorial control. Anne Rice, in her multi-platform self-fashioning through fiction and non-fiction, pursuing and promulgating her derivations from the Gothic authors of the past in all media, and acknowledging (however reluctantly) her inspiration of the authors of the present and future, is a transmedia vampire herself.

The term serves not only as a series title linking certain of her novels, from *Interview* to *Blood Communion* (2018), but I suggest that we can now also write, or construct from existing textual sources, a Vampire Chronicle of Anne Rice the author.

Works Cited

Bertens, Hans. 2019. "Postmodernist Authorship." *The Cambridge Handbook of Literary Authorship*, edited by Ingo Berensmeyer, Gert Buelens and Marysa Demoor, Cambridge: Cambridge University Press, pp. 183–200.
Cancel, Nola. 2014. *Anne Rice, the Interviews*. CreateSpace Independent Publishing Platform: Chunkie Productions. Kindle ebook.
Cherry, Brigid. 2016. *Cult Media, Fandom, and Textiles: Handicrafting as Fan Art*. London: Bloomsbury.
Cortés, Camille. 2007. *The New Face of the Vampire: Autobiographical Fiction in Anne Rice's the Vampire Chronicles*. Unpublished M.A. thesis, University of Puerto Rico.
Dahlberg-Dodd, Hannah E. 2019. "The Author in the Postinternet Age." *Transformative Works and Cultures*, vol. 30.
Editorial. 1790. *The Ladies' Monthly Museum*, vol. 2, November 9.
Fessier, Bruce. 2018. "Vampire Chronicles Lands at Hulu. Anne Rice Said She Sees It Becoming 'Prestige TV' in Insightful Interview." *Palm Springs Desert Sun*, July 18, https://eu.desertsun.com/story/life/entertainment/books/2018/07/17/hulu-present-anne-rices-vampire-chronicles-prestige-tv/793066002/.
Guttzeit, Gero. 2018. "Authoring Monsters: Mary Shelley, Edgar Allan Poe and Early Nineteenth-Century Figures of Gothic Authorship." *Forum for Modern Language Studies*, vol. 54, no. 3, July, pp. 279–292.
Haggerty, George E. 1999. *Men in Love: Masculinity and Sexuality in the Eighteenth Century*, New York: Columbia University Press.
Hogle, Jerrold E. 2002. "Introduction: The Gothic in Western Culture." *The Cambridge Companion to Gothic Fiction*, edited by Jerrold E. Hogle, Cambridge: Cambridge University Press.
Jaszi, Peter. 1991. "Toward a Theory of Copyright: The Metamorphosis of 'Authorship.'" *Duke Law Journal*, vol. 40, no. 2, pp. 455–502.
Jekkal. 2001. *Corporate Bandwagon Issue 8*. Fanfiction.net, May 31, https://web.archive.org/web/20010609233505/http://www.fanfiction.net:80/index.fic?action=column-read&columnEntryID=417.
Jenkins, Henry. 2008. *Convergence Culture: Where Old and New Media Collide*. New York: New York University Press.
Kutzuba, Kerry. 1997. "'Lestat, C'est Moi': Anne Rice's Revelation of Self Through the Vampire Chronicles." *The Review: A Journal of Undergraduate Student Research*, vol. 1, pp. 37–48.
Lyall, Sarah. 2004. "The People Have Spoken, and Rice Takes Offense." *New York Times*, 11 October, https://www.nytimes.com/2004/10/11/books/the-people-have-spoken-and-rice-takes-offense.html.
Macfarlane, Robert. 2007. *Original Copy: Plagiarism and Originality in Nineteenth-Century Literature*. Oxford: Oxford University Press.
Ramsland, Katherine. 1994. *Prism of the Night: A Biography of Anne Rice*. New York: Plume Books.
_____. 1997a. "Let the Flesh Instruct the Mind: A *Quadrant* Interview with Anne Rice." *The Anne Rice Reader*, edited by Katherine Ramsland, New York: Ballantine Books. Kindle ebook.

———. 1997b. "*Interview with the Vampire*: How the Movie Finally Got Made." *The Anne Rice Reader*, edited by Katherine Ramsland. New York: Ballantine Books. Kindle ebook.
Rice, Anne. 1976. *Interview with the Vampire*. New York: Ballantine Books.
———. 1986. *The Vampire Lestat*. New York: Ballantine Books
———. 1992. *The Tale of the Body Thief*. London: Chatto and Windus.
———. 2000. "Important Message from Anne on "Fan Fiction." *Anne Rice: The Official Site*, April 7, http://annerice.com/ReaderInteraction-MessagesToFans.html.
———. 2003. *Blood Canticle*. New York: Alfred A. Knopf.
———. 2010. "Philosophical Influences." Uploaded on 8 April 2010,' Youtube video. 1.15 min., https://www.youtube.com/watch?v=v0eIfqmQhcU.
Riley, Michael. 1996. *Conversations with Anne Rice*. New York: Ballantine Books.
Rose, Lisa. 2010. "Interview with Anne Rice: 'Vampire' Writer Talks About Creating Characters and Stories You Can Sink Your Teeth Into." *New Jersey.com*, Oct. 31, 2010, https://www.nj.com/entertainment/arts/2010/10/interview_with_anne_rice_vampi.html.
Roth, Jenny, and Monica Flegel. 2014. "It's Like Rape: Metaphorical Family Transgressions, Copyright Ownership and Fandom." *Continuum*, vol. 28, no. 6, pp. 901–913.
Skarda, Patricia L. 1989. "Vampirism and Plagiarism: Byron's Influence and Polidori's Practice." *Studies in Romanticism*, vol. 28, no. 2, Summer, pp. 249–269.
Smith, Jennifer. 1996. *Anne Rice: A Critical Companion*. Westport, CT: Greenwood.
Stern, Marlow. 2016. "Anne Rice Opens Up: 'I Feel Like I'm Gay.'" *Daily Beast*, December 22, https://www.thedailybeast.com/anne-rice-opens-up-i-feel-like-im-gay.
Trout, Jenny. 2014. "Jenny Trout: Gangster Bully." *Trout Nation* (blog), April 28, http://jennytrout.com/?p=7532
Tushnet, Rebecca. 2011. "Scary Monsters: Hybrids, Mashups, and Other Illegitimate Children." *Notre Dame Law Review*, vol. 86, no. 5, pp. 2133–2156.
Williamson, Milly. 2005. *The Lure of the Vampire*. London: Wallflower Press.

About the Contributors

Katarzyna **Ancuta** is a lecturer at the Department of Languages, Faculty of Liberal Arts, King Mongkut's Institute of Technology Ladkrabang in Thailand. Her research interests include the interdisciplinary contexts of contemporary Gothic/Horror, with a strong Asian focus. She has contributed to *The Cambridge Companion to the Modern Gothic* (2014) and *Ghost Movies in Southeast Asia and Beyond* (2016).

Simon **Bacon** is an independent scholar based in Poznań, Poland. He has edited various books including *Gothic: A Reader* (2018), *Horror: A Companion* (2019), *Monsters: A Companion* (2020), Nosferatu *in the 21st Century* (2022), and *The Palgrave Handbook of the Vampire* (forthcoming). And published a series of books on vampires in popular culture, including *Becoming Vampire* (2016), *Dracula as Absolute Other* (2019), *Eco-Vampires* (2020), *Vampires from Another World* (2021), and is working on *1000 Vampires on Screen* (forthcoming).

Verena **Bernardi** is an Academic Administrator & Senior Lecturer in the Department of English and American Studies at Saarland University, Germany. She holds a PhD in North American Cultural Studies and is the author of *Us versus Them, or We? Post-2000 Vampiric Reflections of Family, Home and Hospitality in* True Blood *and* The Originals. Her work is in the field of vampire studies, cultural studies, television studies and U.S. southern/Louisiana regionalism. She has published in *Hospitality, Rape and Consent in Vampire Popular Culture* (2017). She is a coeditor of *All Around Monstrous* (2019).

Cathleen Allyn **Conway** is a creative writing PhD student at Goldsmiths, University of London. Her research interests and publications include Sylvia Plath, experimental poetics, the Gothic, vampires, feminism, science fiction and pop culture. She is a creative writing lecturer and the author of four poetry pamphlets. Her first full collection, *Bloofer*, an experimental work exploring the female vampire and the creative component of her PhD thesis, will be published by Broken Sleep Books in 2023.

Laura **Davidel** is a doctoral candidate and member of the research group Interdisciplinarity in English Studies (IDEA) at the Université de Lorraine, France. Her dissertation focuses on the construction of monstrosity through performativity and performance, liminality, and queerness in Anne Rice's *The Vampire Chronicles*. Her research interests include monstrosity, vampire fiction, psychoanalysis, and gender studies. Her "Agency in the Rician Vampire's Compulsion to Feed" was published in *Preternature*.

Shawn **Edrei** is a researcher of digital narratology, exploring how new technologies have changed our perspectives on storytelling and authorship. In addition to publishing numerous articles, he has coedited *Crossing Channels, Crossing Realms* and two collections on science fiction studies, and is working on a book exploring the latest developments in transmedia interactive fiction. He teaches at Tel-Aviv University.

Evan **Hayles Gledhill** PhD, teaches at the University of Reading. Their research interests include the body of the reader, and the social gendering of authors, readers, and text. They have recently published chapters on monstrosity and romance in NBC's *Hannibal*, and on the development of Gothic genre fandom in *Women's Periodicals and Print Culture in Britain, 1690–1820s* (2018).

Alexandra **Heller-Nicholas** is an Australian film critic, author and academic who has published nine books on cult, exploitation and horror films, including *Masks in Horror Cinema: Eyes Without Faces* (2019) and *1000 Women in Horror, 1895–2018* (2020), both which were finalists for the Bram Stoker Awards. She is an adjunct professor at Deakin University, a member of the Alliance of Women Film Journalist, a consultant for a number of film festivals around the world and is on the advisory board for the Miskatonic Institute of Horror Studies.

Derek **Newman-Stille**, Ph.D. ABD, teaches at Trent University where they research representations of disability in Canadian speculative fiction. They are a creator of the digital humanities hub Speculating Canada and have published in *Mosaic, The Canadian Fantastic in Focus, The Canadian Journal of Disability Studies, Creative Teamwork*, and *Misfit Children*. They are the editor of the fiction collections *Over the Rainbow* and *We Shall Be Monsters*.

Lorna **Piatti-Farnell** is a professor of film and popular culture at Auckland University of Technology, where she is also director of the Popular Culture Research Centre. Her research interests lie at the intersection of Gothic studies, screen media studies, food studies, and cultural history, and she has published widely in these areas, including *The Vampire in Contemporary Popular Literature* (2014) and *Consuming Gothic* (2017).

Wayne Derek **Pigeon-Coote** has been a devotee of the Gothic since childhood, captivated in his formative years by *Frankenstein, or the Modern Prometheus* and especially *Dracula*. This was coupled with early access to many an '80s horror film. His research interests primarily lie within Victorian Gothic, Stoker, Stevenson, Wilde and Le Fanu, and particularly the fin de siècle period. He is the author of *Constructing Horror in Dracula: Novel, Stage and Screen*.

Svetlana **Seibel** is an associate professor of North American literary and cultural studies at Saarland University. She teaches courses on a variety of topics, from Indigenous literatures and media in North America to geek feminism in contemporary television. She is working on an edited volume on Indigenous popular culture across the globe.

Jeffrey Andrew **Weinstock** is a professor of English at Central Michigan University and an associate editor for *The Journal of the Fantastic in the Arts*. He is the author or editor of 24 books, including *The Monster Theory Reader* (2020), *The Mad Scientist's Guide to Composition* (2020), and *The Cambridge Companion to the American Gothic* (2018). Visit him at JeffreyAndrewWeinstock.com.

Natalie **Wilson** teaches literature and women's, gender, and sexuality studies at California State University San Marcos. She is the author of *Willful Monstrosity* (2020), an intersectional analysis of contemporary horror and its monsters, and *Seduced by Twilight* (2011), an examination of the *Twilight* saga from a feminist perspective. Her article, "Rules for Surviving Rape Culture in *The Walking Dead*," appears *The Politics of Race, Gender, and Sexuality in* The Walking Dead.

Gina **Wisker** is currently an Associate Professor at the University of Bath, supervising doctoral students, Professor 11, University of the Arctic, Tromso, and also a Professor Emeritus of Higher Education & Contemporary Literature at the University of Brighton. She has published 26 books (some edited) more than 140 articles: *Key Concepts in Postcolonial Literature* (2007); *Horror Fiction: An Introduction* (2005); *Margaret Atwood, an Introduction to Critical Views of Her Fiction* (2012); *Contemporary Women's Gothic Fiction* (2016); She was chair of the Contemporary Women's Writing Association and is one of an editor trio for Palgrave's Contemporary Women's Writing series, on the editorial board for Palgrave's Gothic series, and Anthem's Gothic series. She co-edits online dark fantasy journal *Dissections* (since 2006) and *Spokes* poetry magazine (since the 1990s) and hosts the "words and worlds" readings for ICFA. She has just finished *Contemporary Women's Ghost Stories* for Palgrave, lives in Cambridge, has two sons and a feisty poodle.

Index

abject 14, 36, 45, 55, 92, 95, 96, 100, 110–1
abuse 54, 64, 70, 71, 73, 142
active 4, 6, 14, 77, 84, 85, 91, 97–9, 122, 147, 163, 166, 183, 211
activism 98, 99
adaptation 3–4, 10–1, 16, 21, 23, 25–6, 31, 37, 48–9, 50, 51, 52, 56, 57–8, 62–3, 65–6, 77, 97, 122, 126, 128, 135, 136, 138, 163, 164, 175, 182, 201, 210, 213
advertising 4, 9, 63, 105, 106, 107, 108, 109–12, 114, 115, 158
affect 35, 38, 64, 84, 96, 135, 159
affection 31, 32, 41, 80, 141, 14, 172
African American 97, 98, 112
agency 7, 16, 50, 51, 57, 78, 84, 85, 91, 98, 100, 103, 104, 172, 178
archetype 22, 23, 24, 52, 76, 77, 79, 80, 81, 81
asexual 82
audience 4–7, 11–4, 15, 23, 24, 25, 35, 45, 47, 48, 49, 50, 54, 60, 61–3, 65, 68, 77, 79, 81, 89, 95, 96, 97, 104, 115, 122, 146, 155, 157, 174–6, 177, 178–9, 190, 192, 194, 198, 209
Auerbach, Nina 5, 13, 39, 44, 60, 89, 185, 189
augmentation 4
authenticity 61, 112, 121, 123, 129, 131, 193, 196, 197, 203
author 1, 4, 7, 16, 23, 25, 37, 47, 48, 52, 53, 62, 68, 84, 90, 135, 137, 202, 212
authorial control 7, 15, 16, 63, 64, 66, 158, 164, 171, 172, 188, 198, 201–2, 204–10, 212
avatar 31, 81, 82, 85

Bathory, Elizabeth 168
binary 56, 83, 85; non 213, 214
Black Magic 154, 157
blog 4, 7, 13, 201, 210
blood 9, 11, 26, 27, 29, 32, 38, 39, 44, 45, 52, 53, 54, 64, 67, 72, 73, 78, 81, 83, 84, 88, 89, 92, 100, 106, 109, 111, 114, 115, 123, 132, 147, 149, 150, 153, 154, 157, 158–9, 160, 167, 171, 176, 179, 192, 206, 209; memory 12; sucking 10, 41, 42
bloodline 57
Bram Stoker's Dracula (1992) 14, 21, 23, 28, 31, 33, 35, 39, 42, 53, 88, 133

branding 8, 15, 90, 92, 103, 104–6, 112, 114–5, 120, 146, 160, 204
brides 36, 52, 55–7
broadcast 191, 193, 196
Browning, Tod 37, 82, 152
bully 93, 97, 100, 101, 213
burial 66, 147, 150, 151
Byron, Lord 10, 21, 41, 66, 209

canonical 1, 25, 76, 77, 82, 83, 84, 98, 100, 138
capitalism 12, 205, 208
Carmilla 11, 12, 16, 52, 103–7, 108, 110–7, 140, 162–72, 180
censorship 47, 167
cinema 8, 14, 21–2, 24–5, 32, 39, 42, 76, 77, 122, 131, 136, 137, 147, 149, 151–2, 153, 154, 157, 187, 188
cinematograph 12, 21, 33,
collaborative 16, 99, 108, 109, 110, 135, 148, 158, 177, 196, 204
comics 4–5, 25, 33, 47, 147, 174
commerce 105, 106, 110, 115, 121, 123, 131
commune 29, 164, 188, 215
communication 12, 41, 82, 135, 146, 150
community 4, 13, 65, 67, 99, 125, 176, 181, 189, 196, 209
consumer 6, 48, 61, 62, 90, 91, 96, 98, 99, 110, 112, 115, 177, 189, 190, 193, 196, 197–8, 199, 202
consumerist 12, 106, 123, 132
convergence 3, 4, 6, 12, 26, 177, 197
cosplay 4, 7, 147
creation 3–9, 11, 12, 13–6, 24, 39, 48, 63–5, 68, 70, 77, 88, 90, 93, 94, 97–100, 104, 106, 121, 123, 130, 136, 139, 144, 147, 150, 151, 153, 163, 169, 171, 175, 176, 179, 186, 188, 194, 198, 201, 205, 208–9, 214
creator 4, 6, 24, 52, 117, 199, 203
creature 11, 21, 27, 29, 31, 35, 41, 53, 77, 79, 127, 132, 139, 147–8, 150, 151, 153–60, 173, 175, 178, 186, 188, 194, 204
culture 13, 14, 15, 22, 23, 26, 63, 65, 70, 86, 91, 96–9, 107, 111, 115, 120, 121, 123–7, 130–3, 135, 138, 141, 143, 144, 147, 153, 156, 194, 208, 214; indigenous 15, 136, 218; material 89, 91;

221

222 Index

media 65, 96; popular 28, 58, 94, 108, 113, 122, 123, 127, 131, 147, 155, 159, 193; rape 52; sub 14, 196; trans 120, 144

demon 30, 31
demonic 29, 30, 35, 154, 192
desire 1, 32, 36, 38, 49, 52, 56–7, 61–2, 63, 66, 88, 100, 104, 126, 132, 146, 148, 158, 172, 175–6, 180, 182, 183, 192, 193, 194, 198, 203, 204, 206, 207, 209, 214
device 8, 3–5, 7, 13, 53–5, 117, 122, 138, 153, 170, 196
devil 29, 31, 43, 194, 214
diary 49, 50, 51, 56, 197
digital 99, 100, 104, 116, 163, 171
disability 99
disease 27, 66, 73, 82, 84, 170
dissemination 12, 187, 188, 189, 190, 193, 196, 198, 210
dissonance 5, 9, 14, 16
distribution 108, 190, 191
Dracula (character) 7, 8, 9, 11, 13, 20, 22–33, 35–45, 47–8, 50, 51–8, 72, 74, 76, 77, 125–8, 130–2, 138, 140, 162, 168, 170–3, 178, 180, 193
Dracula (1897) 1, 2, 9, 11, 14, 23, 25, 27, 28, 31, 47, 79, 88, 124, 125, 134, 136, 143, 163, 192
Dracula (1931) 4, 37, 125, 126, 133, 156
Dracula (1979) 23, 39, 75
Dracula's Castle 6, 74, 128–30
Dracula's Daughter (1936) 188, 196
Draculaura 15, 89, 92–3, 95, 100–1

economics 6, 64, 66, 68, 71, 73
education 46, 48, 71, 91, 108, 214
emotions 5, 11, 39, 50, 99, 144, 148, 150, 159, 176, 177–9, 180, 182, 183, 184, 206, 207
engagement 1, 4, 6, 7, 8, 11, 13–5, 27, 48, 51, 100, 114, 172, 174, 179, 197, 202, 205, 209
environment 6, 98, 179, 183
environmental 13, 151
ethnicity 127

Facebook 6, 198
fan 1, 4, 6, 8, 13, 98–100, 113, 115, 128, 148, 174, 176, 177, 178, 182, 185, 186, 194, 198–9, 203; fiction 7, 9, 11, 16, 188, 201–2, 209–14
fandom 16, 98, 99, 100, 111, 115, 120, 147, 203–5
fangs 11, 38, 51, 60, 93, 153, 155, 157, 166
fangtasia 6, 122
fantastic 60, 64, 68, 70, 71, 103
fantasy 60, 62–3, 65–7, 68, 70–1, 82, 121, 127, 158, 159, 181, 202
femininity 91–3, 95, 106, 166
forum 8, 13, 158, 201, 204
franchise 4–5, 8, 9, 13, 14–6, 26, 32, 63, 65, 79, 86, 89, 93, 96, 97, 99–100, 159, 201
Frankenstein 22, 24, 27, 32, 34, 198, 218

gaming 4, 6, 9, 26, 77–86, 147, 148, 156, 174
Gelder, Ken 5, 8, 62, 63, 65–6, 125, 127

gender 1, 50, 60, 63, 64, 66, 67, 70, 71, 73, 91–2, 110, 112, 114, 214, 217, 218
geography 64, 120, 121, 126, 129
ghost 10, 16, 32, 61, 62, 80, 120, 146, 147–9, 151, 152, 153, 154, 157, 191
gothic 1, 2, 60, 61, 63, 65, 76, 120, 123, 128, 129, 132, 137, 151, 190, 195, 202–4, 205–7, 214–5

Hammer films 7, 11, 37, 74, 76, 153
haunt 35, 36, 56, 71, 104, 120, 126, 152, 172, 179, 202, 214
heteronormative 73, 165, 172
heterosexual 112, 158, 180
history 9, 10, 14, 15, 22, 24, 32, 35, 37–9, 42, 44, 45, 60, 64, 65, 68, 69, 71, 76, 78, 79, 89, 98, 105, 107, 110, 115, 120–3, 127–8, 129, 130–2, 135, 137, 138, 142, 143, 157, 162–4, 166, 168–9, 171, 187, 189, 196, 199, 202, 207, 208, 214
homophobia 101
homosexual 11, 52, 88, 158
Horror of Dracula (1958) 23, 25, 76
humanity 36, 37, 39, 45, 85, 89, 155, 175, 178, 185, 214
humanize 14, 35, 39, 43, 45, 158, 175, 186
hysteria 175

identification 10, 13, 14, 35, 45, 78, 79, 129, 131, 140, 160, 204, 211, 213
identity 3, 6, 9, 16, 27, 29, 38, 68, 95, 96, 97, 111, 112, 123, 130, 131, 133, 169, 199, 202, 203, 204, 205, 206, 207, 208, 210, 212, 214
imaginaries 3, 16, 67, 69, 168
immersion 3, 4, 6, 7, 61, 62, 77, 132, 164, 177, 183, 186, 191, 192
inequality 64, 66
intelligent 146, 148, 157, 158
interact 5, 6, 96, 97, 100, 144, 148, 171, 186, 198
interactive 77, 100, 115
internet 103, 130, 158, 200, 201
interpretation 13, 36, 47, 48, 49, 73, 90, 97, 112, 135, 164, 166, 168, 189; reinterpretation 47, 98, 167

Jekyll and Hyde 27, 33
Jenkins, Henry 4, 6, 8, 12, 98, 163, 164, 166, 177, 188, 189, 196, 197, 201
jouissance 45, 166

King, Stephen 24–5, 180

Lee, Christopher 7, 25
Le Fanu, Sheridan 11, 52, 79, 104, 106, 107, 111, 113, 140, 162–3, 164, 165–8, 170–2
lesbian 64, 104, 111, 165
license 63
liminal 48, 55, 63, 195
Lucy (Westenra) 31, 38, 41, 42, 45, 48, 49, 51–2, 54, 57
Lugosi, Bela 32, 82, 125–6

Index   223

magic 61, 62, 72, 77, 78, 80, 83, 84, 123, 124, 126, 154, 157, 176, 183
mapping 82
masculinity 50, 206
media 1, 3–5, 6–7, 10–1, 22, 26, 35, 37, 45, 57, 65, 76–7, 78, 78, 86, 89–91, 95–6, 98–103, 104, 105, 123, 132, 135, 147, 156, 164, 174–5, 177, 182, 187–9, 190, 193, 196–7, 199, 204, 215; multi 89, 163, 171, 194, 196, 199; social 8, 10, 111, 112, 115, 174, 198, 201
medical 10, 107, 138, 147, 166
megatext 14, 23–31, 33
memory 7, 12, 23, 36, 50, 56, 131, 139, 140, 167, 169, 171, 181, 189, 198, 209
menstrual 103, 105–8, 109, 110–2, 114–5
merchandise 7, 8, 15, 47, 62, 66
metafiction 189–90
migration 9, 15, 35, 44, 45, 55, 153, 154, 183, 198
Mina (Harker) 14, 21, 27, 29, 31, 33, 36, 37, 38, 41–2, 47–58, 170, 171, 192,
monster 13, 15, 22, 26, 27, 32, 33, 34, 36, 37, 38, 39, 41, 43–5, 65, 76, 77, 85, 86, 88, 91, 92, 93–4, 124, 126, 127, 143, 145, 149, 254, 157, 158, 168, 186, 189, 190, 194, 198, 202, 203, 207, 208, 210
monstrous 33, 38, 39, 43, 68, 81, 85, 93, 147, 151, 178, 188, 202, 206, 209, 212, 213; feminine 91, 92, 104, 195
morality 61, 73, 84, 85, 97, 137, 160, 214
Murnau, F.W. 4, 9, 15, 22, 76, 134, 135, 136, 138, 143
music 1, 4, 89, 154, 189, 190, 191, 193–5, 199, 201
myth 9, 22, 30, 31, 67, 70, 71–2, 96, 110, 121, 122, 124, 125, 126, 129, 164, 170, 194, 195, 199, 209

narrative 3–9, 10, 11, 12, 13–6, 23–6, 28, 29, 30–1, 33, 48, 51, 52, 58, 61, 75, 77–8, 79, 80, 81, 82–3, 84, 85–6, 90–1, 95–9, 101, 103, 105, 112, 114, 120–5, 126–7, 128, 130–2, 134, 135, 136–7, 138, 139, 144, 162–7, 168–9, 171, 173, 174–5, 179, 186, 187, 188–90, 197, 199, 201, 202, 204, 206, 207, 210, 211, 212–3
network 4, 5, 63, 84, 113, 127, 128
New Media 10, 16, 76, 90, 163
non-human 35, 36, 37, 39, 151
Nosferatu (1922) 4, 9, 15, 25, 37, 76, 88, 134–9, 142–4, 154

occult 166, 195
online 4, 5, 6, 158, 177, 201, 204, 213
oral 10, 89, 189
original 4, 8, 9, 13, 15, 21, 22, 47, 50, 52, 65, 90, 96, 105, 106, 110, 141, 154, 157, 159, 162, 164, 166, 167, 169, 171–2, 188, 203, 205–7, 209, 210, 213
The Originals 16, 122, 174–83, 185–6, 198
Orlok 76, 138

ownership 1, 16, 52, 68, 136, 201, 202, 204–5, 210, 212, 214

participation 4, 6, 7, 11, 12–4, 20, 28, 77, 98, 111, 132, 147, 163, 167, 202, 203
participatory 98, 99, 192
perform 50, 52, 64, 65, 69, 77, 83, 85, 146, 151, 176, 193, 213
performance 4, 21, 33, 61, 62, 63, 126, 194, 210
performative 7, 61, 66, 67, 126
performer 8
phenomenon 1, 3, 5, 8, 16, 88, 108, 112, 115, 138, 143, 164, 177, 201
philosophy 105, 147, 202, 205, 208, 214
platform 3, 4, 9, 11, 14, 178, 213; cross 8, 12, 14, 164; media 65, 163, 174, 177, 193, 201; multi 6, 163, 193, 201, 214
play 15, 23, 24, 27, 32, 33, 50, 52, 63, 89, 90–1, 96–100, 163, 167, 214
play (theatre) 4, 10, 15, 57, 60, 61, 62, 64–71, 73–4
player 4, 6, 7, 63, 77, 78–86
Polidori, John 4, 10, 11, 66, 69, 73, 75, 209
politics 43, 64, 71, 86, 105, 107, 110, 112, 123–5, 128, 131, 137, 172
progeny 56, 206, 209
psychoanalysis 36, 43

queer 2, 60, 104, 105, 112, 163, 165, 169, 172

radio 191–2, 193, 194, 199, 200
reader 1, 4, 6, 11, 16, 23, 24, 28, 48, 50, 53, 57, 78, 93, 98, 124, 129, 135, 137, 139, 141, 162, 163, 164, 166–8, 171–2, 174, 177, 179, 181–6, 188, 190, 191–3, 201, 203, 204, 206, 208–10, 213, 214
reality 5, 6, 14, 32, 37, 38, 67, 71, 74, 91, 98, 121, 135, 143, 149, 160, 171, 181, 187, 190, 191, 192, 196, 214
recreate 6, 198, 204
reimagining 15, 22, 23, 33, 91, 100
religious 25, 141, 142, 147, 153
Renfield 2, 21, 27, 28
resistance 15, 16, 66, 77, 78, 100, 210
retroactive 78
Rice, Anne 7, 16, 30, 68–9, 71, 88, 100, 122, 175, 178, 187–99, 201–14
ritual 106, 147, 150, 151, 155, 157, 176

screenplay 47, 49, 51, 53, 54, 56, 201
sexual 11, 36, 45, 51, 52, 53, 57, 64, 66, 69, 82, 93, 99, 105, 111–3, 142, 147, 148, 159; hyper 55, 160
sexuality 13, 36, 49, 70, 88, 96, 111, 112, 201
society 12, 36, 37, 70, 95, 97, 155, 175, 193, 196
space; cultural 137, 138, 141; domestic 70, 204; dream 60; narrative 23, 56, 60, 77, 85, 94, 95, 96, 202, 204; outer 23; real 61, 62, 64, 65, 144; safe 96, 100, 103, 115; virtual 15
Stoker, Bram 2, 3, 4, 5, 8, 11, 12, 14, 15, 21, 23,

224 Index

24, 25–8, 29, 30–1, 33–9, 41, 42, 45–8, 49, 50–8, 72, 79, 88, 124–6, 128–33, 134, 135, 136–8, 140, 163, 165, 170, 171, 172, 173, 192
storytelling 61, 65, 134, 143, 163, 174, 179, 189
storyworld 22, 23, 24, 204
supernatural 30, 32, 35, 36, 37, 38, 44, 79, 80, 84, 86, 103, 121, 124, 126, 127, 128, 130, 137, 147, 151, 157, 158, 160, 179, 185, 191, 192, 194, 195, 213, 214
surveillance 197

technology 12, 50, 69, 77, 78, 86, 105, 112, 125, 163, 164, 166, 171, 177, 186, 189, 191–5, 199; convergence 3, 12
television 5–6, 8, 9, 13, 23, 32, 39, 76, 77, 89, 90, 92, 95, 98, 113, 122, 143, 156, 171, 174–5, 177, 178, 179, 183, 185, 195, 198, 201
temporal 14, 37, 51, 60, 61, 67–8, 70–1, 73, 136, 143, 144, 169, 184, 188, 208
theater 4, 21, 60, 61, 62, 65–7, 188, 194, 199
transgender 112
transgression 11, 36, 39, 48, 51, 88, 165
transmedia 3, 5, 7, 8, 10, 11, 12–7, 47, 48, 63, 99–100, 105, 107, 110, 112, 115, 120, 126, 128, 132, 134, 137, 144, 147, 163–6, 171, 172, 174–5, 177, 178, 185–91, 193–9, 202
Transylvania 6, 15, 56, 72, 86, 94, 121, 123, 124–8, 130–2
trauma 38, 69
True Blood (2008–14) 3, 6, 13, 32, 46. 76, 122, 163, 173, 174, 175, 177, 198, 199, 204
Twilight Saga 8–9, 13, 26, 32, 42, 66, 69, 132, 159, 174
Twitter 115

urtext 16, 90
user 6, 7, 16, 78, 99, 115, 152

vampire: child 68, 71, 192, 197; female 11, 15, 16, 25, 38, 52, 55, 56, 62, 64, 66, 68, 70, 74, 77, 80, 92, 95, 103, 106, 111–2, 139, 140, 141, 157, 166, 168, 179, 180, 203; folklore 9, 10, 13, 64, 72, 88, 121, 137, 147, 151; genre 5, 8, 9, 14, 15, 24, 25, 26, 29, 30, 31, 48, 51, 63, 68, 72, 76, 77, 82, 89, 110, 121, 123, 124–5, 134, 143, 164, 174; hunters 12, 25, 39, 58, 83, 157, 176, 180; transmedia 5, 7, 10, 11, 13, 14, 16, 121, 132, 178
The Vampire Diaries 8, 76, 175–6, 178, 179, 182, 186
Vampirella 25
Vampirina 15, 88–90, 94–7, 99–101
Vampyr (game) 82, 84–5
The Vampyre 4, 10, 66, 69
Van Helsing 25, 26, 27–8, 37, 38, 39, 48, 50–1, 54–8, 83, 170, 172
Varney the Vampire 11, 25, 27
victim 11, 12, 41, 48, 51, 53, 54, 64, 67, 68, 69, 84, 104, 151, 153, 154, 155, 168, 175, 204, 209, 211, 213
video 4, 5, 15, 25, 77–9, 81, 82, 86, 99, 103–4, 105, 111, 114–5, 189–90, 191, 193, 194, 213
viewer 4, 21, 25, 27–8, 31, 94, 98, 104, 134, 174, 176–80, 182–4, 185–6, 189, 192–3, 205, 213
violence 53, 67, 84, 142, 143, 145, 170
virtual 4, 5, 6, 14, 15, 16, 77, 84, 86, 99
Vlad 14, 21, 28, 35, 37–9, 40, 41–6, 130–1
vlog 103, 174

web series 15, 103, 104, 106, 107, 110–3, 116–7, 163
werewolf 20, 22, 28, 29, 31–3, 47, 71, 80, 82, 93, 176, 178–9, 181, 183–4
Whitby 6, 15, 31, 49, 72, 132, 136
witch 39, 142, 157, 178–9, 181–4, 204

xenophobia 88

YouTube 99, 103, 105

zombie 145, 158, 178

www.ingramcontent.com/pod-product-compliance
Ingram Content Group UK Ltd.
Pitfield, Milton Keynes, MK11 3LW, UK
UKHW041950140426
5217IPUK00014B/732